THE WORLD OF THE GALLOGLASS

The World of the Galloglass

*Kings, warlords and warriors in Ireland and
Scotland, 1200–1600*

Seán Duffy

EDITOR

FOUR COURTS PRESS

Typeset in 11pt on 13pt EhrhardtMt by
Carrigboy Typesetting Services for
FOUR COURTS PRESS LTD
7 Malpas Street, Dublin 8, Ireland
e-mail: info@fourcourtspress.ie
and in North America for
FOUR COURTS PRESS
c/o ISBS, 920 N.E. 58th Avenue, Suite 300, Portland, OR 97213.

A catalogue record for this title is available
from the British Library.

ISBN 978–1–85182–946–0

Printed in England
by MPG Books, Bodmin, Cornwall.

Contents

Illustrations

Contributors

DAVID H. CALDWELL is Keeper of Scotland and Europe, National Museums of Scotland.

ALISON CATHCART is a lecturer in the Department of History, University of Strathclyde.

SEÁN DUFFY is co-director of the Centre for Irish-Scottish Studies at Trinity College, Dublin.

DAVID EDWARDS is a senior lecturer in the Department of History, University College, Cork.

R. ANDREW McDONALD is Director of the Centre for Medieval and Renaissance Studies at Brock University, Canada.

WILSON McLEOD is a senior lecturer in Celtic and Scottish Studies, School of Literatures, Languages and Cultures, University of Edinburgh.

KENNETH NICHOLLS is an emeritus senior lecturer in the Department of History, University College, Cork.

ALASDAIR ROSS teaches in the Department of History, University of Stirling.

KATHARINE SIMMS is a senior lecturer in the Department of History, Trinity College, Dublin.

ALEX WOOLF is a lecturer in the School of History, University of St Andrews.

Editor's preface

The papers in this volume arise from a conference held in the University of Edinburgh in March 2003. The conference was organized by the Centre for Irish-Scottish Studies at Trinity College Dublin, in conjunction with the School of Languages, Literatures & Cultures and the School of History & Classics at Edinburgh University. The conference would not have been possible without the financial support of the above (and/or their constituent Departments), and without the organizational input of Dr Wilson McLeod (Edinburgh) and Dr Susan Foran (Dublin), who received much-appreciated assistance on the ground from Ms Christina Strauch. I would also like to express my gratitude for their interest and support to my fellow co-directors, past and present, of the Trinity Centre for Irish-Scottish Studies, David Dickson, Damian McManus, Cathal Ó Háinle, Ian Campbell Ross, and Katharine Simms.

The Edinburgh conference was constructed around the first public trial demonstration of the Galloglass Project database. The project, which is ongoing, aims to establish a comprehensive record of all known galloglass individuals and activities from the time of their first recorded appearance in Ireland in the thirteenth century to the end of the Middle Ages. The project is based in the Department of History, TCD, under the aegis of the Centre for Irish-Scottish Studies and has been supported to date as part of a cluster of related research projects funded by the Higher Education Authority under the Programme for Research in Third Level Institutions (PRTLI). The database will shortly go 'live' and will be accessible online to interested researchers. Such a database, almost by definition, can never be complete and it is hoped to secure a recurrent funding stream for its future development. Enquiries are welcome to sduffy@tcd.ie.

I am one of, by now, an entire generation of medievalists (to say nothing of those toiling in other fields) privileged to have had their work published by Michael Adams and Four Courts Press. I thank him for his personal interest in this volume, and I thank too Martin Fanning for the ever judicious (and I trust not too torrential) spilling of red ink thereon. Lastly, I am especially grateful to the patient contributors to this volume. The only mitigating factor in the delay of its publication until now is that it means *The world of the Galloglass* makes its appearance exactly seventy years after the landmark study upon which it hopes to build, G.A. Hayes-McCoy's *Scots mercenary forces in Ireland* (Dublin, 1937).

SEÁN DUFFY

A note on the orthography of personal names

In a volume such as this it is not possible to arrive at a standardized form of orthography for personal names that will please all, or perhaps even most, readers. The primary editorial objective must be consistency between contributions, and this I hope I have achieved. As to guiding principles, I have adopted the following practices rather than hard and fast rules.

I have sought to avoid *imposed* Latinized and Anglicized forms. At least in the first instance of usage, names of Scandinavian origin are rendered in Old Norse format (and, in so far as my very limited expertise permitted, I have attempted to produce patronyms using the suffix *–son* or *–dóttir* added to the genitive). And where a name of Scandinavian origin has clearly been adopted into Gaelic and developed its own Gaelic orthography, I have used the latter. By way of illustration, in the case of the celebrated twelfth-century ruler of Argyll, I have avoided the Latinized/Anglicized *Somerled* in favour of Old Norse *Sumarliði*, but for later Gaelic dynasts given this name (perhaps in his honour) I have used the appropriate Gaelic form.

With regard to the latter, this volume has core temporal termini of AD1200 and AD1600, with occasional excursions back to earlier centuries and forward as late as the eighteenth. Therefore, the following principles are adopted. Names are generally rendered in Classical Early Modern Irish form, e.g. *Aodh* rather than *Áed*, *Domhnall* rather than *Domnall*, *Maolmhuire* rather than *Máel Muire*, *Toirdhealbhach* rather than *Toirdelbach*, etc. But as this practice has less validity the further an individual's floruit extends beyond the 1200–1600 central timeframe, there are a small number of instances where the Early Modern Irish form has been abandoned in favour of a more appropriate orthography. For example, therefore, Middle Irish orthography has been applied to the famed tenth-century poet Cináed ua hArtacáin, while it seemed faintly absurd to standardize into Classical Irish the name of Patrick Randal McDonnell, a galloglass descendant and populist politician in Co. Mayo murdered in the 1780s.

It should be noted also that Scottish Gaelic forms are generally avoided before the seventeenth century.

SD

Abbreviations

AC	A.M. Freeman (ed.), *Annala Connacht: the Annals of Connacht* (Dublin, 1944)
AClon	*The annals of Clonmacnoise, being annals of Ireland from the earliest period to A.D. 1408*, ed. Denis Murphy (Dublin, 1896)
AFM	*Annála Rioghachta Éireann: annals of the kingdom of Ireland by the Four Masters, from the earliest period to the year 1616*, ed. and tr. J. O'Donovan, 7 vols (Dublin, 1851)
AI	*Annals of Inisfallen (MS Rawlinson B. 503)*, ed. and trans. Seán Mac Airt (Dublin, 1951)
ALC	*The Annals of Loch Cé: a chronicle of Irish affairs from A.D. 1014 to A.D. 1590*, ed. and tr. W.M. Hennessy, 2 vols (London, 1871)
Anderson, *Early sources*	*Early sources of Scottish history, A.D. 500–1286*, ed. and trans. A.O. Anderson, 2 vols (Edinburgh, 1922, rpr. Stamford, 1990)
Anderson, *Scottish annals*	*Scottish annals from English chroniclers*, ed. A.O. Anderson (London, 1908; rpr. Stamford, 1991)
APC	*Acts of the privy council of England, 1542–1631*, 46 vols (London, 1890–1964)
ATig	'The annals of Tigernach', ed. Whitley Stokes, in *Revue Celtique*, 16 (1895), 374–419; 17 (1896), 6–33, 119–263, 337–420; 18 (1897), 9–59, 150–97, 267–303; rpr., 2 vols (Felinfech, 1993)
AU	*Annala Uladh: Annals of Ulster: otherwise, Annala Senait, Annals of Senat: a chronicle of Irish affairs*, ed. and trans. with notes by W.H. Hennessy and B. MacCarthy, 4 vols (Dublin, 1887–1901)
Bergin, *Irish Bardic Poetry*	Osborn Bergin, *Irish Bardic Poetry*, ed. David Greene and Fergus Kelly (Dublin, 1970)
BIHR	*Bulletin of the Institute of Historical Research*
BL	British Library
Cal. papal letters	*Calendar of entries in the papal registers relating to Great Britain and Ireland: letters*, ed. W.H. Bliss *et al.* (London, 1893–)
CDI	*Calendar of documents relating to Ireland, 1171–1307*, ed. H.S. Sweetman, 5 vols (London, 1875–86)
CDS	*Calendar of documents relating to Scotland*, 5 vols, vols 1–4 ed. Joseph Bain (London, 1881–8); vol. v (Supplementary), ed. G.G. Simpson and J.D. Galbraith (Scottish Record Office, Edinburgh, 1986)
Chron. Man	*Cronica Regum Mannie & Insularum. Chronicles of the Kings of Man and the Isles, BL Cotton Julius Avii*, transcribed and translated with an introduction by George Broderick (2nd ed. Douglas, 1995; rpr. 1996)
CMCS	*Cambrian [formerly Cambridge] Medieval Celtic Studies*

CSPI	*Calendar of the state papers relating to Ireland … 1509–[1606]*, ed. H.C. Hamilton et al. (London and Dublin, 1860–2000)
CSPS	*Calendar of the state papers relating to Scotland and Mary, Queen of Scots, 1547–1605*, 12 vols in 14 (Edinburgh, 1898–1952)
CSPV	*Calendar of state papers and manuscripts relating to English affairs existing in the archives and collections of Venice and in other libraries of northern Italy* , ed. Rawdon Brown, G. Cavendish Bentinck, Horatio F. Brown, et al., 38 vols (London, 1864–1940)
DIAS	Dublin Institute for Advanced Studies
DNB	*Dictionary of national biography*, ed. Sir Leslie Stephen et al., rev. ed., 22 vols (London, 1908–9)
EHR	*English Historical Review*
ER	*Rotuli scaccarii regum Scotorum. The exchequer rolls of Scotland [1264–1600]*, ed. John Stuart and George Burnett et al., 22 vols (Edinburgh, 1878–1908)
Expugnatio	Giraldus Cambrensis, *Expugnatio Hibernica. The conquest of Ireland*, ed. and trans. A.B. Scott and F.X. Martin (Dublin, 1978)
G.E.C., *Complete Peerage*	G.E. Cokayne, *Complete peerage of England, Scotland, Ireland, Great Britain and the United Kingdom*, ed. V. Gibbs et al., 12 vols (London, 1910–59)
HMC	Historical Manuscripts Commission
IoMNHAS Proc.	*Proceedings of the Isle of Man Natural History and Antiquarian Society*
Irish faints	*The Irish faints of the Tudor sovereigns during the reigns of Henry VIII, Edward VI, Philip & Mary, and Elizabeth I*, ed. K.W. Nicholls, 4 vols (Dublin, 1994)
JMM	*Journal of the Manx Museum*
LCS	*Leabhar Chlainne Suibhne. An account of the Mac Sweeney families in Ireland, with pedigrees*, ed. Pól Breatnach [Fr Paul Walsh] (Dublin, 1920)
Letters of James V	*Letters of James V*, ed. R.K. Hannay and D. Hay (Edinburgh, 1954)
LMG	An Dubhaltach MacFhirbhisigh, *Leabhar mór na ngenealach. The great book of Irish genealogies*, ed. Nollaig Ó Muraíle, Nollaig, 5 vols (Dublin, 2004)
LP Henry VIII	*Letters and papers, foreign and domestic, of the reign of King Henry VIII*, ed. J.S. Brewer et al., 21 vols (London, 1862–1932)
Misc. Ir. annals	*Miscellaneous Irish annals (A.D. 1114–1437)*, ed. Séamus Ó hInnse (Dublin, 1947)
NAI	National Archives of Ireland
NHI, ii	*A new history of Ireland. Volume II: medieval Ireland, 1169–1534*, ed. Art Cosgrove (Oxford, 1987)
NLI	National Library of Ireland
NLS	National Library of Scotland

Oliver, *Monumenta*   *Monumenta de Insula Manniae or a collection of national documents relating to the Isle of Man*, trans. and ed. with an Appendix by J.R. Oliver, 3 vols (Douglas, 1860–2)

Orkneyinga Saga   *Orkneyinga Saga. Legenda de Sancto Magno. Magnús Saga Skemmri. Magnúss Saga Lengri. Helga Þáttr Úlfs*, ed. F. Guðmundsson. (Reykjavík, 1965), ch. 110; trans. H. Pálsson and P. Edwards, *Orkneyinga Saga. The History of the Earls of Orkney*. (London, 1981)

ODNB   *Oxford dictionary of national biography*, ed. H.G.C. Matthew et al., 60 vols (Oxford, 2004)

PRO   Public Record Office (now National Archives), Kew, London

PSAS   *Proceedings of the Society of Antiquaries of Scotland*

RCAHMS   The Royal Commission on the Ancient and Historical Monuments of Scotland

RIA   Royal Irish Academy

RIA Proc.   *Proceedings of the Royal Irish Academy*

RMS   *Regestrum magni sigilii regum Scotorum*, ed. J.M. Thomson et al. (Edinburgh, 1892–1914)

Rot. Scot.   *Rotuli Scotiae in Turri Londinensi et in Domo Capitulari Westmonasteriensi assertati*, ed. D. Macpherson et al., 2 vols (Record Commission, London, 1814)

RRS   *Regesta regum Scottorum: the acts of the kings of Scotland* (Edinburgh, 1960–)

RSAI Jn   *Journal of the Royal Society of Antiquaries of Ireland*

RSS   *Registrum secreti sigilli regum Scotorum*, ed. J. Thomson et al., 11 vols (Edinburgh, 1882–1914)

Scotichronicon   *Scotichronicon by Walter Bower in Latin and English*, gen. ed. D.E.R. Watt, 9 vols (Aberdeen, 1987–98)

SHR   *Scottish Historical Review*

Song of Dermot (Mullally)   *The deeds of the Normans in Ireland: la geste des Engleis en Yrlande*, ed. Evelyn Mullally (Dublin, 2002); this edition and translation supersedes the longstanding edition generally known as *The song of Dermot and the earl*, ed. G.H. Orpen (Oxford, 1892), although the latter remains indispensable for the quality of its historical annotation.

SP   State papers

SP Henry VIII   State papers *of King Henry the eighth*, 11 vols (London, 1830–52)

TA   *Accounts of the Lord High Treasurer of Scotland*, ed. T. Dickson and J. Balfour Paul, 12 vols (Edinburgh, 1877–1916 (1970))

TCD   Trinity College Dublin

TGSI   *Transactions of the Gaelic Society of Inverness*

UJA   *Ulster Journal of Archaeology*

WHN & Q   *West Highland Notes and Queries* (formerly *Notes and Queries of the Society of West Highland and Island Historical Research*)

The prehistory of the galloglass

SEÁN DUFFY

As has long been recognized, the first recorded instance of the use of the term *gallóglach* – usually translated 'foreign warrior', but in fact a shorthand for 'warrior from Innse Gall (the Hebrides)' – occurs in the Irish annals as late as the year 1290. In this year, Toirdhealbhach Ó Domhnaill (whose mother was a daughter of Aonghus Mór mac Domhnaill of Islay) seized the kingship of Tír Chonaill from his half-brother Aodh 'through the power of his mother's kin, the Clann Domhnaill, and of many other galloglass'.[1] But it is generally accepted that galloglass had been present in Ireland, at least intermittently, for a generation or more by that stage: the marriage in 1259 of Aodh na nGall Ó Conchobhair, to a daughter of Dubhghall mac Ruaidhri, lord of Garmoran in Argyll, is taken to be a more likely admission-point, since the annals tell us that Aodh na nGall received a dowry of 160 *óglaigh* under the command of Dubhghall's brother, Alan.[2] These are assuredly galloglass, albeit minus the prefix *gall*, who presumably then entered into military service with Ó Conchobhair. That said, the role of Alan mac Ruaidhri can hardly have differed much from that of a kinsman of his, surnamed 'Mac Somhairle' by the Irish annals, who was killed fighting alongside Maoilsheachlainn Ó Domhnaill, at the battle of Ballyshannon in 1247; in all probability Mac Somhairle did not die alone, and doubtless commanded a troop of warriors, having either been hired or voluntarily recruited to help Ó Domhnaill counter the emerging threat of English encroachment into Tír Chonaill.[3]

It seems, then, that we must learn to look earlier than the second half of the thirteenth century for the origins of the galloglass. In what follows, I examine some of the prior evidence for Irish contacts with political and military figures in the West Highlands and Islands, and speculate (for frequently that is as much as one can do) on the earlier history of the deployment of galloglass or galloglass-type warriors on Irish soil.

If we turn the clock back a full century to the autumn of 1149, we find Muircheartach Mac Lochlainn, overking of the Northern Uí Néill, beginning to contend with his rival provincial kings for the kingship of all Ireland.[4] His progress was rapid, and in 1154 the annals report that he led

---

1 *AC* 1290. 2 *AC; ALC* 1259. 3 *AC* 1247. 4 For his career, see Seán Duffy (ed.), *Medieval Ireland: an encyclopedia* (New York and London, 2005), pp 295–8.

his armies as far as Dublin, where 'the foreigners of Áth Cliath submitted to him as their king, and he gave the foreigners 1,200 cows as their wages (*ina ttuarastal*)'.[5] It was a very substantial sum and suggestive of a city whose fortunes were flourishing, its would-be master obliged not merely to do without receiving the customary tribute (*cáin*) but having to pay heavily in wages (*tuarastal*) for their services.[6] And we see what those services entailed, and why they were so essential to Mac Lochlainn's purposes, from a noteworthy incident that occurred that same year. The Four Masters record that in 1154 the elderly king of Connacht, Toirdhealbhach Ó Conchobhair, not yet willing to cede the high-kingship to Mac Lochlainn, gathered together all the shipping available along the Connacht coast; he sent them up the western seaboard under the command of Cosnamhach Ó Dubhda (from a family that regularly provided admirals of the Connacht fleet), and they raided Tír Chonaill and the Inishowen peninsula. Thereupon Mac Lochlainn

sent over sea to hire, and did hire, the fleet of Galloway, Arran, Kintyre, Man, and the territories of Scotland besides (*centair Alban archena*), with Mac Scelling in command of them. And when they arrived near Inishowen, they fell in with the other fleet, and a naval battle was fiercely and spiritedly fought between them … and a great number of the men of Connacht, including Cosnamhach Ó Dubhda, were slain by the overseas men (*las na hallmhurachaibh*). The overseas host (*an sluagh nallmhurach*) was defeated and slaughtered; and they left their ships behind, and Mac Scelling's teeth were knocked out.[7]

It says something of the contacts which the Mic Lochlainn had in the Isles and Scotland if they were able to assemble such a disparate flotilla of vessels at such apparently short notice. The identity of Mac Scelling, its commander, is uncertain, but a late source has it that the ruler of Argyll, Sumarliði (Somhairle, Somerled) mac Giolla Bhrighde mhic Ghiolla Adhamhnáin, whose descendants traced (or fabricated) their descent from the northern Irish kings of Airghialla,[8] had an illegitimate son of this name.[9]

Those whom Mac Scelling led were not galloglass *senso stricto* since, as we have seen, the term *óglaigh*, applied to Hebridean troops, is not recorded before 1259, while the express term *gallóglaigh* does not make an appearance until 1290. Yet in these instances, as in later usage, the Hebridean and West Highland warriors in question play the role of troops whose commanders were militarily and politically allied to a particular

5 *AFM* 1154. 6 For Dublin's relations with the Irish kings in this period, see Seán Duffy, 'Irishmen and Islesmen in the kingdoms of Dublin and Man, 1052–1171', *Ériu*, 43 (1992), 93–133. 7 *AFM* 1154. 8 See W.D.H. Sellar, 'The origins and ancestry of Somerled', *SHR*, 45 (1966), 123–42; cf. Alex Woolf, 'The origins and ancestry of Somerled: Gofraid mac Fergusa and "The Annals of the Four Masters"', *Mediaeval Scandinavia*, 15 (2005) 199–213. 9 See 'The Book of Clanranald', in *Reliquiae Celticae*, ed. Alexander Cameron, 2 vols (Inverness, 1892–4), ii, pp 148–59.

Irish dynast, and that is without doubt the function performed here by Mac Scelling a century earlier. Furthermore, assuming Mac Scelling was indeed a member of Clann Somhairle, so too were those who sent galloglass into action in Ireland in 1259 and 1290 (respectively, Dubhghall mac Ruaidhri and Aonghus Mór mac Domhnaill). Mac Scelling is surely therefore a galloglass commander in all but name.

And if Mac Scelling *was* a son of Sumarliði, the formation of an alliance between this important family and Mac Lochlainn of Cineál Eoghain was an event of some significance. Sumarliði was bitterly opposed to the Manx king Guðrøðr Óláfsson (Gofraidh mac Amhlaoibh), whose reign in Man and the Isles is said to have commenced in 1154.[10] The Manx chronicle records that both sides fought a naval battle in 1156 which resulted in the kingdom of the Isles being divided between them.[11] If one is right to see Sumarliði and Muircheartach Mac Lochlainn as allies at this juncture, this would presumably have put the latter too at loggerheads with King Guðrøðr. Mac Lochlainn had been, as mentioned above, overlord of Dublin since 1154, but the Manx chronicle places in 1156 an extraordinary development whereby the populace of Dublin sent for Guðrøðr of Man to rule over them: he assembled a large fleet and army, sailed to Dublin, and was warmly received by its citizens who elevated him to the kingship by common assent. In accepting Guðrøðr as overlord, the Dubliners were repudiating their declarations of fealty to Muircheartach Mac Lochlainn, who, we are told, collected a vast army and hastened towards Dublin to expel Guðrøðr and to subject the town once more to his suzerainty. However, the Dubliners along with Guðrøðr and his army of Islesmen attacked a troop of Mac Lochlainn's cavalry sent to parley with them, and put them to flight, causing Muircheartach to abandon the whole expedition.[12]

If the episode is to be believed, it was a humiliating climb-down by the highking, but no such event is recorded in Irish sources for 1156. However, it is possible, in light of the confused chronology of the Manx chronicle, that this is the same expedition recorded in the Annals of Ulster for 1162, when we hear of 'a hosting by Muircheartach Mac Lochlainn with most of the Leath Cuinn', that is, an army drawn from most of the provinces of the northern half of Ireland. They came to an unidentified place called Magh Fitharta, apparently near Dublin,[13] but the foreigners killed several of their cavalry, so that the Irish 'did not get their demand

---

10 *Chron. Man*, fo. 37r.   11 *Chron. Man*, fo. 37v.   12 See Duffy, 'Irishmen and Islesmen'.
13 The Irish army is said to have spent a week 'burning the corn and townlands of the foreigners (*ic loscad arba 7 bailed Gall*)' which would indicate a location in Fine Gall; but cf. Edmund Hogan, *Onomasticon Goedelicum* (Dublin, 1910), p. 520.

(*a réir*) on that occasion'. Both the Manx chronicle and the Annals of Ulster, therefore, refer to an unsuccessful cavalry expedition by Muircheartach Mac Lochlainn targeted at the Ostmen of Dublin, and hence both may be describing the same event. And if there is any truth in the version preserved in the Manx chronicle, the men of Dublin were able to cast off the overlordship of Muirchertach Mac Lochlainn by enlisting the support of King Guðrøðr of Man and the Isles and, more particularly, a large Insular army and fleet. Again, these are not galloglass, but they are in a strictly literal sense *gallóglaigh*, warriors from the Isles, and they serve much the same function as galloglass: they are recruited by one important element of the contemporary Irish political landscape, the Ostmen of Dublin, to help strengthen their opposition to the apparently unwelcome suzerainty of the king of Cineál Eoghain.

The Four Masters also record these events, confirming the Manx chronicle's description of Mac Lochlainn leading a vast host to Dublin to lay siege to it (*co hÁth Cliath, dforbais for Ghallaib*). They admit, likewise, that the expedition was a failure and that Muirchertach returned home without obtaining the Ostmen's submission, but having done some raiding in Dublin's hinterland, Fine Gall. They claim, though, that

he left the men of Leinster and Midhe at war with the foreigners [i.e., the Ostmen of Dublin]. A peace was afterwards concluded between the foreigners and the Irish, and seven score ounces of gold were given by the foreigners to Mac Lochlainn.

It appears, then, that a negotiated settlement was reached with the Dubliners, who again acknowledged the highking's authority, handing over a tribute, purportedly, of 140 ounces of gold. The price of peace can only have been an agreement by the citizens to have Guðrøðr withdraw: the Manx chronicle makes no further allusion to his kingship of the city, and says that 'after a few days Guðrøðr returned to Man, and let all the chieftains of the Isles (*omnes principes insularum*) return home'.[14] The compromise may have been sealed by a face-saving marriage-pact: the Manx chronicle later reveals that Guðrøðr's queen, Fionnghuala, was a granddaughter of Muirchertach.[15]

According to the Annals of Ulster, there occurred at this point the pillaging (*argain*) of the foreigners of Dublin by the Leinster king, Diarmait Mac Murchadha, and 'great power was obtained over them, such as was not obtained over them for a long time' (*nert mór do gabáil forro, amail ná rogabad reime re céin móir*). Diarmait enjoyed mastery over the city for the next four years until 1166, when he was ejected from the

14 *Chron. Man*, fos. 37r–v.   15 *Chron. Man*, fo. 40r.

overkingship of Leinster by a crushing alignment of his opponents: the Dubliners rebelled against him at this point, and played a significant role in sealing Diarmait's fate.[16] As is well known, Mac Murchadha sailed off into a brief overseas exile while he mustered Anglo-Norman and Cambro-Norman military aid, and by 1170 he had secured a complete restoration. In September 1170 he and his foreign allies marched on Dublin where he wreaked harsh vengeance on the Ostmen, his overseas allies slaughtering them inside their fortress, carrying off their cattle and goods.[17] Their king, however, Áskell Mac Turcaill (Þorkellsson), managed to make good his escape, along with the bulk of the inhabitants: according to Gerald of Wales 'the greater part of them, led by Áskell, went on board ship, taking their most precious belongings, and sailed off to the northern isles (*boreales ad insulas se navigio transtulerunt*)'.[18]

By the time Áskell attempted to reinstate himself in Dublin, within weeks of the death of Diarmait Mac Murchadha about Mayday 1171,[19] he had recruited a substantial army described by Gerald of Wales thus:

> They were warlike figures, clad in mail in every part of their body after the Danish manner (*Danico more undique ferro vestiti*). Some wore long coats of mail (*alii loricis longis*), others iron plates skilfully knitted together (*alii laminis ferries arte consutis*), and they had round red shields protected by iron round the edge (*clipeis quoque rotundis et rubris circulariter ferro munitis*). These men, whose iron will matched their armour, drew up their ranks and made an attack on the walls at the eastern gate.[20]

They hailed, we are told, from Man, the Western Isles, the Orkneys, and even Norway,[21] the latter led by a man whom Gerald calls 'Johannes nicknamed *þe Wode*', meaning 'mad'; the poem generally known as *The Song of Dermot and the Earl* calls him 'Johan le Devé', which carries a similar meaning, and says that the fleet came from 'the islands and from Man', and that John was 'a highly reputed fighter', who was 'the nephew of the mighty king of Norway, according to the Irish'.[22] The annals of 'Tigernach' call him 'Eoan Lochlandach', which could refer to Norway or simply mean 'the Viking', since the Four Masters add to this nickname the detail that he hailed from the Orkneys. Given the imperfect state of our knowledge of the equipment and appearance of a typical galloglass warrior, or of how these may have developed over the centuries,[23] it is impossible to

16 See Seán Duffy, 'Ireland's Hastings: the Anglo-Norman conquest of Dublin', *Anglo-Norman Studies XX*, ed. Christopher Harper-Bill (Woodbridge, 1998), 69–86.   17 *AFM* 1170; *Song of Dermot* (Mullally), ll. 1570–97; *Expugnatio*, pp 66–9.   18 *Expugnatio*, pp 68–9.   19 *Expugnatio*, p. 304, n. 105; *ATig* 1171.   20 *Expugnatio*, p. 77.   21 *Song of Dermot* (Mullally), ll. 2257–72; *Expugnatio*, pp 76–7.   22 *Expugnatio*, pp 76–7; *Song of Dermot* (Mullally), ll. 2257–2452. 23 See chap. 8 below.

make any valid comparison between the fighting-men here described by Gerald at second hand (he, of course, did not personally witness the battle of Dublin in 1171) and the galloglass that emerge as a significant factor in Irish warfare a century later. But at least his account is evidence that heavily-armoured Hebridean troops were not entirely strangers to Ireland generations before the true age of the galloglass dawned.

Despite their warlike appearance, Áskell's army failed in its objective, John the Wode was slain, and Áskell himself captured and later executed.[24] It was after this disaster, and in a more concerted attempt to dislodge the English garrison from Dublin, that Ruaidhri Ó Conchobhair instated his famous siege of the city. Ruaidhri and also the archbishop of Dublin, Lorcán Ó Tuathail, are said by Gerald to have sent letters to Guðrøðr, the king of Man, and the other men of the Isles (*alios insulanos*), asking them to besiege the port, 'letters in which a generous promise of financial reward accompanied persuasive arguments (*tam verborum invitant persuasione quam larga quoque stipendiorum promissione*)'.[25] This observation, albeit Gerald's and his alone, is not without interest in light of the subsequent Insular contribution to military combat in Ireland. Like the later galloglass, the pursuit of a mercenary reward was part and parcel of the existence of those in receipt of these letters (though the same is probably true of most military men of the age) but they were motivated by more than mere financial acquisitiveness and could be persuaded by political considerations. And Gerald goes on to explain that Guðrøðr's response to the letters sent by King Ruaidhri and Archbishop Lorcán was one stimulated by what he calls 'the threat of English domination, inspired by the successes of the English'.[26]

Apparently, King Guðrøðr gathered together 'the men of the Isles' and 'they immediately sailed about thirty ships full of warriors into the harbour of the Liffey', to assist the highking's blockade of the town. But the blockade was a failure and Dublin stayed in English hands. The English king himself, Henry II, landed in Ireland that same year.[27] Henry now took charge of the programme of conquest and colonization, confirming many of the early invaders in their recent acquisitions, taking the Ostman towns of Dublin, Waterford and Wexford into his own hands, and granting the once great province of Midhe, stretching from the Irish Sea in the east to the Shannon in the west, to one of those who accompanied him to Ireland, Hugh de Lacy.[28] As the Shannon alone separated Midhe

24 *Expugnatio*, pp 76–7; *Song of Dermot* (Mullally), ll. 2257–2452.   25 *Expugnatio*, pp 78–9.
26 Ibid., pp 78–9.   27 The best modern account of Henry II's expedition to Ireland is M.T. Flanagan, *Irish society, Anglo-Norman settlers, Angevin kingship* (Oxford, 1989), chap. 6.   28 See Colin Veach, 'Henry II's grant of Meath to Hugh de Lacy in 1172: a reassessment', *Ríocht na*

from Connacht, the preserve of the highking, Ruaidhri O Conchobhair, its grant to de Lacy may have been made in annoyance at Ruaidhri's refusal (unlike most of the other province-kings) to submit to Henry's overlordship. But with the invaders almost on his doorstep the conquest had come too close for comfort and King Ruaidhri set about its reversal.

In the summer of 1173 (or 1174), he assembled an army comprised of almost all the kings of the Leath Cuinn (the northern half of Ireland) intent upon bringing to a halt the encastellation of Midhe. One of the most remarkable facets of this vast gathering of recruits is that it is quite likely also to have had a component from the Scottish Highlands or the Isles. *The Song of Dermot* lists the kings who accompanied Ó Conchobhair.[29] The list contains the names of more than twenty kings and lords from Leath Cuinn. While it is clear the author did not have before him a written source (the orthography being poor), he supplies a faithful phonetic rendition of the names as undoubtedly related to him by an oral source. This is done with exceptional precision,[30] and because of the meticulousness in the reproduction of the names in the litany, one has to give more than a little credence to the occurrence of one particular name: 'Mac Scilling'. The only other time that this name features, to my knowledge, in a medieval Irish source, is, as earlier noted, in the Annals of the Four Masters when referring to the leader of a Scottish fleet that aided the northern king, Muircheartach Mac Lochlainn, in 1154; and the only time it features in a Scottish source is in an admittedly late one that identifies a certain 'Mac Scelling' as a bastard son of Sumarliði of Argyll.[31] One cannot be certain, but there must surely be grounds for believing that Ruaidhri Ó Conchobhair had enlisted Hebridean aid in this massive if ultimately unsuccessful attempt to turn the tide of English conquest in his favour.

One other piece of evidence from *The Song* may just be relevant here. Having recorded the leaders of Ruaidhri's army, the poem tells us that:

> Assembles erent les Norreis
> E de Leth Choin trestut les rois.

Midhe, 18 (2007) 67–94.   **29** *Song of Dermot* (Mullally), ll. 3236–59.   **30** Indeed, this catalogue of names, like many other proper names in *The Song*, merits thorough linguistic analysis as an insight into the transition from Middle to Classical (Early Modern) Irish, particularly, it seems to this inexpert writer, as regards lenition, and the time-lag between, on the one hand, this crucial shift in the spoken language and, on the other, the acknowledgment of the shift in the language as written.   **31** See above, n. 9.

The same phrase is repeated almost verbatim in the narrative several lines
further along:

> … Que assembles erent les Norreys
> E de Leth Coin trestut les rois …[32]

The editors of the poem, G.H. Orpen and latterly Evelyn Mullally, have
translated 'les Norreis/Norreys' as 'the northerners' and 'de Leth C(h)oin
trestut les rois' as 'all the kings of Leath Cuinn'. Now, it appears to me
that the author of *The Song* knew what Leath Cuinn meant, and knew that
by definition it *included* 'the northerners', and that what he is doing here is
making a distinction between two quite separate groups, one of which is
'les Norreis/Norreys', the other 'de Leth C(h)oin trestut les rois': and if
they are distinct, then 'Norreis/Norreys' must mean something other than
'northerners'. Elsewhere in the poem the author uses the word 'Norwiche'
to mean Norway,[33] and there must be a real possibility that by 'Norreis/
Norreys' he means 'Norse', or, given the contemporary haziness about the
region (a Welsh source of similar date refers to the Hebrides as 'the islands
of Denmark'),[34] he is referring to warriors drawn from somewhere in the
Scoto-Scandinavian world. If their leader is Mac Scelling/Scilling, and if
he is a son of Sumarliði – admittedly, a lot of 'ifs' – then it can be posited
that Ruaidhri Ó Conchobhair had indeed procured Hebridean military
support at this point.

We know that at least two of Ruaidhri's sons followed suit. After
Ruaidhri was deposed as king of Connacht, his sons and grandsons vied
for the kingship with Ruaidhri's younger brother, Cathal Croibhdhearg. It
was a contest from which Cathal emerged victorious, but Ruaidhri's
offspring, sons of the last highking of Ireland, did not easily resign themselves to permanent exclusion from power. Hence, the annals record that
Toirdhealbhach son of Ruaidhri (d. 1239) gave his daughter Beanmhidhe
(d. 1269) in marriage to Maolmhuire, a member of Clann Suibhne of
Knapdale in Kintyre:[35] one presumes that the marriage had political
implications, and that Toirdhealbhach hoped that some of his new son-in-
law's fighting-men would be committed to action arising from the alliance,
in order to bolster his grip on the kingship of Connacht which, with the
aid of Aodh Méith Ó Néill of Tír Eoghain, he had managed to seize
briefly in 1225.[36]

32 *Song of Dermot* (Mullally), ll. 3258–9, 3268–9.   33 Ibid., ll. 2262, 2266.   34 See D. Simon
Evans (ed.), *A medieval prince of Wales. The life of Gruffud ap Cynan* (Lampeter, 1990), passim;
see also, Seán Duffy, 'Ostmen, Irish and Welsh in the eleventh century', *Peritia*, 9 (1995),
378–96.   35 *AC*, 1269.   36 *AC*, 1225.

Another of Ruaidhri's sons, Diarmait, went to greater lengths, the annals reporting for 1221 that he 'was coming from the Isles, and he assembling a fleet [in order] to take the kingship of Connacht (*ag teacht a hInnsi Gall, 7 é ag tinól chabhlaigh do ghabhail righe Connacht*)', when disaster struck because the fleet was attacked by Thomas of Galloway, and Diarmait was killed.[37] Despite its failure, this enterprising exploit is proof that when Cathal Croibhdhearg's grandson Aodh na nGall Ó Conchobhair (as mentioned above) enlisted the support of what were, for all intents and purposes, galloglass in 1259, as part of a marriage-alliance with Dubhghall mac Ruaidhri of Clann Somhairle, he was not the first aspirant to the kingship of Connacht to contemplate such action: indeed, Aodh na nGall might well have been an also-ran in the race for power if, more than a third of a century earlier, his father's first-cousins, Toirdhealbhach and Diarmait, sons of King Ruaidhri Ó Conchobhair, had accomplished their goal of securing and retaining the Connacht kingship by deploying, and apparently not for the first time, galloglass-type Hebridean warriors on the battlefields of the west of Ireland.

The cause of Diarmait's quarrel (if quarrel it was – it certainly had a deadly outcome) with Thomas of Galloway is not immediately apparent. It may just be relevant that the man whom Diarmait Ó Conchobhair wished to oust from the kingship of Connacht, his uncle Cathal Croibhdhearg, employed throughout this period, as did his son and successor Aodh, as one of their most senior household officers (their *reachtaire* or, in Latin, *senescallus*),[38] a man with a name Latinized in a charter as Torbertus and appearing in the Irish of the annals as Toirberd.[39] This is emphatically not a Gaelic name, and is otherwise unknown in Irish-language sources of this period, the annals, significantly, adding that his surname was 'mac Gallghaeidhil'. Although this could mean something like 'son of a "foreign-Irishman"' (that is, son of someone who was part Gael and part Gall) or son of an individual with the nickname Gallghaedheal, in light of his odd forename it seems more likely to be a reference to Galloway. When Thomas of Galloway's father Roland died in 1201, the annals describe him as *rí Gallgaidhel*, as they do in the case of Thomas's brother Alan in 1234.[40] This translates as 'king of the Gallowaymen', and hence Toirberd mac Gallghaeidhil's surname may be 'son of a Gallowayman'. The Four Masters amended the name to *mac rígh Gallghaeidhil*, 'son of *the king of*

---

37 *ALC* 1221; *AFM* 1220. 38 For the terms, see Katharine Simms, *From kings to warlords*, chap. VI, esp. pp 79–82; for Toirbert in particular, see ibid., pp 65, 71, 80. 39 For the charter, see Marie Therese Flanagan, *Irish royal charters. Texts and contexts* (Oxford, 2005), pp 349–55; for the annals, see *AFM* 1209 (recte 1210); *ALC* 1210, 1211; *AU* 1211. 40 *AU* 1201; *ALC* 1199 (recte 1201); *AU* 1234.

the Gallowaymen' but as nobody of the name Toirberd/Torbert(us) is attested in the ruling family of Galloway at this point, this seems to be without foundation. Perhaps the most we can say with safety is that it is a most curious coincidence that when Diarmait Ó Conchobhair, Cathal Croibhdhearg's nephew and enemy, was killed (while recruiting an invasion-fleet in the Isles) by a man called Thomas of Galloway, back in Connacht the overseer of Cathal's household was a man called Torbert, quite possibly, if not probably, also of Gallovidian extraction.

Thomas of Galloway maintained his own fleet of galleys which, from time to time, he put at the service of the kings of England, and for which he was well rewarded:[41] he was, in fact, a tenant of the crown in Ulster, where he was attempting to build up a presence in the Coleraine area.[42] Thomas appears on record in Ireland for the first time in 1212. He did so at the head of a motley invasion-fleet made up of seventy-six ships under his own command and that of two famous grandsons of Sumarliði, Ruaidhri mac Raghnaill (a quo the Mic Ruaidhri) and his brother, probably Domhnall (a quo the Mic Dhomhnaill).[43] Their target in 1212 was the ecclesiastical centre at Derry, where they wreaked great havoc. Derry was a Cineál Eoghain possession but during this period it and the entire Inishowen peninsula were the subject of dispute between the kings of Cineál Chonaill and Cineál Eoghain. The Irish poet Muireadhach Albanach Ó Dálaigh has left us a poem in which he flatters Cineál Conaill pretensions over the Inishowen area by calling its reigning king, Domhnall Mór Ó Domhnaill, 'rí Dhoire (king of Derry)'.[44] In this same poem Muireadhach refers to Cineál Chonaill connections with Scotland (requesting that he be allowed to return to Ireland on the first ship that Ó Domhnaill sends to Scotland). It is notable that when Thomas of Galloway and Clann Somhairle left Derry but continued their depredations in Inishowen, they were joined by the Cineál Chonaill.[45] The latter were clearly exploiting Hebridean and Gallovidian manpower in pursuit of their own local objective. In 1214, Thomas of Galloway and Ruaidhri mac Raghnaill again launched a crippling assault on Derry and seized from its church a valuable collection of ornaments and jewels.[46] If in their previous assault on the city they had the backing of the Cineál Chonaill, this time Thomas and Ruaidhri were

---

41 CDS, i, 357–60, 382, 405, 409, 426, 442, 497.   42 CDI, i, 564–5, 567; CDS, i, 625–7.   43 It was perhaps this alliance with Thomas and, accordingly, his older brother Alan, lord of Galloway and constable of Scotland, that caused Ruaidhri to name one of his sons Alan, well known for his role as the first named commander of galloglass in Ireland (AC 1259). 44 Printed in Brian Ó Cuív, 'Eachtra Mhuireadhaigh Uí Dhálaigh', Studia Hibernica, 1 (1961), 56–69 (at p. 61).   45 AU 1212 (ALC; AFM 1211).   46 AU 1214 (ALC; AFM 1213).

either employed by or had the support of the Uí Chatháin of Fir na Craoibhe, who launched an all but simultaneous attack on the city.[47]

Two years later, in 1216, the chief of Cineál Fhearghusa, a small territory in the northwest of the Inishowen peninsula, was killed (we are not told where), along with his brothers and many others, by Muireadhach, a son of the earl of Lennox in Scotland.[48] The annalist offers not a hint of explanation as to why the son of a Scottish earl should do battle with an Inishowen dynast, so there is room for speculation. According to a legend stitched into the Annals of the Four Masters, the poet Muireadhach Ó Dálaigh was banished from Ireland in 1213 for a crime against Domhnall Mór Ó Domhnaill, king of Tír Chonaill. He fled to Scotland (hence his soubriquet *Albanach*) where he spent a lengthy period in exile and apparently founded the Scottish bardic family of MacMhuirich. He appears to have found refuge in the Lennox, with its ruling family,[49] and since his forename, Muireadhach, is one already found in the family of the earls of Lennox, this may suggest an earlier Ó Dálaigh family association with the rulers of the area.[50] It is possible, therefore, in light of Muireadhach Albanach's links with both Tír Chonaill and the Lennox, that the lords of the latter were involved with Cineál Chonaill in their effort to subdue Inishowen to their sway. And therefore the Muireadhach, son of the earl of Lennox, who killed the chief of Cineál Fhearghusa in 1216, may have been in Inishowen in consequence of a recruitment-campaign in Scotland by the ambitious Domhnall Mór Ó Domhnaill.

The evidence, scattered and uncertain as it is, is sufficient to suggest that a close affinity existed in this age between certain forces within Ireland and those whose affairs dominated society in western Scotland and the Isles. That relationship had been placed under threat after the creation of a strong Anglo-Norman state with pretensions to rule throughout Britain and Ireland. Irish prospects of obtaining hegemony over the Isles (such as that wielded by the Leinster and Munster kings a hundred years or more earlier, through their involvement with Dublin)[51] had receded. But other forms of contact were maintained and may actually have increased. The fractious nature of power in later medieval Ireland meant that even the smaller fry could have access to such advantages as Hebridean mercenaries, an access which was perhaps denied them in the days when diplomatic channels were monopolized by the provincial kings.

---

47 *AU* 1214.   48 *AU* 1216 (*AFM*; *ALC* 1215).   49 Derick S. Thomson, 'The MacMhuirich bardic family', *Trans. Gaelic Society of Inverness*, 43 (1960–3), 276–304 (at pp 280–1).   50 For his Lennox verse, see Lambert McKenna, *Athdioghluim dána. A miscellany of Irish bardic poetry*, 2 vols (London, 1939–40), no. 42; RIA MS 743 (A iv 3), p. 863; Ó Cuív, 'Eachtra Mhuireadhaigh Uí Dhálaigh', 67.   51 For which, see Duffy, 'Irishmen and Islesmen'.

For instance, an annal-entry for 1213 preserved only by An Dubhaltach Mac Fhirbhisigh, records that the petty king of Tír Amhalghaidh (Tirawley in Co. Mayo), Donnchadh Ó Dubhda (a successor to Cosnamhach Ó Dubhda, who featured in the 1154 naval expedition against Muircheartach Mac Lochlainn discussed above), brought from the Isles a fleet of 56 ships, and so managed to wrest his lands free from the tribute imposed by Cathal Croibhdhearg Ó Conchobhair:

Donnchadh Ua Dubhda go g-cobhlach 56 long á h-Innsibh Gall, gut ghabh cuan I n-Inis Raithin ar Insibh Modh, i n-Umhall, gur bhean a fhearoinn fén soar gan chain do Chathal Chraoibh-dherg Ua Concabhair.

Donnchadh Ó Dubhda [sailed] with a fleet of 56 ships from the Western Isles, and landed on Inishraher, one of the Innse Modh [Clew Bay islands], in the Owles, and wrested his own land free of tribute from Cathal Croibhdhearg Ó Conchobhair.[52]

If true, and Mac Fhirbhisigh is a reputable source, it demonstrates the effectiveness of the Insular input into Irish warfare even at that stage. Were we to halve the annalist's claim that Donnchadh recruited a fleet of 56 ships, and to assume a complement of, let us say, no more than ten men per vessel, one could have something in the region of 250 Hebridean troops in north Connacht in 1213, successfully assisting the lord of Tír Amhalghaidh in challenging the claim to tribute (cáin) being made by the provincial overking. That the mission proved a success is testimony to the strength and effectiveness of the forces enlisted. Surely this represents archetypal galloglass activity in west Connacht almost a half-century before Aodh na nGall Ó Conchobhair's famous dowry-grant of 160 óglaigh in 1259.

Several years later, in 1221, Donnchadh's successor, Maol Ruanaidh Ó Dubhda, was also in the Western Isles, as part of Diarmait Ó Conchobhair's ill-fated expedition there. The operation proved to be devastating also for Maol Ruanaidh Ó Dubhda who, the annals tell us, 'drowned while assembling the same fleet (do badhad ac tinól in cabhlaigh cedna)'.[53] But the Uí Dhubhda seem to have maintained their links with the Isles. In 1246, when their chief killed an Ó Conchobhair he 'was banished overseas after that murder (do indarba tar muir d'eis in marbta-sin)'.[54] One can only presume that if exiled 'overseas' from his patrimonial lands in northwest Mayo, he headed for the Western Isles. In the following

52 The genealogies, tribes and customs of Hy-Fiachrach, commonly called O'Dowda's Country, ed. John O'Donovan (IAS, Dublin, 1844), p. 302: O'Donovan proposed that Mac Fhirbhisigh obtained the entry from the lost 'Annals of Lecan'.   53 O'Donovan (ed.), Tribes and customs of Hy-Fiachrach, p. 302.   54 AC; ALC; AFM 1246.

year, the Annals of Connacht record that '*longes mor do techt d'h. Dubda 7 d'h. Baigill*'; the editor suggests that *do techt*, 'came to', may be a scribal error for something like *do timsugad*, and hence has translated the entry to the effect that 'a great fleet was collected by' Ó Dubhda and Ó Baoighill.[55] But there is surely no need to mistrust the text here, and every likelihood that this 'great fleet' came from the Isles to Ó Dubhda and his ally, Ó Baoighill, an under-king of Tír Chonaill; they plundered Carbury in Co. Sligo, although the annals note that the crew of one of the ships was drowned.

Some months if not weeks before Diarmait Ó Conchobhair sailed to the Hebrides, in November 1220, the then king of Man and the Isles, Rögnvaldr Guðrøðarson (Raghnaill mac Gofraidh) had informed Henry III of a menace that imperilled him: the king of Norway, his letter states, 'lays snares for him and threatens his land with evil' because he had rendered homage to the English king.[56] There is no evidence that the appearance of Diarmait Ó Conchobhair in the Western Isles shortly thereafter was connected to this Norwegian harassment and, it seems, suspected invasion, but it is not impossible that it was (just as Diarmait's cousin, Aodh na nGall Ó Conchobhair, hearing of the arrival in the Isles in 1263 of King Hákon IV of Norway, tried to procure his aid).[57] King Rögnvaldr's concerns about a Norwegian threat were not confined to him alone and were shared in England, where they were combined with worries that Hugh de Lacy, who had been personally ejected from his earldom of Ulster by King John ten years earlier, was about to seek to recover it by force.[58] As it transpired, Hugh's bid for power did not begin until the latter half of the year 1223.[59] At this point, the Scots queen informed her brother Henry III that the king of Norway was rumoured to be planning an assault on Ireland in the summer of 1224 to help de Lacy.[60]

Now, Thomas of Galloway, and his older brother Alan, were intent upon keeping Hugh de Lacy out in the cold because they had acquired a substantial share of the earldom of Ulster after his forfeiture. And in or after September 1224, Alan of Galloway wrote to Henry III, saying that he had been in the Western Isles, going from island to island with his army in his galleys, ready to cross to Ireland, when, on the very eve of sailing, a

55 *AC* 1247 (pp 92–3). 56 *CDI*, i, 976. 57 See the 'Frisbôk' *Haakon Haakonsson's saga*, in Anderson, *Early sources*, ii, 611, 617, 625–6, 635. 58 For some skilfully textured insights into the de Lacy manoeuvrings at this point, see Robin Frame, 'Aristocracies and the political configuration of the British Isles', in R.R. Davies (ed.), *The British Isles: contrasts, comparisons and connections* (Edinburgh, 1988), pp 141–59 (at pp 147–9). 59 For a discussion, see James Lydon, 'The expansion and consolidation of the colony, 1215–54', in *NHI*, ii, 158–9. 60 *CDI*, i, 1179; *CDS*, i, 852 (dated *c.*Mar./Apr. 1224).

messenger arrived with the news that an agreement had been reached between the king's justiciar of Ireland and Hugh de Lacy. As a result, Alan states, he did not cross to Ireland, but, in view of his preparedness to do so, sought confirmation of his and his brother's Ulster lands.[61] One of the important points to note here is that Alan of Galloway implies that his perambulations about the Western Isles were indicative of his good faith, were, in other words, a sign of his opposition to Hugh de Lacy. This seems to mean that the latter was expected to make his return to power in Ulster using Hebridean manpower. We do not know whether Hugh did enlist Hebridean support. Queen Joan of Scotland, in her letter to Henry III, had stated that her husband Alexander II had told her that 'he did not wish any of his horse or foot to go from Scotland to Ireland to injure the [English] king's subjects, and any who did so should if possible be intercepted and punished',[62] but this is unlikely either to have referred to Islesmen or, if it did, to have had much effect. What we *can* say is that de Lacy sailed to Ulster possibly as early as the summer of 1223, and conducted a vigorous campaign that lasted over a year until October 1224; at some stage he joined forces with the north's most powerful Irish king, Aodh Méith Ó Néill, and together they targeted the lands of their mutual enemies, including Thomas of Galloway's castle at Coleraine; we also know that Hugh besieged Carrickfergus Castle by land and sea, a siege in which he deployed the services of eight vessels in an unsuccessful attempt to prevent its relief.[63] De Lacy may or may not have procured these vessels and their crews in the Isles, but, at the least, Alan of Galloway's petition for a reward for time spent navigating his way from island to island in the Hebrides, suggests that that is where contemporaries *expected* Hugh to have looked for military and naval assistance.

The Connacht chronicler, writing over a decade later, observed that since Hugh de Lacy's invasion of 1223–4 pillage and lawlessness had been the order of the day: 'frequent assaults and routs on the churches by Irishmen and foreigners, and churches used as dormitories this year and for the space of twelve years ever since [de Lacy's and] Ó Néill's war; Irishmen and foreigners plundering by turns; no kingship or government, but Connacht lying open for foreigners to ruin whenever they come into it'.[64] By the late 1240s that situation had worsened further. We are told that a '*cocad mór* (great war)' was waged in Connacht in 1247 led by Toirdhealbhach Ó Conchobhair, nephew of the reigning King Feidhlimidh.[65]

61 *CDI*, i, 1218; *CDS*, i, 890 (dated shortly after 8 September 1224). 62 *CDI*, i, no. 1179; *CDS*, i, no. 852. 63 G.H. Orpen, *Ireland under the Normans, 1169–1333*, 4 vols (Oxford, 1911–20), iii, p. 43 (rpr. in one vol., Dublin, 2005), p. 302. 64 *AC* 1236. 65 *AC* 1247.

Other princes then joined in the general uprising that ensued. It was a war on a slightly more destructive scale than previously: 'the foreigners of Connacht had not experienced for many a long year the like of the war these sons of kings waged against them in this year, for they did not forbear to ravage a single tract or territory of the foreigners of Connacht'.[66]

In that same year, 1247, Maurice fitz Gerald, to whom Hugh de Lacy had granted the manor of Sligo and what was in effect an exploratory licence to conquer the lands of Fir Manach and Cineál Chonaill, led an invasion of the latter. His army, a large force by all accounts, made it only as far as Ballyshannon on the Erne where a standoff ensued for an entire week. When both sides finally came to blows, the annals record that:

… marbthur Maelsechlainn h. Domnaill ri Ceneoil Conaill ann sin 7 in Gilla Muinelach h. Baigill 7 Mac Somurli ri Airir Gaidil 7 maithi Ceneoil Conaill archena.

Maoilsheachlainn Ó Domhnaill, king of Cineál Chonaill, was killed there and An Giolla Muinealach Ó Baoighill, and Mac Somhairle, king of Argyll, and the nobles of Cineál Chonaill as well.[67]

Doubt remains as to the precise identity of the Mac Somhairle killed in the battle of Ballyshannon,[68] but for the purposes of this essay that uncertainty is neither here nor there. The only points that matter are that nobody doubts that the man killed at Ballyshannon in 1247 was a descendent of Sumarliði, most probably (in light of the latter's not overly premature death in 1164) a grandson. Most probably too, he was a man of some importance: granted, Irish annalists were generous in bestowing titles in their obits, but not excessively so, and if they deemed Mac Somhairle to be 'king of Argyll' we can take it that he was one of the most formidable contemporary figures in the West Highlands and Islands, and certainly somebody with a convincing claim to lordship there. And this brings us to another point: the annal-entry for 1247 that notes Mac Somhairle's death is almost matter-of-fact about it, but not because he was a figure of little consequence. The notice of his death, as quoted above, follows immediately on that of the deaths of Ó Domhnaill and Ó Baoighill (one of the latter's principal under-kings), which were events of great regional magnitude. Mac Somhairle's death is treated in precisely the same way: it was the demise of, in contemporary eyes, a great man, but, much more importantly than that, it was not something that required explanation. As far as the annalist was concerned, no further elaboration was needed. And that can only mean that Hebridean lords and, of course,

---

66 *AC; ALC; AFM* 1247.   67 *ALC; AC; AFM, AU* 1247.   68 See chapter 4 below.

the armed and naval forces they commanded were, by 1247, a quotidian feature of warfare in the northwest of Ireland.

Following his death at Ballyshannon in the company of an unidentified member of Clann Somhairle, Maoilsheachlainn Ó Domhnaill was succeeded by his brother Gofraidh (interestingly, a borrowing of the Norse name Guðrøðr) and he in turn by a third brother, Domhnall Óg Ó Domhnaill.[69] One of the latter's two wives was a daughter of Aonghus Mór, son of Sumarliði's grandson Domhnall (*a quo* Clann Domhnaill).[70] Just *when* this family alliance began is impossible to say. But on 13 February 1256 the English king ordered his officials 'not to allow Aonghus mac Domhnaill or other Scottish malefactors, whose names the king of Scots will communicate, to be received in Ireland'.[71] The instruction was to remain valid for seven years, which was the length of time the fourteen-year-old king of Scots needed to reach maturity. Since it was the latter, Alexander III, who was to supply the names of these troublemakers, he – being a minor and in a vulnerable position – was perhaps the one for whom they were making trouble, the one who had something to fear should they find friends in Ireland. But this is mere conjecture. It is just as plausible that Alexander's father-in-law, Henry III, had got word that Aonghus Mór and others were making mischief in Ireland and had asked King Alexander for a list of names of the likely suspects. If this is the case, one can only suppose that by the mid-1250s Aonghus mac Domhnaill and his men were providing military service to their Irish associates, and serving to undermine the English position in Ireland in the manner that galloglass would before long assume.

Aonghus Mór, judging by the evidence of a poem written for him not long after his succession, was no stranger to Ireland. The poet, in fact, makes direct allusion to the subject: 'Thou hast come round Ireland; rare is the strand whence thou hast not taken cattle'. He continues:

To Lough Foyle, to Erris [Co. Mayo], thy path is straight from the Hebrides:
the haven of Erris, 'tis a true preparation, thou hast found the host of Islay there.

The host of Islay has been with thee beside Aran, to test their shooting as far as Loch Con [Co. Mayo]:
that fair host of Islay takes cattle from smooth Innse Modh [in Clew Bay].

69 For a history of the Uí Dhomhnaill in these and later years, see Katharine Simms, 'Late medieval Donegal' in *Donegal: history and society*, ed. W. Nolan, L. Ronayne and M. Dunlevy (Dublin, 1995), pp 183–202.   70 Paul Walsh, 'O Donnell genealogies', *Analecta Hibernica*, 8 (1938), 377.   71 *CDS*, i, 2041; *CDI*, ii, 490.

Corcomroe [Co. Clare] thy fleet has reached, Corca Bascinn beside it:
from Bun Gaillmhe [Co. Galway] to Cúil Chnámha [Co. Sligo] thou art a salmon that
searches every strand.

Elsewhere in the poem Aonghus is called 'champion of the Bann', 'lion of
Loch Cé', 'king of Tuam', 'lord of Fál', and 'scion of Tara'.[72] Even
allowing for exaggeration, Aonghus mac Domhnaill was obviously a man
with a reputation in Ireland. The catalogue of places along Ireland's west
coast is perhaps not quite the usual *caithréim* (or list of the dedicatee's
battle-triumphs) found in such poems, but it is nevertheless indicative of a
career spent scouring the Irish coast in pursuit of plunder. Judging from
the targets, though, it may be worth considering whether Aonghus's
activity amounted to more than indiscriminate hit-and-miss: several of the
locations were the scenes of recent English attempts at settlement, and it
is not beyond the bounds of possibility that Aonghus was engaged by
some Irish comrade-in-arms to challenge the colonization of these areas.[73]

In 1258, what at first sight appears to be just the sort of piratical raid
described in the poem to Aonghus Mór took place along Connacht's coast.
As with the battle of Ballyshannon in 1247, the annals supply no more
precise name for its leader than the patronymic 'Mac Somhairle'. He came
with a great fleet from the Hebrides (*longus mór do tocht a hInsib Gall*),
sailing around the west coast as far as Connemara, where he robbed a
merchant ship of her goods. The English settlers in the area were the
victims of the assault and it was the sheriff of Connacht, Jordan d'Exeter,
who took to the seas to oppose Mac Somhairle. The Islesmen, having put
ashore on an island, were challenged to battle by d'Exeter, who was killed
along with many of his men, and Mac Somhairle 'went back to his land,
joyful and laden with spoil'.[74] Annalists seldom place events in their
context, and this episode may well be no more than a random old-
fashioned Viking-style raid. However, the very next entry in the annals is
the following:

Aodh mac Feidhlimidh [Ó Conchobhair] and Tadhg Ó Briain held a great meeting with
Brian Ó Néill at Caol Uisce, where they all concluded a peace and gave the kingship of the
Irish of Ireland to Brian Ó Néill (*rige do thabairt ar Gaidelaib Erenn do Brian h. Neill*).[75]

This gathering at Caol Uisce on the Erne, which saw the son of the king
of Thomond (heir to Brian Bóroimhe and the Ó Briain highkings) and the
son of the king of Connacht (successor to the Ó Conchobhair highkings)

72 Bergin, *Irish bardic poetry*, no. 45.   73 Orpen, *Ireland under the Normans*, iii, pp 190–251=pp
377–408 (2005 edn).   74 *AC* 1258.

abandon their claim to 'the kingship of the Irish of Ireland' in favour of
Brian Ó Néill, has rightly been viewed as a major development.[76] It must
have taken quite some negotiation, planning, and time, and was part of a
broad programme of action by the parties concerned. Ó Néill and
Feidhlimidh Ó Conchobhair's son Aodh na nGall had been allies since
1255, when the latter undertook a mission to Tír Eoghain 'and made peace
between his own father and the north of Ireland'.[77] Together they cooper-
ated in an assertion of Ó Conchobhair suzerainty over Bréifne;[78] as for
Ó Néill, it was part of Brian's aim to annex the former kingdom of Ulaid,
now largely subsumed into the earldom of Ulster, and he had the support
of Aodh na nGall Ó Conchobhair in attempting to do so.

It is hard to believe that the appearance of 'Mac Somhairle' off the
Galway coast – where he was so stoutly opposed by the Connacht settlers
that the sheriff of Connacht lost his life in the confrontation – was not
somehow connected with the Caol Uisce assembly of that same year. And
the probability must be that the member of Clann Somhairle in question
was Aonghus mac Domhnaill's first-cousin, Dubhghall mac Ruaidhri of
Garmoran. This is because, from an annal-entry of the following year,
1259, we get firm evidence of Dubhghall's association with both Ó Néill
and Ó Conchobhair, when he disembarked at Derry, the chief port of
Ó Néill's kingdom, with his daughter and a contingent of 160 warriors
(*óglaigh*) led by his brother Alan. There they were met by Aodh na nGall
Ó Conchobhair who had travelled all the way from Connacht for the
occasion: Aodh married the daughter, and received the warriors as
dowry.[79] This marriage alliance and dowry settlement were, likewise,
arrangements that called for considerable preparation and coordination,
and one assumes that some of the groundwork was lain at the time of the
naval expedition to Connacht by 'Mac Somhairle' the previous year.

Within a matter of months, on 14 May 1260, all of their preparations
and plans turned to dust when Brian Ó Néill advanced the armies of the
North and West of Ireland on the city of Down, only to meet with
catastrophe when confronted in the field by the English settlers of the
locality;[80] Brian himself lay among the slain, along with many of the
under-kings and lords of Leath Cuinn, and Irish plans were set at nought.

It was in the spring of that year, 1260, that Alexander III took full
personal control of the government of Scotland.[81] One of his first acts
upon doing so was to dispatch a letter to Henry III seeking help in dealing

75 *AC* 1258.   76 The pioneer in this regard was Eoin Mac Néill, *Phases of Irish history* (Dublin, 1919), pp 330–1.   77 *AC* 1255.   78 *ALC* 1255; *AC* 1256.   79 *ALC*; *AC* 1259.   80 Orpen, *Ireland under the Normans*, iii, p. 275=p. 419 (2005 edn).   81 A.A.M. Duncan, *Scotland: the making of the kingdom* (Edinburgh, 1975), p. 576.

with a pressing problem. We do not know the contents of the letter, but we have Henry's response, dated 29 April 1260, just over a fortnight before the battle of Down, which was to order the Irish justiciar not to permit 'persons from Scotland to be received in Ireland to the King of Scots' damage'; if he found any people 'seeking confederacies with the Irish or compassing other damages against said king [of Scots]', he was to arrest them and keep them in custody until further orders.[82] The array of Irish kings and lords who lined up behind Ó Néill two weeks later (from Ulster, Ó Catháin, Ó hAnluain, Mac Lochlainn, Mac Cana, Ó Goirmleadhaigh, Ó Cairre, Ó hInndheirghe; and from Connacht, Ó Conchobhair, Mac Diarmata, Ó Maolruanaidh, Ó Gadhra, Mac Donnchadha, Ó Cuinn, and Ó Muireadhaigh)[83] was such that the campaign, disastrous as it was, must have been weeks if not months in the planning. In all probability, therefore, Henry's letter refers to those plans, and to the involvement of men from Scotland in Brian Ó Néill's campaign to annex the earldom of Ulster by taking its capital, Down.

Did Ó Néill have what was effectively galloglass support at the battle of Down? There is no evidence to this effect, although Aodh na nGall Ó Conchobhair was present and presumably deployed the best weapon in his arsenal, the 160 *óglaigh* under the command of Alan mac Ruaidhri that had come into Aodh's service in the previous year. For what it is worth, one might also mention at this point that according to a late genealogical tract on the Uí Mhórdha of Laoighis, Brian Ó Néill married Julia, daughter of John Campbell, earl of Lorne and prince of Argyll.[84] We can no doubt dismiss the Campbell connection as they had yet to come to prominence, but the ruler of Lorne at this juncture *was* a John, that is, Eoghan son of Donnchadh mac Dubhghaill (*a quo* Clann Dubhghaill), and it is just possible that the tract preserves a garbled recollection of a marriage between Brian Ó Néill and Eoghan Mac Dubhghaill's daughter.[85] There exists also another source that claims that Brian was married to Egidia, daughter of Donnchadh mac Dubhghaill.[86] Whether these dubious traditions reveal anything about the possible deployment of West Highland manpower at the battle of Down it is quite impossible to say and most unsafe to conjecture. Nonetheless, one cannot underestimate the significance of Alexander III's letter to Henry III in April 1260, and the

---

82 *CDI*, ii, 652; *CDS*, i, 2185. 83 *AC*; *AFM*; *ALC*; *AU* 1260; *Misc. Ir. annals* 1261 (recte 1260). 84 D. O'Byrne, *History of Queen's County* (Dublin, 1854), p. 94. 85 See M.K. Simms, 'Gaelic lordships in Ulster in the later Middle Ages' (unpublished PhD thesis, University of Dublin, 1976), ii, 663. 86 W.D.H. Sellar, 'Hebridean sea kings: the successors of Somerled, 1164–1316', in *Alba: Celtic Scotland in the medieval era*, ed. E.J. Cowan and R.A. McDonald (East Linton, 2000), p. 202.

latter's response, both of which suggest that recent developments in Ulster were a cause of deep concern to the Scots king. And the implication appears to be that the achievement of Ó Néill's ambition would have had damaging repercussions for Scotland as much as for England, arising directly from the identity of the men from Scotland who were seeking 'confederacies' with the Irish rebels.

One Scottish family who may have been a cause of worry to Alexander were the Mic Suibhne of Knapdale in Argyll. They had recently been ejected from Knapdale, with Scottish royal backing, by the Stewarts of Menteith. Maurice fitz Gerald (d. 1257) had capitalized on his victory at Ballyshannon in 1247, in which Mac Somhairle king of Argyll had died, by persevering in the effort to conquer the far northwest of Ireland. But at the very point of Maurice's death in 1257 the Geraldine advance into the northwest was forestalled by the defeat of their forces at Credrán (near Drumcliff, Co. Sligo) by Gofraidh Ó Domhnaill, king of Cineál Chonaill.[87] In the following year Gofraidh died of the wounds he received in the battle,[88] and was replaced by his brother, Domhnall Óg. The Four Masters have an elaborate and highly fictionalized account of the youth's arrival in Tír Chonaill from Scotland, announcing in Scottish Gaelic (*san nGaoidilcc nAlbanaigh*) his intention of defending his people from the onslaughts of their enemies. The story is a legend incorporated into the text in order to glorify the deeds of the Uí Dhomhnaill, but the kernel is probably true: that Domhnall Óg was fostered in Scotland. A contemporary poem written by Giolla Bhrighde Mac Con Midhe to commemorate his accession, while confirming that Domhnall Óg did indeed return to Tír Chonaill from overseas (*táinig don chuan a-muigh macámh*), adds that he was reared with the Mic Suibhne in Scotland: 'since the young ox of Bruidhean Dá Bhearg was reared in Suibhne's house in the east (*ó do tógbhadh i dtoigh Suibhne/ toir ógdhamh Bruidhne Dá Bhearg*)'.[89] And it may be of significance that within a decade of Domhnall Óg's return from his foster-home in Knapdale, Clann Suibhne make their first recorded appearance in Ireland: Murchadh Mac Suibhne was captured by an Ó Conchobhair somewhere in the Owles, Co. Mayo, and handed over to the English lord of Connacht (and, since 1263, earl of Ulster), Walter de Burgh, in whose prison Murchadh later died.[90] If, since 1258, Domhnall Óg Ó Domhnaill had been providing a haven in northwest Ireland for members of Clann Suibhne, it may have been the coalition of these two families that the Scots king sought to undermine in 1260.

---

87 *AC* 1257. 88 *AC* 1258. 89 *The poems of Giolla Brighde Mac Con Midhe*, ed. N.J.A. Williams (London, 1980), no. VII, qtt. 2, 22. 90 *AC*; *AFM*; *ALC*, 1267.

If Alexander III feared this development, his reasons for doing so are fairly transparent: they had to do with his attempts to extend royal authority over the western seaboard of Scotland and the Isles.[91] And there were others who stood in the way of this project. The reigning king of Man and the Isles was Magnus son of Óláfr *Dubh*, who had successfully invaded the Isle of Man in 1252 and was proclaimed king; but he appears to have done so with Irish support. On 14 November 1251 Henry III informed the justiciar of Ireland, that 'Magnus Mac Olave Duff proposed to raise a force in Ireland to invade the territory of the king of Norway in the Isle of Man', and ordered him to prevent any force leaving Ireland for that purpose.[92] One can only assume that the justiciar proved unable to do so, and that Magnus managed to set himself up in Man using Irish arms. At some date in 1252 the justiciar came north, rebuilt the castle of Magh Cóbha in Iveagh, Co. Down, and forced Brian Ó Néill into submission.[93] This expedition, coming within months of the royal instruction to prevent Magnus's invasion of Man, was either an attempt to pre-empt it, or a punishment attack on Magnus's Irish supporters.[94]

But by 1260 the young and energetic Alexander III sought nothing short of the annexation of Magnus's kingdom, and the latter's Irish allies presumably stood in the way. If those allies included the loose coalition of forces put together by Brian Ó Néill, it soon became clear that they also included Dubhghall mac Ruaidhri of Garmoran and his brother Alan. The Scots opened negotiations with the Norse, sending an embassy to Bergen in 1261, in the hope of persuading them to cede the Isles peacefully; when this failed, they invaded Skye in the following year.[95] The Islesmen reported to Hákon IV of Norway what was most assuredly the case, 'that the Scottish king intended to lay under himself all the Hebrides'.[96] It was in response to these displays of Scottish intentions, and in an effort to prevent them coming to fruition, that Hákon IV made his expedition to the Western Isles in 1263.[97] From an Irish perspective, one of the most remarkable things about Hákon's western expedition is this: we only know the identity of three Islesmen who supported him without reservation, and all three were heavily involved in Irish affairs –

---

91 *CDS*, i, 2157.   92 *CDI*, i, 3206.   93 *AU*; G.H. Orpen, 'The earldom of Ulster', *RSAI Jn.*, 43 (1913), 35.   94 For Brian Ó Néill's career, see Katharine Simms, 'The O'Hanlons, O'Neills and the Anglo-Normans in thirteenth-century Armagh', *Seanchas Ard Mhacha*, 9 (1978–9), 78–82.   95 According to the saga of Hákon Hákonarson, printed in translation in Anderson, *Early sources*, ii, pp 601–2, 605; see also, A.A.M. Duncan and A.L. Brown, 'Argyll and the Isles in the early Middle Ages', *PSAS*, 90 (1956–7), 212–13.   96 The 'Frisbók' *Haakon Haakonsson's saga*, in Anderson, *Early sources*, ii, 605.   97 See E.J. Cowan, 'Norwegian sunset – Scottish dawn: Hakon IV and Alexander III', in *Scotland in the reign of Alexander III*, ed. N.H. Reid (Edinburgh, 1997), 103–31.

King Magnus of Man who seems to have won his kingdom using Irish manpower, possibly supplied by Brian Ó Néill; Dubhghall mac Ruaidhri whose daughter was married to Aodh na nGall Ó Conchobhair, and the latter's brother, Alan, who was commander of Aodh's West Highland *óglaigh*. Of its very nature, their unequivocal support for Hákon is testimony to (indeed, a last-ditch attempt to prevent) Scottish expansion along the western seaboard. These are surely the men from Scotland whom Alexander III sought to prevent from reaching Ireland in the run-up to the battle of Down; and by inference, therefore, the Ó Néill-Ó Conchobhair confederacy was conspiring with them to thwart Alexander's plans.

Because Ó Néill was killed at Down, in the aftermath of that disaster Aodh na nGall Ó Conchobhair found it very difficult to maintain the supremacy over Bréifne which, with Ó Néill's help, he had won,[98] and it became an uphill struggle to withstand renewed pressure from the colonists.[99] The prospect of recruiting additional Scoto-Scandinavian military aid must have been tempting. When, therefore, King Hákon came west in 1263 to help Aodh na nGall's father-in-law, Dubhghall mac Ruaidhri, Ó Conchobhair seized his chance. Even after Hákon arrived in the Isles it was far from clear to observers just what his intentions were; it was by no means certain that he intended confining himself to pursuing his quarrel with the Scots king over the future of the Isles. One report that reached the English government in the summer stated that the Norse king and his fleet were now 'in the outer islands of Scotland, but where they are bound is not yet known'.[1] So, while the Norwegian king was in the Hebrides, 'messages reached him from Ireland, to the effect that the Irish offered to place themselves under his power, if he would rid them of the trouble to which English men had subjected them; because [the English] had then occupied all the best places by the sea'. Hákon then sent a Hebridean fleet to Ireland on a mission 'to discover on what grounds the Irish wished to call him thither'. When they returned, they 'told him that the Irish offered to maintain his whole army, until he freed them from the power of English men'. The Norse king was anxious to take up the offer, but was dissuaded from doing so by his army.[2] If this story is true, we can say with a good deal of confidence that the invitation to Hákon came from Aodh na nGall Ó Conchobhair of Connacht, for two reasons: first, because of their mutual allies, the Mic Ruaidhri, and second, because we have confirmation that there were indeed plans afoot to bring Hákon to

98 *AC* 1261.   99 *AC* 1262.   1 *CDS*, i, 2351; *Diplomatic documents preserved in the Public Records Office, vol. I, 1101–1272*, ed. Pierre Chaplais (London, 1964), 226–7: '... [rex] Norewaye cum magna multitudine navegii in forencecis insulis Scocye applicuit, set quo proponant divertere nondum scitur'.   2 Anderson, *Early sources*, ii, 622, 634.

Ireland, and that confirmation comes from the main corpus of Irish annals,[3] which were at this period compiled in Connacht. As is well known, Hákon's expedition ended in failure, and as winter approached he set about the journey back to Norway, but died unexpectedly in the Orkneys en route.[4] But the Connacht-based author of the annals instead reports that King Hákon died 'in the Orkneys on his way to Ireland (*a nInsib Gall Orc ar sligid ag techt a nErinn*)'.[5] Clearly the annalist was aware that a plan was afoot to bring the Norwegian king to Ireland (even if he had not heard news of its cancellation), and it is more than likely the case therefore that the plot to bring Hákon there was one that was hatched locally.

The proposal to bring the king of Norway to Ireland is one of the most innovative moves to emerge from Gaelic Ireland in the thirteenth century. One may perhaps conclude that the scheme had little to recommend it in the first place, and was doomed to failure. But of greater significance than the practicality of the thing is its motivation. Hákon IV, in coming west in 1263, had shown himself willing to collaborate with the rulers of Argyll and the Isles to withstand the aggrandizement of the king of Scots. It was an extension of that policy to assist the Islesmen's Irish allies in seeking to slow up, if not reverse, the expansion of the English colony in Ireland. The appeal to Hákon, on whomsoever's behalf it was made, demonstrates a breadth of vision not always discernible in the seemingly petty squabbles that have tarnished the reputations of most Irish rulers in that era. One would be foolish to imagine that the project had very widespread appeal – those who had swallowed past differences in rallying to Brian Ó Néill's banner shortly beforehand were probably its only supporters – but it does indicate that there were individuals in Ireland sufficiently despairing of the country's plight to contemplate radical solutions, and it likewise shows that some of them lifted their gaze from the ostensibly puny wranglings that clutter the pages of the annals, to set their sights on greater goals, goals that in effect included the overthrow of the English lordship of Ireland. It was in pursuit of that goal, and, admittedly, more local squabbles, that Gaelic Ireland thenceforward embraced – if it had ever been otherwise – the world of the galloglass.

3 *AC*; *ALC* 1263. 4 Anderson, *Early sources*, ii, 634. 5 *AC*; *ALC* 1263.

Moray, Ulster, and the MacWilliams[1]

ALASDAIR ROSS

Over the last 300 years historians have been united in agreement that the MacWilliam kindred were of royal descent from William fitz Duncan, son of King Donnchadh mac Maoil Choluim (Duncan II, 1094). Although various members of this kindred pressed their claim for inauguration as kings of Scotia over a number of decades between c.1180 and 1230, in historiography they have largely become relegated to the position of an annoyance in the inevitable 'progress' of the kingdom of Scotia, probably because they were not descended from St Margaret, but from the first wife of King Maol Choluim mac Donnchadha (Malcolm III, 1058–93), Queen Ingibjörg of Orkney.

Historians have also been united in linking the MacWilliams to Moray. The only recorded marriage of William fitz Duncan was to Alice de Rumilly, a Cumbrian heiress, with whom he had one son (also called William) and three daughters. Yet, it has been clear for some time that the MacWilliam kindred were not descended from Alice. In 1876 W.F. Skene suggested that William fitz Duncan had made a previous marriage to a Scottish woman.[2] G.W.S. Barrow then took this suggestion one stage further and argued that William fitz Duncan's first wife was a cousin or sister of Aonghus of Moray (d. 1130) and that their son, Domhnall Bán Mac Uilliam, thus inherited a better claim to the kingship through his mother as a descendant of King Lulach mac Giolla Chomhgháin (Lulach, 1058) than that which he received from his father. This suggestion answered two thorny problems. Firstly, it explained why William fitz Duncan was named *comes de Murray* in a thirteenth-century Cumbrian genealogy.[3] Presumably, he held the title by right of his wife. Secondly, it explained why Domhnall Bán Mac Uilliam possessed a claim to the earldom of Moray in the 1180s and why Moray was closely connected to the various MacWilliam risings.[4] This Barrovian thesis regarding the close links between the MacWilliams and Moray has held sway in historiography for

1 My thanks to Sonja Cameron and Richard Oram for reading this paper prior to publication and for making many helpful suggestions.   2 W.F. Skene, *Celtic Scotland: a history of ancient Alban*, 3 vols (Edinburgh, 1876–80), i, p. 477.   3 J. Wilson (ed.), *The register of the priory of St Bees* (Durham, 1915), p. 532.   4 G.W.S. Barrow (ed.) with W.W. Scott, *RRS*, ii, pp 12–13.

some numbers of years now and during the last decade its most prolific proponent, in both a number of articles and in a recent monograph, has been R. Andrew McDonald.[5]

Yet another popular theory is that the MacWilliams launched their various invasions of Scotia from Ireland. In 1993, for example, Keith Stringer remarked: '[...] it is difficult to resist the conclusion that the MacWilliams traditionally used Gaelic Ulster as a haven and a place where large bodies of troops could readily be recruited [...].'[6] While the latter point seems incontrovertible, there is still some doubt as to the actual role of Moravians in the MacWilliam invasions of north Britain and whether the MacWilliams were permanently based in Ulster as guests and allies of Cineál Eoghain between *c.*1179 and *c.*1230.

HISTORIOGRAPHY AND THE MAC WILLIAMS

Over the last 800 years or so many writers have been careful to stress the illegitimacy of the MacWilliam claim to the throne. These aspersions regarding the ancestry of William fitz Duncan actually first appear in an English source, *Gesta regum Anglorum* by William of Malmesbury, written *c.*1126, where King Donnchadh mac Maoil Choluim was described as *nothus*.[7] This description fed into a number of other works although it should be noted that later kings of Scotia never described William fitz Duncan's father in such terms in their own charters.[8] The reason behind this unexpected description of King Donnchadh mac Maol Choluim as *nothus* after *c.*1125 in an English source may have everything to do with the fact that he was not a son of King Maol Choluim mac Donnchadha and Queen Margaret, but a scion of King Maol Choluim mac Donnchadha's first marriage to Ingibjörg of Orkney. Given the continued English interest in and military support for the sons of Maol Choluim and Margaret, this labelling of King Donnchadh as a *nothus* in an English source is perhaps less than surprising and should probably be regarded as

5 For example, R. Andrew McDonald, 'Monk, bishop, imposter, pretender: the place of Wimund in twelfth-century Scotland', in *TGSI*, 58 (1993–4), 247–70; idem, 'Treachery in the remotest territories of Scotland: northern resistance to the Canmore dynasty, 1130–1230', in *Canadian Journal of History*, 33 (1999), 161–92; idem, *Outlaws of medieval Scotland: challenges to the Canmore kings, 1058–1266* (East Linton, 2003). 6 Keith J. Stringer, 'Periphery and core in thirteenth-century Scotland: Alan son of Roland, lord of Galloway and constable of Scotland', in Alexander Grant and Keith J. Stringer (eds), *Medieval Scotland: crown, lordship and community. Essays presented to G.W.S. Barrow* (Edinburgh, 1993), pp 82–113, at p. 87. 7 R.A.B. Mynors and Rodney M. Thomson (eds), *Gesta Regum Anglorum*, 2 vols (Oxford, 1998–9), i, p. 725. 8 For example, Cosmo Innes (ed.), *Registrum episcopatus Moraviensis* (Edinburgh, 1837), no. 36.

English-driven propaganda to ensure and advance the claims of just one
segment of the royal kindred of Scotia, the one descended from Queen
Margaret. It is also probably no coincidence that the claim regarding the
ancestry of William fitz Duncan appeared around the time of the
inauguration of David I in 1124, when David's right to be inaugurated
may have been challenged both by William fitz Duncan and Maol
Choluim, son of King Alexander I.[9]

Two later Scottish sources, *Gesta annalia I* and *Scotichronicon*, followed
William of Malmesbury. They justified their denigration of the MacWilliam
claims by asserting that the progenitor of the MacWilliam kindred,
Donnchadh mac Maoil Choluim, was a 'bastard son', and that it was
therefore absurd that any of his descendants should have considered themselves as suitable candidates for the kingship of Scotia.[10] The effects of
this propaganda continued to be felt in the nineteenth century and the
easiest method of disparaging the claims of the MacWilliam kindred was
to label them as 'impostors' and 'bastards' at every opportunity. Since
King Donnchadh mac Maoil Choluim was frequently called 'the bastard
king of Scotland',[11] this meant that his descendants became doubly damned:
they were the bastard sons and bastard grandsons of a bastard king.

As if allegations of bastardy were not bad enough, John Mair, writing
in the sixteenth century, introduced a new dimension to MacWilliam
historiography when he presented them as 'wild Scots' or Highlanders. In
his opinion, men like this were rebels and should be executed for their
actions.[12] Perhaps characteristically, Hector Boece also added some new
elements into the story when he discussed the MacWilliams: he stated that
these men lived as pirates in the Hebrides.[13] In addition, Boece made

9 For a re-evaluation of the career of Maol Choluim, son of King Alexander I, see Alasdair
Ross, 'The identity of the prisoner of Roxburgh: Malcolm son of Alexander or Malcolm
MacEth?' in S. Arbuthnot and K. Hollo (eds), *Fil súil nglais – a grey eye looks back: a festschrift
for Professor Colm Ó Baoill* (Clann Tuirc, 2007).   10 For example, W.F. Skene (ed.), *Johannis de
Fordun chronica gentis Scotorum* (Edinburgh, 1871–2) [*GA* 1], p. 268. The text of *Chronica gentis
Scotorum* has recently been re-examined by Dauvit Broun, in 'A new look at *Gesta annalia*
attributed to John of Fordun', in Barbara E. Crawford (ed.), *Church, chronicle and learning in
medieval and early Renaissance Scotland* (Edinburgh, 1999), pp 9–30. In this article Broun
convincingly demonstrates that the text of the work known as *Chronica gentis Scotorum* also
preserves two earlier texts that Broun called *Gesta annalia I* (completed before April 1285 but
probably based on an earlier Dunfermline work) and *Gesta annalia II* (completed by 1363).
Accordingly, only the first five books, together with the unfinished sixth book, of *Chronica gentis
Scotorum* are likely to have been Fordun's work, completed sometime between 1371 and the
mid–1380s. Consquently, I have chosen to use *Chron. Fordun (GA I)* when referring to the first
Gesta annalia section of *Chronica gentis Scotorum*.   11 George Chalmers, *Caledonia: or a
historical and topographical account of North Britain*, 8 vols (new ed., Paisley, 1887), ii, p. 631.
12 Archibald Constable (trans. and ed.), *A history of Greater Britain as well England as Scotland*
(Edinburgh, 1892), p. 166.   13 R.W. Chambers, E.C. Batho and H.W. Husbands (eds), *The*

absolutely no reference to the MacWilliams being members of the royal kindred who wanted to have their claims recognized. This must have had the effect, whether intentional or not, of greatly lowering the status of this segment of the royal kin-group. Because the MacWilliams had no special status in his history of Scotland, their efforts in opposing successive kings of Scotia became just one small part of a greater picture of recurring Highland unrest in Scotland.[14] It is possible that this is why John Leslie, for example, completely ignored the various members of the MacWilliam kindred in favour of other examples of Highland unrest. To him, the MacWilliam 'revolts' were obviously of no particular interest or significance.

In contrast to Leslie, George Buchanan included two MacWilliam 'revolts' in his work even though one of these was not directly associated with the MacWilliams by the author.[15] In addition, Buchanan rightly recognized that the MacWilliams had a claim to the throne and this would imply that he had checked Boece's version of events against either *Chronica gentis Scottorum* or Bower. Nevertheless, Buchanan also continued to describe the MacWilliam kindred as Hebridean pirates who raided Scotland from the sea. One final important adjustment made to MacWilliam 'history' by Buchanan was that his description of their piracy was shifted from the Hebrides and Ross into Moray. Perhaps not too much emphasis should be put on this change of scenery since Buchanan regarded the river Spey as the 'utmost boundary of Ross-shire'.[16] However, it is just possible that Buchanan was heavily influenced by the writings of Boece who had stated that a number of serious rebellions had occurred in Moray, virtually since recorded history had begun.

In fact, it must have made sense to many historians to associate closely Moravians and the MacWilliams since the inhabitants of medieval Moray have an equally bad reputation. Much of this has been derived from the enigmatic entry in the Holyrood chronicle for 1163: *Et rex Malcolmus Murevienses transtulit.*[17] The author of *Gesta annalia I*, for example, took this phrase to mean that King Maol Choluim (Malcolm) IV had removed the entire treacherous population of Moray, just as Nebuchadnezzar had once done to the Jews.[18] Later writers adopted this explanation to account for the fact that the the medieval Moravians were such bad people.

It should come as no surprise, then, that for many historians the people of Moray had been rebellious subjects since recorded history had begun.

---

chronicles of Scotland compiled by Hector Boece, 2 vols (Edinburgh, 1936–41), ii, pp 206–7. 14 Ibid., pp 282–3. 15 J. Aikman (trans.), *The history of Scotland*, 6 vols (Glasgow and Edinburgh, 1827–9), i, pp 371 and 376. 16 Ibid., p. 349. 17 M.O. Anderson with A.O. Anderson (eds), *A Scottish chronicle known as the chronicle of Holyrood* (Edinburgh, 1938), p. 142. 18 Skene (ed.), *Chron. Fordun (GA I)*.

But, since they were sure that Moray had never been an independent kingdom, these historians had to find a reason why the Moravians excelled at organizing regular rebellions. Ethnographic differences were one possible answer: Highland Celts fighting against Teutonic Lowlanders. This solution was further aided by the imposition of a perceived nineteenth-century Highland/Lowland divide onto early medieval Moray. For example, according to Charles Rampini, writing in 1897, the Picts of Moray were really Gaels who sided with their Celtic brethren against Norman (and Flemish) incomers. After losing their lands in the Laich of Moray to these settlers, the previous inhabitants had no other choice than to live in the Highlands and harass civilized (Lowland) people, thus becoming 'caterans' (usually Anglicized as 'kern(e)s' in Ireland, from Gaelic *ceithearn*, a band of mercenary foot-soldiers). This explanation allowed him to class the original inhabitants of Moray as: 'a warlike and impetuous race [...] who [...] were wholly responsible for spreading a fear of any Gaelic speaking people in lowland northern Scotland.'[19] In fact, medieval Moravians were supposedly so inclined to mayhem and slaughter that they even possessed their own origin-legend to explain exactly how they first achieved such notoriety in Pannonia during the reign of the Emperor Nero.[20]

A second possible answer as to why Moravians frequently liked to rebel was politics. Both David Dalrymple and Andrew Lang preferred to class twelfth- and thirteenth-century kindreds associated with Moray as proto-Jacobites. Lang, in particular, compared various leading representatives of the MacWilliam kindred to Prince Charles Edward Stuart and continually referred to them as 'pretenders' who 'raised their standards' whenever they were 'out'.[21] While it is perhaps difficult to excuse Dalrymple and Lang's use of emotive Jacobite terminology, there is little doubt that Rampini's commentary was influenced by the ethnographic debate over the different merits of Teutonic and Celtic ancestry, which took place in Scotland in the eighteenth and nineteenth centuries.[22]

All of the above probably helps to explain why R. Andrew McDonald, for example, has recently described the MacWilliams and Moravians as being at the forefront of an anti-feudal and anti-Canmore resistance movement in northern Scotland. Essentially, according to McDonald, these people resented the intensive process of internal colonization and

---

19 Charles Rampini, *A history of Moray and Nairn* (Edinburgh, 1897), p. 5 and pp 121–3.
20 Walter Bower, *Scotichronicon*, ed. D.E.R. Watt et al., 9 vols (Aberdeen, 1987–98), i, pp 236–9. This origin legend is discussed in more detail in a forthcoming paper of mine called 'Pannonians, pirates, and Pictish princesses'.   21 David Dalrymple, *Annals of Scotland* (Edinburgh, 1776), p. 43; Andrew Lang, *A history of Scotland*, 4 vols (Edinburgh, 1900–7), i, pp 88–118.   22 Colin Kidd, 'Teutonist ethnology and Scottish nationalist inhibition, 1780–1880', in *SHR*, 74 (1995), 45–68.

feudalization that was undertaken by the crown in Moray between 1175 and 1200.[23] Other historians clearly share this view even though it assumes *prima facie* that a process of internal colonization and feudalization took place in Moray in the first instance. Alan Young, for example, has claimed: 'Moray had proved to be a consistently difficult region to control throughout the twelfth century. Despite the planned settlement of Moray in David I's time, Highland rebellions continued to be a danger to the throne [...] The lordship of Badenoch, perhaps part of the estates forfeited by Gillescop MacWilliam [...] was in the highest part of Moray [...]'.[24] This is a persuasive and popular group of theories about the MacWilliams and Moray. But how much of it can be supported from the documentary record?

THE MAC WILLIAMS AND MORAY

Although it has recently been argued that Bishop Wimund claimed to be a MacWilliam,[25] the various careers of members of this kindred really only begin to be recorded in detail by chroniclers in the 1170s. Between 1179 and 1186 sources indicate that Domhnall Bán Mac Uilliam may have invaded Scotia on three different occasions. Under the year-date 1179 Bower commented:

Hoc eciam anno Willelmus rex Scocie cum fratre suo David comite de Huntyngdon' et exercitu magno perrexit in Ross' contra Makwilliam, sed vero nomine Donald ban, ibique duo castella firmavit scilicet Dunschath et Edirdovar, quibis firmatis ad australes regni sui partes remeavit ...

Also in this year William king of Scotland, together with his brother David earl of Huntingdon and a great army, advanced into Ross against Mac Uilliam, whose real name was Domhnall Bán. There he [the king] fortified two castles, Dunskeath and Etherdouer [Redcastle]. Having fortified these, he returned to the southern parts of his realm.[26]

In this invasion there is no mention of either Moray or of any Moravian involvement. Ross is clearly the centre of the events in question. In fact, by implication Moray must have remained loyal to the king otherwise it would clearly have been a strategic error to advance further north into

23 McDonald, 'Treachery in the remotest territories of Scotland', 181.   24 Alan Young, *Robert the Bruce's rivals: the Comyns, 1212–1314* (East Linton, 1997), pp 23–7.   25 Alex Woolf, 'The diocese of the Sudreyar', in Steinar Imsen (ed.), *Særtrykk fra Ecclesia Nidrosiensis 1153–1537, Søkelys på Nidaroskirkens og Nidarosprovinsens historie* (Trondheim, 2003), pp 171–81.
26 Translation taken from *Scotichronicon*, ed. Watt, iv, pp 336–7, although this was clearly borrowed from *Gesta annalia I*. Whenever there is a very close textual relationship between Bower and *Gesta Annalia*, I have preferred to use *Scotichronicon*. The reason for this is that the text of Fordun has not yet been edited to modern historical standards.

Ross without first having secured the country between the Strathbogie/
Lochaber line and the river Beauly. Domhnall Bán may have undertaken a
second expedition into Scotia in 1181. Of that year a well-informed
English source, Roger of Howden, remarked that:

Interim dum rex Scotiae moram faceret cum domino suo rege Angliae in Normannia,
Duvenaldus filius Willelmi filii Duncani, qui saepius calumniatus fuerat regnum Scotiae, et
multoties furtivas invasiones in regnum illud fecerat; per mandatum quorundam potentum
virorum de regno Scotiae, cum copiosa multitudine armata applicuit in Scotiam, devastans
et comburens totam terram quam attingebat; et homines fugabat, et omnes quos capere
potuit interficiebat.

Meanwhile, while the king of Scotland tarried with his lord the king of England in
Normandy, Domhnall the son of William son of Donnchadh, who had very often claimed
the kingdom of Scotland, and had many a time made insidious incursions into that
kingdom, by a mandate of certain powerful men of the kingdom of Scotland landed in
Scotland with a numerous armed host, wasting and burning as much of the land as he
reached; and he put the folk to flight, and slew all whom he could take.[27]

This extract is important because it provides the first indication that
Domhnall Bán possessed a fleet, and presumably a base of naval oper-
ations outwith Scotia. Once again, though, there is no mention either of
Moray or of Moravian involvement.

The final recorded expedition into Scotia by Domhnall Bán took place
in 1186:

Sed transactis inde septem annis eo solitam continuante nequiciam rex cum exercitu
copioso et manu pervalida profectus est in Moraviam adversus eundem inimicum suum
Donaldum ban qui se regio ortum | semine ac filium se fore Willelmi filii Duncani bastardi
qui fuit filius magni Malcolmi regis viri Sancte Margarete. Is prodicione nonnulorum
fretus perfidorum primum quidem totum comitatum Rossensem importunitate tirannidis
sue a rege suo extorserat. Ac deinde totam Moraviam non parvo tempore detinens
maximam partem regni cedibus et incendiis occupaverat, totum ambiens et ad totum
aspirans. Cumque rex cum eius exercitu ad oppidum de I[n]virnes moram faceret et
Donaldum ban ac suos adherentes cotidianis predis inquietasset et rapinis, contigit una
dierum ut cum homines suos more solito ad duo milia numero per saltus et pagos ad
explorandum et predandum emisisset ecce subito et inopinate quidam commilitones
exercitus regis super Macwilliam cum suis copiis in mora que dicitur Makgarby prope
Moraviam delitescentem offerunt. Quos de exercitu regis ut vidit paucos respectu suorum
repente congressum faciens in regios irruit. Cui toto conamine viriliter resistentes et in
justicia sue partis confidentes intrepidi propterea persistentes, Macwilliam cum quingentis
suorum opitulante Deo ceteris fugatis dignum sibi pro meritis premium conferentes ii kal'
augusti feria sexta occiderunt, cuius caput regi ad tocius spectaculum exercitus detulerunt.

27 William Stubbs (ed.), *Gesta Regis Henrici Secundi Benedicti Abbatis*, 2 vols (London, 1867), i,
pp 277–8. On Roger of Howden in Scotland, see A.A.M. Duncan, 'Roger of Howden and
Scotland, 1187–1201' in Crawford (ed.), *Church, chronicle and learning*, pp 135–59.

But seven years after that, since Domhnall Bán continued in his customary wickedness, the king advanced into Moray with a large army, a very strong force, against this same adversary Domhnall Bán. Domhnall Bán [boasted] that he was of royal descent, the son of William, the son of Duncan the Bastard, who was the son of the great king Malcolm, the husband of St Margaret. Relying on the treachery of some disloyal subjects, he had first of all by insolent usurpation forcibly removed from the king the whole earldom of Ross. He subsequently held the whole of Moray for a considerable time, and by employing fire and slaughter had seized the greater part of the kingdom, moving about all of it, and aspiring to have it under his control. While the king with his army was staying in the town of Inverness, and had been harrying Domhnall Bán and his supporters with daily raids for booty and plunder, it chanced one day that when he had sent out his men as usual, up to two thousand strong, to reconnoitre and take booty across the moors and countryside, some of those who were serving with the king's army suddenly and unexpectedly came upon Mac Uilliam as he was resting with his [exhausted] troops on a moor near Moray called 'Makgarby'. When Mac Uilliam saw that the king's troops were few in comparison with his own, he hurriedly joined battle with them, and charged the royal forces. They bravely resisted all his efforts, and because they trusted in the righteousness of their cause, continued to resist courageously. With God's help they cut down Mac Uilliam and five hundred of his men, and put the rest to flight, on Friday 31 July, thus repaying him with a just reward for his evil deeds. They sent his head to the king to be displayed to the whole army.[28]

In this extract we see that Moray is mentioned for the first time in connection with MacWilliams, though only after the conquest of Ross had already taken place. Once again, there is no mention of Moravian support for Domhnall Bán. In fact, Domhnall Bán is recorded as capturing only one castle in Moray. This was when Giolla Choluim the royal marshal, a man with strong Perthshire connections, surrendered 'Heryn' (probably Auldearn) to Domhnall Bán and then fought for the MacWilliams against the king.[29]

Roger of Howden had also heard about the MacWilliam expedition of 1187 and it is from his account that speculation has arisen regarding a marriage between William fitz Duncan and a female relative of Aonghus of Moray:

Interim Willelmus rex Scotiae, magno congregato exercitu, profectus est Moraviam, ad debellandum quendam hostem suum qui nominabatur Mach Willam: qui etiam dicebat se regia stirpe genitum, et de jure parentum suorum, ut asserebat, regnum Scotiae calumniabatur, et multa et incommoda faciebat saepe Willelmo regi Scotiae, per consensum et consilium comitum et baronum regni Scotiae.

Meanwhile William, king of Scotland, collected a great army, and set out for Moray, to subdue a certain enemy of his, who was named Mac Uilliam; who also said that he was born of the royal stock, and by right of his parents, so he affirmed, claimed the kingdom of Scotland, and often did many and harmful things to William, king of Scotland, through consent and council of the earls and barons of the kingdom of Scotland.[30]

28 *Scotichronicon*, ed. Watt, iv, pp 336–7. 29 *RRS*, ii, no. 258. 30 Stubbs (ed.), *Gesta Regis Henrici*, ii, pp 7–9.

In this passage Roger of Howden stated that Domhnall Bán claimed the kingdom of Scotia in right of his *parentes*. This statement, which is almost certainly accurate given the time that the author spent in Scotia towards the end of the twelfth century, has been taken to mean that the mother of Domhnall Bán was important in her own right. As we have already seen Barrow suggested that this woman was either a cousin or sister of Aonghus of Moray.[31] Oram further developed this theory in 1999 and noted that as a descendant of King Lulach mac Giolla Chomhgháin, Domhnall Bán would have inherited membership of the royal kindred of Clann Chustantín mic Chionaoith. Furthermore, Oram argued that the marriage of William fitz Duncan to a Moravian woman may have been deliberately encouraged by King David I as a means of 'tying-off' the claims of two collateral branches of the royal kindred, although such a calculation was predicated on the gamble that any children of such a union would be uninterested in pursuing their own claims.[32]

To a large extent this theory depends on the belief that Domhnall Bán actually received support from Moray between 1179 and 1186. As we can see, there is not a shred of evidence to suggest that this was the case. Accordingly, William fitz Duncan's first marriage could have been to any female member of the royal kindred. More importantly perhaps, the theory that the mother of Domhnall Bán was closely related to Aonghus of Moray depends on translating the Latin word *parentes* as 'parents', rather than 'ancestors' or 'kindred'. The use of either of these latter two meanings suggests that there need be no parental link between Domhnall Bán and an important Moravian woman. In fact, this word may simply refer to his paternal descent from King Donnchadh mac Maoil Choluim and the fact that he belonged to the royal kindred.[33]

The death of Domhnall Bán must have been a heavy blow to the aspirations of the wider MacWilliam kindred as they clearly did not manage to gather enough resources to invade Scotia again until 1211:

Anno domini m cc xi rex Scocie Willelmus misit exercitum infinite multitudinis cum omnibus optimatibus regni sui in Ros contra Gothredum Macwilliam, et ipse rex secutus est ut potuit inter Nativitatem Sancti Johannis et autumpnum. Quo dum perveniret duo castella edificavit, et totam terram Rossensem fere destruxit, et fautores dicti Gothredi quotquot invenire potuit cepit vel occidit. Ipse autem Gothredus semper regis exercitum declinavit, sed interim quocienscumque potuit diebus ac noctibus exercitui regis clam insidiabatur et predas de terra domini regis abigebat. Tandem dominus | rex electorum quatuor milia hominum de exercitu misit ut ipsum Gothredum quererent ubi eum latere

31 *RRS*, ii, p. 13.   32 Richard D. Oram, 'David I and the Scottish conquest and colonisation of Moray', in *Northern Scotland*, 19 (1999), 1–19, at p. 10.   33 To date only A.A.M. Duncan seems to have translated *parentes* as 'kin' (cf. Duncan, 'Roger of Howden', p. 141).

putabant. Quibus in campidoctores prefecit quatuor militares comites videlicet Adolie et de Buchan, Malcolmum Morigrond et Thomam de Londi hostiarium suum. Qui pervenientes in quandam insulam in qua ipse Gothredus victualia congregaverat, et thesauros suos inde asportaverat, cum Gothredicis congressi sunt, ubi utrimque ceciderunt interfecti multi, plures tamen ex parte rebellium, quorum qui remanserunt ad proximum nemus et loca tuciora pro tempore declinarunt. Dominus autem rex circa festum Sancti Michaelis rediens inde cum manu valida Malcolmum comitem de Fife Moravie custodem dereliquit. Sed incontinenti post regis recessum dictus Gothredus obsessit unum de castris paulo ante per regem in Ros extructis, et ingeniis paratis, cum iam capturus esset illud, timentes qui intus erant sponte illud tradiderunt ut vitam suam tantum salvarent. Hoc eis Gothredus concessit, et apposito igne castrum combussit. Quod cum audisset rex ira incanduit, sed propter hiemis asperitatem expedicionem distulit. Sed in sequenti estate dominus Alexander filius domini regis de precepto patris paulo ante Nativitatem Sancti Johannis profectus est de Laudonia versus Ros cum grandi exercitu, quem ipse rex post modicum subsequi cum alio terre sue exercitu disponebat. Interea Gothredus Macwilliam prodicione suorum captus et vinculatus ad Willelmum Comyn comitem Buchanie justiciarium domini regis adductus est usque Moraviam. Erat enim tunc temporis ipse custos Moravie nam comes de Fiffe Malcolmus non multum ante venerat ad regem cum ipso locuturus. Justiciarius autem volens ipsum Gothredum vivum regi presentari pervenit usque Kincardin, ubi cum audisset voluntatem regis scilicet quod nollet eum vivum videre, cum et ipse Gothredus iam pene defecisset quia postquam captus fuerat refici victu renuit, decollatum et trac- | tum per pedes suspenderunt. Qui Gothredus anno precedenti circa Epiphaniam de consilio ut dicitur thanorum de Ros venit ad partes illas ex Hibernia, queque obvia conculcans, et in plerisque locis regnum infestans.

In 1211 William king of Scotland sent a huge army together with all the nobles of his kingdom into Ross against Guðrøðr Mac Uilliam. The king himself followed when he was able some time between the Nativity of St John and the autumn. On his way he built two castles, laid waste pretty well all of Ross, and took or killed as many of the said Guðrøðr's supporters as he could find. But Guðrøðr himself always avoided the king's army, meanwhile laying ambushes for it whenever he could by night or day, and driving off booty from the lord king's land. At last the lord king sent 4000 men picked from his army to seek out Guðrøðr in the area where they thought he was hiding. He put in command of them four military men: the earls of Atholl and of Buchan, Malcolm Morgrund and his door-ward Thomas de Lundie. They came to an island on which Guðrøðr himself had gathered together provisions, and from which he had carried off his treasure, and there they engaged Guðrøðr's men. Many were killed on both sides, but more from among the rebels. Those of them who remained retreated for the moment to the nearest forest and to safer places. About Michaelmas the lord king returned from there with a strong force and left Malcolm earl of Fife as guardian of Moray. But no sooner had the king departed than the said Guðrøðr besieged one of the castles built by the king in Ross just a little earlier. He had made ready his siege engines and was just on the point of capturing it, when the garrison within lost their nerve and surrendered it of their own accord to save their lives, if nothing else. This Guðrøðr granted them, and setting fire to the castle burned it down. The king was enraged on hearing of this, but put off making any expedition because of the severe winter weather. But next summer Sir Alexander the lord king's son on his father's orders set out from Lothian for Ross with a large army a little before the Nativity of St John. The king intended to follow him after a short interval with another army drawn from his territory. Meanwhile Guðrøðr Mac Uilliam was betrayed by his own followers, captured, put in chains and taken to Moray to William Comyn earl of Buchan, the lord king's justiciar, for he was guardian of Moray at that time, since Malcolm earl of Fife had not long since gone to the king to discuss matters with him. The justiciar, who wanted Guðrøðr brought before the king alive, got as far as Kincardine. There when he learned the king's will, which was that he did not want to see him alive, they beheaded Guðrøðr, dragged him along by the feet and hung him up. He was already very close to death, for he had refused food ever since his capture. This Guðrøðr had come to those parts from Ireland in the previous year around Epiphany, as part of a plot (as is commonly said) [hatched by] the thanes of Ross. He trod underfoot everything he encountered and plagued many parts of the kingdom of Scotland.[34]

However, this extract does not tell the whole story. A contemporary English source, the so-called Barnwell chronicle, provides an even clearer exposition of what King William had to do in order to defeat Guðrøðr (Gaelic Gofraidh):

Scottorum rex Willelmus jam aetatis provectae, cum interiores regni sui partes seditione turbatas pacificare non posset, ad Anglorum [regem] confugiens, se et regnum, filiumque quem unicum habebat, ejus commisit provisioni. At ille cingulo militari commendatum sibi donans, in partes illas cum exercitu proficiscens, dimissis per interiora regni suis, Cuthredum cognomento MacWilliam seditionis ducem cepit, et patibulo suspendit. Erat hic de Scottorum regum antiqua prosapia, qui Scottorum et Hibernensium fretus auxilio, longas contra modernas reges, sicut et pater suus Dovenaldus, nunc clam, nunc palam, exercuit inimicitias.

Since William, king of Scots, who was now of advanced age, was not able to pacify the interior districts of his kingdom, disturbed by revolt, he fled to the king of the English and entrusted to his care himself, and his kingdom, and the only son whom he had. And [King John] presented [the son] who was commended to him with the belt of knighthood, and set

34 *Scotichronicon*, ed. Watt, iv, pp 464–7. At least half of this extract was copied from *Gesta annalia I* (cf. Skene (ed.), *Chron. Fordun* (*GA I*), pp 278–9): 'Gothredus, filius Macwilliam, proditione suorum captus et vinculatus, domino Alexandro filio regis apud manerium regis et castrum de Kyncardin praesentatus, ibidem capite truncato per pedes est suspensus. Idem autem Gothredus, filius Macwilliam, anno praecedente circa Epiphaniam Domini, de consilio, prout dicebatur, thanorum de Ross, venit in partes illas ex Hibernia, conculcans obvia quaeque, et in pluribus regnum Scociae infestans. Contra quem repente missus est regis exercitus, ut aut ipsum occideret aut agitaret ex patria. Quem ipse rex Willelmus secutus, eadem aestate sequenti illis in partibus duo extruxit oppida, quorum alterum, post decessum regis, Godhrede cum suis succendit, ultro tradentibus se custodibus (Guðrøðr, the son of Mac Uilliam, by treason of his followers was captured and chained, and presented to the Lord Alexander, the king's son, at the king's manor and castle of Kincardine, and was there hanged by the feet after his head had been cut off. The same Guðrøðr, son of Mac Uilliam, had in the previous year, about the Lord's Epiphany [6 January 1211] by counsel, it was said, of the thanes of Ross, come into these parts from Ireland, overcoming all obstacles, and in many ways molesting the kingdom of Scotland. Against him, the king's army was sent in haste, either to kill him, or to drive him out of the land. King William himself followed the army, and in the same summer following, he built two fortresses in those parts. Of these, Guðrøðr with his followers burned down the one, after the king's departure, the guards surrendering of their own accord)'.

out with an army to those parts; and sending his men through the interior of the kingdom he seized the leader of the revolt, Guðrøðr, surnamed Mac Uilliam, and hanged him on the gallows. [Guðrøðr] was of the ancient line of Scottish kings; and, supported by the aid of the Scots and Irish, had practised long hostility against the modern kings, now in secret, now openly, as had also his father Domhnall.[35]

From these two extracts it is obvious that King William mounted two expeditions against Guðrøðr during 1211 and 1212. The first of these expeditions had only limited success, even though King William wasted much of the province of Ross. After the king left the area, Guðrøðr seems to have regained territory he had previously lost to the king's forces. Indeed, it might be speculated that Guðrøðr actually obtained more local support because of the king's actions in wasting Ross in 1211.[36] Such a scenario could also account for the reason why King John also sent Brabantine mercenaries under the command of an English noble to King William's aid in 1212 to fight against Guðrøðr.[37] Perhaps one reason why the Scottish sources do not mention King William's use of English military aid is that Fordun and Bower were editing and writing their respective texts both during, and in the aftermath, of the wars of independence. To them it may no longer have seemed appropriate to state that a King of Scots needed English aid to regain his kingdom.

These descriptions of the events of 1211 and 1212 are also unanimous in stating that the local lords in Ross were somehow involved in the conspiracy against King William. Like the invasions of Guðrøðr's father, Domhnall Bán, between 1179 and 1186, there is no mention of any Moravian support for Guðrøðr. Indeed, when Guðrøðr was finally captured it was stated that he was taken 'to Moray'. This surely demonstrates that both Moray, and the Moravians, had remained loyal to King William I. Instead, it was local lords in Ross that were blamed for supporting the MacWilliams.

The accounts of the events of 1211 and 1212 also introduce a new element into the equation. This is that it is explicitly stated that Guðrøðr and his forces had set out from Ireland to invade Scotia and it is the first time that Ireland is mentioned in connection with the MacWilliam kindred. Fortunately, the Annals of Ulster may provide a clue as to the

---

35 William Stubbs (ed.), *Memoriale Fratris Walteri de Coventria*, 2 vols (London, 1872–3), ii, p. 206. 36 A.O. Anderson and M.O. Anderson (eds), *The chronicle of Melrose from the Cottonian manuscript, Faustina B ix in the British Museum: a complete and full-size facsimile in collotype* (London, 1936), pp 110–12 states: '… et Rex scocie filium macWilliam Guthred .s. persequendo propriosque seductores destruendo. multorum cadauera inanimata reliqrit (… and also the king of Scotland left behind him the lifeless corpses of many men, when he pursued the son of Mac Uilliam, Guðrøðr, and destroyed those responsible for perverting him)'. In this and in the following quotations all contractions have been silently expanded. 37 Thomas Arnold (ed.), *Memorials of St Edmund's abbey*, 3 vols (London, 1890–96), ii, p. 20.

source of this Irish support for the MacWilliams. Under the year date
1212 they record that:

Tomas, mac Uchtraigh, co macaibh Raghnaill, mic Somarligh, do thaidhecht do Dhaire
Coluim-cille co ré longaibh rechtmogadh ocus in baile do mílliudh doibh co mór ocus Inis-
Eogain co huilidhi do milliudh doib do Cheniul-Conaill.

Thomas, son of Uchtrach, with the sons of Raghnall, son of Somhairle, came to Daire of
Colum-cille with six and seventy ships and the town was completely destroyed by them and
by the Cenel-Conaill.[38]

The 1212 raid was followed by a second in 1214:

Tomás, mac Uchtraigh ocus Ruaidhri, mac Raghnaill, do argain Dairi go huilidhi ocus do
breith shet Muinntere Daire ocus Tuairceirt Erenn archena do lár tempaill in reiclera
ímach [...] Castel Cula-rathain do dhenum le Tomas, mac Uchtraigh ocus le Gallaibh
Uladh. Ocus roscailedh reilce ocus clachana ocus cumdaichi in baile inle, cenmotha in
tempall amain, cuicesein.

Thomas, son of Uchtrach and Ruaidhri, son of Raghnall, plundered Daire completely and
took the treasures of the Community of Daire and of the North of Ireland besides from
out the midst of the church of the Monastery [...] The castle of Cuil-rathain was built by
Thomas, son of Uchtrach and by the Foreigners of Ulidia. And all the cemeteries and
fences and buildings of the town, save the church alone, were pulled down for that.[39]

These two campaigns have been commented on by a number of historians
and it has been argued that the MacWilliams had a base in Ulster and were
supported by Aodh Ó Néill, king of Tír Eoghain, who was actively
resisting the attempts of the kings of Scotia and England to destroy his
power-base in Ireland. According to Stringer, for example, Anglo-Scottish
campaigns in the north of Ireland in 1212 and 1214 can be construed as
retaliation against the MacWilliam invasion of Ross in 1211. He found it
difficult to resist the conclusion that the MacWilliams had traditionally
used Gaelic Ulster as a haven and a place where large bodies of caterans
(kern(e)) could be readily recruited.[40] More recently, McDonald has
expanded on this theory and stated that given the close links between
Gaelic Ireland, the MacWilliams, and the MacEths, it was hardly surprising
that there were campaigns in Ireland between 1212 and 1214 to destroy
MacWilliam bases in the Irish Sea region. He developed the argument
further and noted that the MacWilliams and MacEths also maintained close
links to the Hebrides where they recruited caterans for their campaigns.[41]

38 *AU*, ii, pp 252–3. 39 Ibid., pp 256–7. 40 Stringer, 'Periphery and core in thirteenth-
century Scotland', pp 87–8. 41 McDonald, 'Treachery in the remotest territories of Scotland',
184.

There are, however, a number of problems with these theories. Firstly, only one member of the MacWilliam kindred is ever expressly described as coming from Ireland. This was Guðrøðr in 1211. There is no indication from where the other members of the kindred set out to invade Scotia. This might suggest that Guðrøðr's invasion was unusual in that he had stopped off in Ireland beforehand to pick up caterans. If this was the case the men of Tír Eoghain could have linked themselves to Guðrøðr's cause because of the pressures being put on them in Ulster by Kings John and William and because they saw Guðrøðr's planned invasion as an opportunity to open a second front against the royal allies, thus diverting the joint military resources of these two kings away from Ulster.

The second, and probably the greatest, problem with the theory that the MacWilliams commonly used Ireland and the Hebrides as a base for their invasions of Scotia is a simple matter of geography. It has long been recognized that the two castles built by King William I in 1179, Dunskeath and Redcastle, respectively protect the sea and land approaches to Moray from the north.[42] In addition, Dunskeath also guarded the strategically important northern end of a sea route that removed the need for long journeys by land round the deeply indented Moray, Beauly and Cromarty Firths. In themselves, these would be quite acceptable reasons for the construction of these fortifications were it not for the fact that before 1211 the MacWilliam fleets were clearly operating in eastern waters. The castle of Auldearn (nearby Loch Loy may have been the southern end of the sea route to Dunskeath) was betrayed by the non-Maravian royal marshal to Domhnall Bán Mac Uilliam sometime between 1179 and 1186,[43] and the seat of the see of Moray was shifted away from its coastal location at Spynie to an inland site during the early thirteenth century.[44]

So, perhaps an additional reason for the geographic siting of these two castles was that before 1211 the bulk of the MacWilliam naval threat was seen to come from the waters off the east coast, rather than the west. If so, it is much more likely that the MacWilliam naval base was situated somewhere outwith Scotia but within easy sailing distance of the east coast since this would avoid repeated journeys through the dangerous waters of the Pentland Firth.

There is no firm evidence with which to locate this base. However, the progenitrix of the MacWilliam kindred was Queen Ingibjörg of Orkney. Furthermore, it has been demonstrated that King David I had interfered in the succession to the earldom of Orkney *c.*1139. In addition, King

---

42 A.A.M. Duncan, *Scotland. The making of the Kingdom* (Edinburgh, 1975), p. 193.   43 *RRS*, ii, no. 258.   44 Innes (ed.), *Reg. Moraviensis*, no. 26.

William I was clearly interfering in the earldom of Caithness, also claimed by Earl Haraldr Maddadsson of Orkney, during the late twelfth and early thirteenth centuries. This interference resulted in at least one Orcadian/ Caithness military expedition into Moray, three royal expeditions into Caithness, and three different submissions by the earls of Orkney/ Caithness to the kings of Scotia until a final settlement between the two sides was reached in 1202.[45]

Bearing these facts in mind, the main MacWilliam base of operations could have been located somewhere in the Northern Isles. This would have been to the advantage of the MacWilliams who could have relied on the kindred of their great-grandmother for protection and support. For the earls of Orkney, and particularly Haraldr Maddadsson, the presence of the MacWilliams in the Northern Isles would have had two advantages. Firstly, the MacWilliams would have been valuable allies in helping to resist the interference by kings of Scotia in northern affairs. Secondly, the earls of Orkney would have earned the goodwill of a number of potential kings of Scotia by sheltering the MacWilliams. Although this is nothing more than speculation, it should be noted that *Orkneyinga saga* is the only medieval source that is actually pro-MacWilliam.[46]

Accordingly, armed with this information it is possible to suggest that before 1202 the MacWilliam kindred had been based in Orkney and received support from the earls of Orkney and Caithness as descendants of Queen Ingibjörg. Thereafter, increasing military pressure from the kings of Scotia could have forced Haraldr Maddadsson to evict the MacWilliams from their northern base as part of a diplomatic settlement with the kings of Scotia. This may have resulted in the MacWilliams opening a new base of operations in the Irish Sea world on the lands of Tír Eoghain in Ulster.

In any event, the two Scottish raids on Ulster, in 1212 and 1214, if they were intended to destroy a MacWilliam base, must have failed in their purpose. One year later, Domhnall Bán Mac Uilliam invaded Scotia, although it is not known where he landed:

Intraverunt in moreviam hostes domini Regis scocie scilicet Dovenaldus ban filius macWali et kennauh mac aht et filius cuiusdam Regem hybernie cum turba malignantium copiosa In quas irruens machentagar hostes regis ualide prostrauit capita detruncauit et nouo regi noua munera presentauit.

The lord king of Scotland's enemies entered Moray, namely Domhnall Bán, the son of Mac Uilliam; and Cionaodh 'mac Heth' [mac Aoidh?]; and the son of a certain king of

45 Barbara Crawford, 'The earldom of Caithness and the kingdom of Scotland, 1150–1266', in *Northern Scotland*, 2 (1974–5), 97–118, at 25–43. 46 H. Pálsson and P. Edwards, *Orkneyinga Saga* (London, 1978), p. 76.

Ireland, with a numerous band of malignants. Mac-in-tSacairt attacked them, and mightily overthrew the king's enemies; and he cut off their heads, and presented them as new gifts to the new king.[47]

The death of Domhnall Bán in 1215 did not end MacWilliam attempts to be recognized as legitimate contenders for the kingship of Scotia. *Gesta annalia I* noted the efforts of other members of the MacWilliam kindred in Scotia during the 1220s:

Per idem tempus emerserunt quidam iniqui de genere MacWilliam scilicet Gillascoph et filii ejus et Rodericus, in extremis Scociae finibus. Qui cum regnum opprimere vi niterentur, tradidit eos Deus cum suis fautoribus in manus regis Alexandri, et sic terra de cetero ab eorum malitia requievit.

During this same period some wicked men of the race of MacWilliam, namely Giolla Easpaig and his sons and Roderick [Ruaidhri?] appeared in the furthest limits of Scotland. But when they strove to overwhelm the kingdom by force, God delivered them and their accomplices into the hands of King Alexander, and thus the land was no longer troubled by their wickedness.[48]

Unfortunately, the internal chronology of this part of *Gesta annalia I* is extremely vague. The editor of the most recent edition of Bower's *Scotichronicon*, which included this passage, tentatively placed this event in 1223.[49] However, matters are further complicated by a later entry by Bower under the year-date 1228:

Anno domini m cc xxviii Scotus quidam nomine Gillescop succendit quasdam municiones ligneas in Moravia et occidit quendam latronem nomine Thoman de Thrislane nocte ex improviso municionem eius invadens. Postea succendit | magnam partem de Invernes et de terris domini regis circumvicinis abduxit predas circa Nativitatem Beate Marie. Dominus autem rex cum paucis suorum illac festinans, cum aliquamdiu illuc moram fecisset, commisit custodiam terre Moravie comiti de Buchan justiciario suo tradens ei magnam peditum multitudinem.

In 1228 a certain Scot called Giolla Easpaig set fire to some wooden defensive works in Moray and killed a certain thief called Thomas de Thirlestane after attacking his castle unexpectedly during the night. Afterwards he burned a large part of Inverness, and about [the time of the feast of] the Nativity of the Blessed Mary [8 September] he plundered some neighbouring lands belonging to the lord king. But the lord king hurried there with a few of his men, and after making a stay there for some time entrusted the custody of the land of Moray to his justiciar the earl of Buchan, providing him with a large number of troops.[50]

---

47 Anderson and Anderson (eds), *Chron. Melrose*, p. 59. 48 Skene (ed.), *Chron. Fordun (GA I)*, p. 290. 49 *Scotichronicon*, ed. Watt, v, pp 116–17. 50 Ibid., pp 142–3.

Bower also referred to a man called Giolla Easpaig in 1229: 'In this year
the Giolla Easpaig who has been mentioned above was killed along with
his two sons, and their heads were brought to the lord king.'[51] While all
three events, in 1223, 1228 and 1229, would seem to refer to the same man
and his kindred, there is one good reason for assuming that the entry for 1223
has been misplaced in Bower's chronology: if Giolla Easpaig had been
captured in 1223, it is surely unlikely that King Alexander II would have
released him since every other captured MacWilliam had been executed.

There is only one entry in English sources that refers to these events.
Under the year-date 1230, the Lanercost Chronicle noted that:

Quo anno emerserunt in Scotia quidam iniqui, de genere Mach William videlicet, et filius
ejus, et quidam Rotherike, insidias agentes in extremis finibus Scotiae, et multum
iniquorum copiam sibi ex eodem regno associantes, volentes regnum vi obtinere; sed traditi
sunt, Deo vindice, et complices eorum, et inimicis prospere subactis, aliquantulum in
sanguinem occisorum crudelius vindicatum est. Nam ejusdem Mac Willelmi filia, adhuc
recens de matris utero edita, ante conspectum sori sub voce praeconia, in burgo de Forfar,
innocens traditur neci, capite ipsius ad columnam crucis eliso et cerebro excusso, e contra
dicente Domino, 'non occidentur filii pro patribus', et caetera.

In this year there arose in Scotland certain wicked men of the race of MacWilliam, and his
son, and a certain Roderick [Ruaidhri?], they raised up treachery in the remotest territories
of Scotia, and wished to obtain the kingdom by force, by allying with themselves a great
number of wicked men of that realm. But, by the vengeance of God, they and their
accomplices were betrayed. And after the enemy had been successfully overcome, a somewhat too cruel vengeance was taken for the blood of the slain. The same Mac Uilliam's
daughter, who had not long left her mother's womb, innocent though she was, was put to
death in the burgh of Forfar, in view of the market-place, after a proclamation by the public
crier; her head was struck against the column of the cross, and her brains dashed out. Yet God
says to the contrary effect, 'sons shall not be slain for their father's', and so on.[52]

This version of the events of the 1220s, in contrast to *Gesta annalia I*,
does not state unambiguously that Roderick was a member of the
MacWilliam kindred. This has led to him being identified as Ruaidhri mac
Raghnaill, lord of Garmoran, who had been expelled from Argyll by King
Alexander II in 1221–22.[53] Because of the proximity of Garmoran to
Lochaber and Badenoch, the identification of Roderick as Ruaidhri mac
Raghnaill has further led to the identification of Lochaber and Badenoch
as lands held by Giolla Easpaig Mac Uilliam, and as the centres of 'revolt'
against the crown in 1229.[54] McDonald, writing in 1999, took this

51 Ibid., pp 144–5.   52 J. Stevenson (ed.), *Chronicon de Lanercost* (Edinburgh, 1839), pp 40–1.
53 A.A.M. Duncan and A.L. Brown, 'Argyll and the Isles in the Earlier Middle Ages', in *PSAS*,
90 (1956–7), 192–220, at 199–200; R. Andrew McDonald, *The kingdom of the Isles: Scotland's
western seaboard, c.1000–c.1336* (East Linton, 1997), p. 82.   54 Young, *The Comyns*, pp 27–8.

identification, together with the apparent support offered by Ruaidhri mac Raghnaill for Giolla Easpaig as proof of the political connections between the western Gaelic kindreds descended from Sumarliði (Somerled), Maol Choluim 'MacHeth' (of 1130), and the MacWilliams.[55]

However, this theory depends on accepting the evidence from the Lanercost Chronicle and rejecting the evidence from *Gesta annalia I*. It may be wrong to do so. While it has been persuasively suggested that *Gesta annalia I* was based on an earlier Dunfermline exemplar, perhaps completed by *c*.1250, the Lanercost Chronicle was written towards the end of the thirteenth century.[56] Accordingly, it is probably wrong to place too much emphasis on the wording of this source and perhaps one should accept instead that *Gesta annalia I* contains the more contemporary and accurate information regarding Roderick; namely, that he was probably another MacWilliam.

In contrast to previous MacWilliam attempts to take the kingship of Scotia, the descriptions of the deeds of the MacWilliam kindred between 1215 and 1230 give no direct indication that they were setting out for Scotland from elsewhere. In common with the pre-1215 MacWilliam invasions there is no specific mention of any Moravian involvement in the MacWilliam expeditions post-1215. The sources are, however, very clear that members of the MacWilliam kindred were still receiving help from people within Scotia, though not from Moray. This would indicate that the domination of the kingship of Scotia by the ruling segment of the royal kindred was still not universally accepted before 1230, even though by this stage some men were clearly finding it more profitable to betray members of the MacWilliam kindred than to support them fully. This perception is strengthened by King Alexander's 'final solution' for disposing of the MacWilliam kindred altogether: the premeditated murder of the last MacWilliam infant at Forfar in 1230.[57] This act was tantamount to the deliberate extinction of a segment of the royal kindred. In ordering this murder King Alexander II ensured that any male heir he might have would be inaugurated without opposition from the kindred of MacWilliam. It worked. When King Alexander III was inaugurated at Scone on 13 July 1249 he was possibly the first king of Alba or Scotia whose reign was free of alternate claimants.

So, to sum up thus far: having examined all of the information relating to the MacWilliams there is no indication that they ever received help or

---

55 McDonald, 'Treachery in the remotest territories of Scotland', 184.   56 Antonia Gransden, *Historical writing in England, c.500–c.1307* (London, 1974), p. 495.   57 Stevenson (ed.), *Chron. Lanercost*, p. 41.

military support from any Moravian between 1179 and 1230. This is something of a problem given the sheer volume of literature aimed at proving a connection between the MacWilliams and Moray. Instead, the focus of the MacWilliam invasions seems to have consistently been the province of Ross. Accordingly, probably the best way of reconciling the unjustified but troublesome reputation of the Moravians between *c.*1170 and 1230 in later texts with the complete lack of evidence that they were rebels, is to suggest that the Moravians were slandered through association. Since William fitz Duncan may have been earl of Moray between *c.*1130 and *c.*1150, and since some of his descendents had repeatedly invaded Scotia, possibly to gain the kingship for themselves, it is easy to see how the following equation could have formed in the minds of many chroniclers: Moray = MacWilliams = trouble and revolt.

If so, royal propaganda may also have helped them form this opinion. Dauvit Broun has recently investigated two king-lists produced between 1198 and December 1214. The first of these, the Verse Chronicle, demonstrates a remarkable dislike of Moravians and claims, untruthfully, that two previous kings of Alba had been murdered in Moray. According to Broun, the basis for this denigrating commentary on Moray and Moravians is revealed in the treatment of King Donnchadh II by the Verse Chronicle, mainly because he is the only king of Scotia whom the author of the Verse Chronicle deliberately discredited. Broun argued that the reasoning behind this treatment could be found in the activities of Donnchadh's descendants, the MacWilliams, who had launched a number of challenges against the descendants of King Maol Choluim. Because many of the MacWilliam kindred landed in Ross or Moray before launching their attacks on the kings of Scotia, the inhabitants of those areas also became closely associated with rebellion against the crown.

The second king-list that Broun examined is found in the Chronicle of Melrose. The first part of this king-list begins with the succession of King Maol Choluim mac Donnchadha and finishes with the birth of Prince Alexander in 1198. This part can therefore be dated to 1198x1214. A continuation in a different hand then carries the list on to the birth of Alexander III's first son and heir, also Alexander, on 21 January 1264. According to Broun, the first part of this king-list was written with the senior male line of the royal family very much in mind. It is the only extant Scottish king-list which deliberately begins with King Maol Choluim mac Donnchadha, and which follows the reigns of the king's descendants from his second marriage to Queen Margaret. There is a heavy emphasis on hereditary rights to kingship and on primogeniture. For example, we are told that King Maol Choluim mac Donnchadha's brother, King Domhnall Bán mac Donnchadha, usurped the kingship sending the legitimate heirs, the sons of Queen Margaret, into exile. Furthermore, the king-list also describes King Donnchadh mac Maoil Choluim as illegitimate, thus damning his progeny and their offspring. Therefore, both of these king-lists are heavily committed to King Alexander II's right to rule in Scotia, to the extent that previous legitimate kings are categorized as either usurpers or illegitimate. As with the Verse Chronicle, Broun argues that the king-list in the Chronicle of Melrose was inspired by the repeated MacWilliam challenges faced by King Alexander II.[58]

There is a third Scottish source that is extremely negative about Moravians. This is found in Book 2 of *Chronica gentis Scottorum*, first compiled by John of Fordun between 1371 and the mid-1380s. It is a quite remarkable story that relates how the Moravians originated in Pannonia and why they were disposed to rebellion. It states that while the Moravians were living in Pannonia they slaughtered a Roman legion and, fearing the consequences of Nero's wrath, built a fleet of ships and sailed down the Danube to the North Sea. They then turned into North Sea pirates, raiding shipping and ports, before forming a treaty of perpetual peace with the Picts. The Moravians were eventually given Pictish daughters as brides and land to cultivate in north Britain.[59] The origin-legend aims to make two key points about Moravians: firstly, it was usual for Moravians to rebel against authority; secondly, the Moravians were pirates who plundered the seas around Britain.

Unfortunately, though, there seems to be no reason why anyone would have wanted to classify all Moravians as rebellious murderers and traitors at the time this text was compiled by Fordun. On this basis, it seems logical to suggest that Fordun copied the Moravian origin-legend from an earlier text that could be dated to a time when it was safe to slander all Moravians. One fact that might support this suggestion is that the leader of the piratical Moravians in the origin-legend and one of the leaders of the last MacWilliam invasion of Scotia share the same name, 'Roderick'. If the name of the Moravian prince in the origin-legend was based on contemporary thirteenth-century events, this would then provide a date of *c*.1214x30 for the original hypothetical text that contained the origin-legend later copied by Fordun.

Of course, formulating this Moravian origin-legend also meant that the received pseudo-history of Scotland was radically altered. From this point

58 Broun, 'Contemporary perspectives on Alexander II's succession: the evidence of king-lists', forthcoming, 8–9. My thanks to Dr Broun for allowing me to read a copy of this article before publication.   59 Skene (ed.), *Chron. Fordun*, pp 57–8.

the Scots were descended from three, not two, separate races. It is just possible that this deliberate alteration in the pseudo-history of the Scots provides a measure of the lengths to which crown propagandists were willing to go in order to denigrate and marginalize one segment of the royal kindred. It is also perhaps a measure of the seriousness of the threat posed by the MacWilliams to kings of Scotia.

In fact, it is just possible that the person, or persons, responsible for creating the Moravian origin-legend realized that he or they were radically rewriting Scottish pseudo-history. This may be why the legend contains the long and curious argument that Pannonia was really part of Lower Scythia. During the medieval period it was believed that the Picts originated in Scythia. Therefore, the author of the origin-tale was attempting to prove that the Moravians were also really just Picts, but from a slightly different region of continental Europe. However, it must have been felt that this argument was weak and this may be why the message is reinforced by the revelation that the Moravians were very rapidly absorbed into the native Pictish population in north Britain, after which they all lived happily ever after. Since everyone reading or hearing this origin-legend, together with the two king-lists examined by Broun, would know that the Moravians and MacWilliams had been Pannonian pirates, rebels and murderers since recorded history began, they would agree that Alexander II was completely justified in utterly exterminating them. In the eyes of many people after 1230, due to royal propaganda it must have seemed that the only good Moravian was a dead Moravian.

Dealing death from Man: Manx sea power in and around the Irish Sea, 1079–1265[1]

R. ANDREW McDONALD

At that time King Rögnvaldr was the greatest fighting man in all the western lands. For three years he had lived aboard longships and not spent a single night under a sooty roof.[2]

This brief but vivid pen portrait of Rögnvaldr Guðrøðarson,[3] the King of Man and the Isles who reigned from 1187 to 1226 and was slain in 1229, was written around 1200 by the anonymous Icelandic author of *Orkneyinga saga*. Coming from a writer whose subject-matter embraced such fearsome and heroic characters as the Orkney Jarls Sigurðr (Sigurd) the Stout, with his sorceress mother and infamous raven banner, Þorfinnr (Thorfinn) the Mighty, bester of Macbeth, Rögnvaldr Kali Kolsson (pilgrim, poet, and warrior), and Haraldr Maddaðsson (one of the three most powerful Orkney jarls), not to mention the 'ultimate Viking', Sveinn Asleifsson (famous for his raiding in the Irish Sea, and himself with Manx connections), the words of the saga-man constituted high praise indeed. But they were by no means unique. In fact, about the same time that *Orkneyinga saga* was composed, hundreds of miles away in Ireland or the Isle of Man a Gaelic bard sang Rögnvaldr's praises in similar terms: 'You will deal death from smooth-plained Man', says the bard, 'slaughter by a great ship's host ... You'll hold a man back, and plunder, you'll burn a house and smash ... You'll plunder disputed Dublin ...'.[4] From Iceland to Ireland, King Rögnvaldr evidently cut quite a figure, principally as a great warlord with substantial military resources at his disposal.

1 The author acknowledges the award of a Chancellor's Chair for Research Excellence from Brock University. He is grateful to Peter Davey, Seán Duffy, Allison Fox, Ben Hudson, Andrew Johnson, Neil Kennedy, Cynthia Neville and Angus Somerville for discussion of the topics covered in this paper (though none of these people bear any responsibility for the use he has made of their advice) and to Mandy Bateman and Candice Bogdanski for research and bibliographical assistance. 2 *Orkneyinga saga*. 3 Rögnvaldr is often variously rendered Reginald(us), Ranald, Rag(h)nall, Ragnvald, etc.; his father Guðrøðr frequently appears as Gothred, Godred, Gofraid(h), etc. 4 Brian Ó Cuív, 'A poem in praise of Raghnall, king of Man', *Éigse*, 8 (1956–7), 283–301; a more recent translation, lacking the critical apparatus of Ó Cuív, is *The triumph tree: Scotland's earliest poetry, AD 550–1350*, ed. and trans. T.O. Clancy (Edinburgh, 1998), pp 236–41.

The same could also be said of other members of the dynasty to which Rögnvaldr belonged, who enjoyed similar reputations. The mysterious Guðrøðr (Godred) Crovan, for example, the Hiberno-Norse conqueror of the Isle of Man in 1079 and founder of the dynasty to which Rögnvaldr belonged, was known in Irish tradition as *meranach*, 'the furious'.[5] This reputation is suggested also by the *Cronica regum Mannie et Insularum* (*Chronicle of the kings of Man and the Isles*) – our major source for the history of the Isle of Man in this period, composed in the second half of the thirteenth century[6] – which said of him that 'he so tamed the Scots [?Irish] that no one who built a ship or boat dared use more than three iron bolts'.[7] Even a century and a half after Guðrøðr's demise, the English kings John (1199–1216) and Henry III (1216–72) engaged Manx fleets for guarding the coasts of England and Ireland: as late as 1235 Rögnvaldr's brother Óláfr II had a commission from Henry III for 'guarding, at his own cost, the coast of the sea of England towards Ireland, and towards the Isle of Man, and likewise the coast of the sea of Ireland towards England, and towards the aforesaid Isle of Man, lest injury might happen to the aforesaid our lands of England and Ireland, by sea, upon these coasts'.[8]

As these chronologically diverse examples suggest, a defining character-istic of the Manx sea-kings descended from Guðrøðr Crovan is their status as formidable warlords in command of substantial galley-fleets, active in and around the shores of the Irish Sea from the late eleventh to the mid-thirteenth century. These kings, rulers of a far-flung maritime kingdom in the islands between Britain and Ireland, remain largely neglected by historians, typically falling through the cracks of British, Irish, and Scandinavian historical writing. Although some modern historians have acknowledged in passing the status of the Manx kings as powers to be reckoned with, the subject of their military muscle and its utilization has received no serious consideration in its own right. This essay offers a start at exploring the military resources of the Manx kings, paying particular attention to the nature of those resources, the spheres within which they were utilized, and the degree to which they were engaged in the practice

---

5 *AU*, ii, pp 52–5 (s.a. 1094, 1095). See B.T. Hudson, *Viking pirates and Christian princes: dynasty, religion, and empire in the North Atlantic* (Oxford, 2005), p. 173, on the derivation, but cf. Ó Cuív, 'A poem in praise of Raghnall', 283–4, n. 6, who suggests *méarach* is derived from *méar*, a finger. The derivation of *Crovan* from Irish *cró-bán*, 'very pale', is suggested in Anderson, *Early sources*, ii, p. 43, n. 6.   6 Broderick, 'Introduction', *Chron. Man*, p. vii; I use the terms Manx Chronicle or simply the Chronicle when referring to this text.   7 *Chron. Man*, fos. 33r–v.   8 *Foedera, conventiones, litterae, et cujuscunque generis acta publica, inter reges Angliae et alios quosvis imperatores*, ed. Thomas Rymer, 10 vols (Hagae Comitis, 1739–45), i, pt i, p. 118; trans. in Oliver, *Monumenta*, ii, pp 72–3. Oliver's dating and interpretations are not always to be relied upon.

of providing fleets and armies to rulers of surrounding lands. It is argued
that by virtue of their extensive connections to surrounding lands,
formidable galley-fleets, and access to Gaelic-Norse troops, the Manx sea-
kings played an important role within the world of the galloglass.

* * *

The Isle of Man is a small (572 sq km) roughly teardrop-shaped island in
the northern Irish Sea basin, roughly equidistant between Strangford
Lough in Ulster to the west and St Bees Head in England to the east. The
nearest landmass is Burrow Head in southwest Scotland, a mere 30km to
the north, while Anglesey in Wales lies some 80km to the south. In clear
weather all of these surrounding lands are visible from the Isle of Man;
little wonder that to a medieval Welsh poet the Irish Sea was 'Môr
Manaw', 'the sea of Man', while one modern historian has christened the
Isle of Man itself 'Midway Island'.[9] Under ideal conditions in the middle
ages travel across the Irish Sea could be quick and uncomplicated. Ireland
and Wales might be reached within about twenty-four hours, while the
journey to England or the nearer parts of Scotland might take even less
time. Hazards to navigation did exist, of course, but the inter-visibility of
surrounding landmasses meant navigation was relatively straightforward.
Unfavourable winds, on the other hand, might cause considerable delays
or lengthen journeys.[10] By virtue of its position in the northern Irish Sea
basin at the southern outlet of the North Channel, the narrow and often
dangerous passage that links the Irish Sea to the North Atlantic, Man was
joined by the sea-road to the Hebrides, the chain of more than 500
topographically diverse islands arcing through some 400km off the west
coast of Scotland. Further north, round the stormy seas off Cape Wrath
(from Old Norse *hvarf*, turning point), lay the Orkney and Shetland
islands – themselves stepping-stones to Norway, Iceland, and Greenland.
Parts of the Hebrides, including the Isle of Skye and some of the outer
Hebridean isles like Lewis fell under the control of the Manx sea-kings;

9 B. Jones, 'Gwriad's heritage: links between Wales and the Isle of Man in the Early Middle
Ages', *Transactions of the Honourable Society of Cymmrodorion*, n.s. [no vol.] (1990), 30; Norman
Davies, *The Isles* (Oxford, 1999), p. 7 (map), p. 9. A. Moffat, *The sea kingdoms. The history of
Celtic Britain and Ireland* (London, 2002), pp 44–5, suggests that the name of the island itself is
derived from the Gaelic root *meadhon*, 'middle'. 10 On sailing times within the Irish Sea, see
Hudson, *Viking pirates*, pp 16–17; there is much of value in Timothy O'Neill, *Merchants and
mariners in medieval Ireland* (Dublin, 1987), ch. 5 and in Rosemary Power, 'Scotland in the Norse
sagas', in *Scotland and Scandinavia, 800–1800*, ed. G.G. Simpson (Edinburgh, 1990), pp 13–24,
esp. pp 20–3.

hence the title 'king of Man and the Isles'. The traffic flowing along the sea-road is exemplified by the spectacular find of 78 chess-pieces (with 14 plain disks and one belt buckle) made at Uig Bay on the island of Lewis in 1831, the so-called Lewis Chessmen. Made of walrus-ivory and crafted, in all likelihood, in Norway, the chess pieces were prestigious items and were probably buried by a merchant travelling the well-established route from Scandinavia to Ireland via the Hebrides.[11] Indeed, 'the strategic value of the island must have been considerable', never more so, perhaps, than in the Norse period under consideration here.[12]

The Isle of Man offered more than simply a strategic location within the Irish Sea and upon the sea-routes to those who controlled it, however: it also represented an economic prize of some consequence.[13] Above all it was renowned for its fecundity, so that a variety of medieval writers ranging from Icelandic saga authors to the Irish bard who sang Rögnvaldr's praises to the author of the Manx Chronicle all celebrated the fertility of the island.[14] Despite a high proportion of uplands, Man contains much good farmland well suited to the grazing of cattle and sheep (King Óláfr II (1226–37) granted the monks of St Bees the right to purchase sixty head of cattle in his lands, or their equivalent value in swine or sheep, for example) and cereal crops could also be grown.[15] Archaeological excavations reveal that even upland areas seem to have been intensively exploited in the period of the late Norse kings, suggesting that the island was 'fairly densely populated at the time, and that all the good, and even medium-quality, farmland was occupied'.[16] Fishing was another important activity, attested in the charters of several Manx kings that granted fishing rights to religious houses, and in the archaeological record. Excavations at Peel Castle in the 1980s showed that fish played a major role in the medieval

11 See J. Robinson, *The Lewis chessmen* (London, 2004), and N. Stratford, *The Lewis chessmen and the enigma of the hoard* (London, 1997).   12 B.R.S. Megaw and E. Megaw, 'The Norse heritage in the Isle of Man', in *The early cultures of North-West Europe*, ed. C. Fox and B. Dickins (Cambridge, 1950), p. 148.   13 Good overviews are P.J. Davey, 'At the crossroads of power and cultural influence: Manx archaeology in the High Middle Ages', in *Mannin revisited. Twelve essays on Manx culture and environment*, ed. P.J. Davey and David Finlayson (Edinburgh, 2002), pp 81–104, and B.T. Hudson, 'The changing economy of the Irish Sea province', in Brendan Smith (ed.), *Britain and Ireland, 900–1300: insular responses to medieval European change* (Cambridge, 1999), pp 39–66.   14 *Orkneyinga saga*, ch. 41; Clancy, *Triumph tree*, p. 236; *Chron Man*, fos. 35r, 41v.   15 *The register of the priory of St Bees*, ed. J. Wilson (Durham and London, 1915), no. 45; C.R. Cheney, 'Manx synodal statutes, A.D. 1230(?)–1351. Part I: introduction and Latin texts', *CMCS*, 7 (Summer 1984), 63–89 at 76–8; idem, 'Manx synodal statutes, A.D. 1230(?)–1351. Part II: translation of Latin texts', *CMCS*, 7 (Winter 1984), 51–63, at 51–3; see also P.S. Gelling, 'Shielings in the Isle of Man', *JMM*, 6/77 (1960–61), 123–5, and idem, 'Medieval shielings in the Isle of Man', *Medieval Archaeology*, 6–7 (1964), 156–72.   16 P.S. Gelling, 'A Norse homestead near Doarlish Cashen, Kirk Patrick, Isle of Man', *Medieval Archaeology*, 14 (1970), 74–82; quotation at p. 81.

economy, with an expansion of fishing activity detected in the eleventh or twelfth century.[17] The island was also well endowed with significant mineral resources: King Haraldr Óláfsson (d.1248) granted the monks of Furness abbey 'the use of all kinds of mines which may be found within my kingdom, both beneath the soil and above', as well as a depot at 'Bakenaldwath' (probably Ronaldsway).[18] Mercantile activity is more difficult to trace in the written sources. A letter of Rögnvaldr's brother, Óláfr, of about 1228 refers specifically to his merchants, presumably Manx, while the Lewis chessmen point to long-distance mercantile activity along the sea-road.[19] All of these resources appear to have been effectively exploited by the Manx kings, who, like other contemporary rulers, regulated commerce in their realm and benefited from customs duties, tolls, and taxes.[20] It is perhaps testimony to the wealth of the island and its efficient exploitation by its rulers that despite its small size it was home to three major power-centres in the late Norse period: St Patrick's Isle on the west coast, guarding the best natural harbour in the island, a multi-period centre with ecclesiastical and secular buildings; Castle Rushen overlooking Castletown Bay in the southeast, a late twelfth- or early thirteenth-century tower keep in contemporary style which, by the mid-thirteenth-century, had become the headquarters of the Manx kings; and Rushen Abbey, a Savignac, later Cistercian, foundation from Furness abbey established in 1134 by Óláfr I, which by the second quarter of the thirteenth century became the mausoleum of the dynasty.[21] Against this evidence of prosperity must be set the fact that the Isle of Man, lacking urban centres until the sixteenth century, did not participate in the 'commercial revolution' of the eleventh to early fourteenth centuries, and there is a rather puzzling

---

17 A.R. Hutchinson and A.K.G. Jones, 'The fish remains', in *Excavations on St Patrick's Isle, Peel, Isle of Man 1982–1988: prehistoric, Viking, medieval and later*, ed. D. Freke (Liverpool, 2002), pp 258–61. An increasing corpus of work by archaeologists like James H. Barrett is shedding important light on this resource: see J.H. Barrett, 'Fish trade in Norse Orkney and Caithness: a zooarchaeological approach', *Antiquity*, 71 (1997), 616–38. 18 *Sir Christopher Hatton's Book of Seals*, ed. L. Lewis and D.M. Stenton (Oxford, 1950), pp xxxii, 298–9 and 302 with accompanying notes; Oliver, *Monumenta*, ii, pp 77–8. See also B.R.S. Megaw, '"Bakenaldwath" and the medieval lead mines', *JMM*, 6/77 (1960–61), 105–7. 19 *CDS*, v, no. 9 (p. 136); on the Lewis chessmen, see note 9 above. 20 See, e.g., *The register and records of Holm Cultram*, ed. F. Grainger and W.G. Collingwood (Kendal, 1929), nos. 265, 266. 21 B.R.S. Megaw, 'St Patrick's Isle: "The Tara of the Isle of Man": its churches, castles, saints and kings', *JMM*, 5/69 (1943), 116–20; R.A. Curphey, *Peel Castle on St Patrick's Isle, Peel* (revised ed., Douglas, 2005); Freke, *Excavations on St Patrick's Isle*; D. Freke, *The Peel Castle dig* (Douglas, 1995); B.H. St J. O'Neil, 'Castle Rushen, Isle of Man', *Archaeologia*, 94 (1951), 1–26; P.J. Davey (ed.), *Rushen Abbey, Ballasalla, Isle of Man: first archaeological report* (Douglas, 1999); see now P.J. Davey and Andrew Johnson, 'Medieval archaeology and architecture', in *A new history of the Isle of Man. Volume III: the medieval period 1000–1405*, ed. Seán Duffy (Liverpool, forthcoming).

lack of coinage on the island between the late eleventh and early fourteenth centuries.[22] Yet clearly the Isle of Man proved to be a considerable
economic, as well as strategic, asset to its medieval rulers.

* * *

The full potential of the Isle of Man as a power centre for a dynasty of
sea-kings was realized with the arrival in Man of Guðrøðr Crovan and his
entrenchment there in 1079, which opened a new era in the history of
Man, the Isles, and indeed the Irish Sea. According to the Manx Chronicle,
Guðrøðr came to the Isle of Man after the battle of Stamford Bridge in
1066, in which he fought on the losing Norwegian side. He was received in
Man by the king, Guðrøðr Sigtryggsson (possibly a kinsman) who died in
1070. The Chronicle then relates how Guðrøðr invaded three times in
1079, ultimately defeating the Manx at the battle of Skyhill overlooking
Ramsey and establishing himself in the island as a conqueror.[23] Guðrøðr's
identity remains shrouded in Irish Sea mists thanks to problems with the
sources, but recent scholarship has linked him to the famous Óláfsson
dynasty of Dublin, and he may have been a son of Ivarr Haraldsson who
died in 1054.[24] Guðrøðr himself died in 1095, when he succumbed to
plague in Islay, and one of his most enduring accomplishments was as the
founder of a vigorous line of sea-kings described by the Irish poet who
sang Rögnvaldr's praises as 'Gofraidh Méarach's fair offspring'.[25] Commonly
referred to by modern historians as the 'Crovan dynasty', Guðrøðr's
descendants presided over something of a golden age in Man and the Isles
until the death of the last Manx king, Magnus, in 1265.

   The kings descended from Guðrøðr are for the most part fairly well
known in the history of the Irish Sea and the Hebrides, though they
remain largely ignored in broader British or Scandinavian contexts.[26] The

22 See Davey, 'Crossroads', passim; also Hudson, 'Changing economy', passim. 23 *Chron.
Man*, fos. 32v–33v. 24 Hudson, *Viking pirates*, pp 171–2; Seán Duffy, 'Emerging from the mist:
Ireland and Man in the eleventh century', in Davey and Finlayson (eds), *Mannin revisited*, pp
55–6; Duffy regards Guðrøðr as a son or nephew of Ivarr Haraldsson. See also George
Broderick, 'Irish and Welsh strands in the genealogy of Guðrøðr Crovan', *JMM*, 8/89 (1980),
32–8. 25 Clancy, *Triumph tree*, p. 239; Ó Cuív, 292. 26 See now Duffy (ed.), *New History III*;
R.A. McDonald, *Rögnvaldr Guðrøðrsson, King of Man and the Isles, 1187–1229* (forthcoming);
R.A. McDonald, *The kingdom of the Isles: Scotland's western seaboard, c.1100–c.1336* (East
Linton, 1997); G.V.C. Young, *The history of the Isle of Man under the Norse, or, now through a glass
darkly* (Peel, 1981); older works include A.W. Moore, *History of the Isle of Man*, 2 vols (London,
1900; rpr. Douglas, 1977); R.H. Kinvig, *The Isle of Man. A social, cultural and political history*
(Liverpool, 1975). There is much of value in W.C. MacKenzie, *History of the Outer Hebrides
(Lewis, Harris, North and South Uist, Benbecula, and Barra)* (Paisley, 1903, rpr. Edinburgh,
1974). I am currently preparing a history of the Crovan dynasty.

dynasty is certainly noteworthy for a series of long-reigning kings through the twelfth and into the thirteenth century: Óláfr Guðrøðarsson (Óláfr I, 1113–53) was followed by his son Guðrøðr (II) (1154–87) who was followed in turn by his sons Rögnvaldr (I) (1187–1226, d. 1229) and Óláfr (II) (1226–37). Then, from 1237 until 1265, the three sons of Óláfr II ruled in turn: Haraldr (I) (1237–48), Rögnvaldr (II) (May 1249) and Magnus (I) (1252–65). These kings endured periodic bouts of kin-strife, challenges from the Hebridean chieftain Sumarliði, better-known as Somerled (d. 1164) and his descendants (Clann Somhairle or the MacSorleys), and the waxing of English, Norwegian, and Scottish naval power in the western seaways. But for the most part the history of the Crovan dynasty is remarkable for its stability and for the manner in which the Manx kings successfully amplified their power, prestige, and status within an intensely competitive arena in British and Irish history, all the while modernizing their kingship along contemporary lines. There can be no doubt that much of their success rested upon their military might, principally the galley-fleets that frequently appear in a variety of eleventh-, twelfth-, and thirteenth-century sources.

* * *

For the rulers of a splintered water-world embracing not just the Isle of Man but extending into the Hebrides as well, survival within this stormy maritime arena required, above all else, large fleets of ships. A Norse king without ships was next to helpless: King Sverre of Norway (1177–1202) recognized this when he opined in the early 1180s that 'from this have come all our distresses, that we lost all our ships'.[27] Giraldus Cambrensis (Gerald of Wales), writing about the Northern and Western Isles and their Norse masters, observed:

> The Norwegians, who keep their eyes ever on the ocean, lead, above any other people, a piratical life. Consequently, all their expeditions and wars are decided by naval engagements.[28]

The Crovan kings would have understood that sentiment perfectly. They were by no means undisputed masters of the seas, although they possessed

27 *Sverris saga*, ed. G. Indrebø (Kristiana, 1920), p. 79 (ch. 73); trans. J. Sephton, *Sverrissaga: the saga of King Sverri of Norway* (London, 1899; rpr. Felinfach, 1994), p. 92. 28 Giraldus Cambrensis, *Opera*, ed. J.S. Brewer, J.F. Dimock, and G.F. Warner, 8 vols (London, 1861–91), v, p. 94; *Topographia Hiberniae: history and topography of Ireland*, trans. J.J. O'Meara (revised ed. London, 1982), pp 65–6.

impressive fleets and evidently knew a thing or two about naval engagements. As would be expected of the rulers of a small island in the midst of
the Irish Sea, within sight of surrounding landmasses, the fleets of the
Manx kings were felt at one time or another, in varying degrees, and in
varying capacities, round the shores of neighbouring lands. We may begin
by evaluating the sphere of operations of the Manx fleet.

Unquestionably Ireland received the most military attention from the
Manx kings, something that is hardly surprising in light of the historic
links between Dublin and Man from at least the eleventh century, and the
close involvement of Manx kings in Irish affairs into the thirteenth century.
Guðrøðr Crovan, who is widely regarded as a member of the Hiberno-
Norse Óláfsson dynasty of Dublin, re-conquered his ancestral home in
1091 and is said by the Manx Chronicler to have 'so tamed the Scots
[?Irish] that no one who built a ship or boat dared use more than three
iron bolts'.[29] The precise meaning of this statement remains rather
puzzling, though the domination of the seas that it implies seems clear
enough. Guðrøðr's domination of Dublin was short-lived, however, as he
was expelled in 1094 and died the next year on Islay,[30] but his successors
maintained Irish connections and aspirations to a revived Dublin-Manx
axis.[31] Manx vessels appeared in Irish waters in 1154 (on which, see
below), and King Guðrøðr II invaded Dublin early in his reign, possibly
around 1156, with a 'large fleet and a substantial army', but withdrew after
a few days.[32] King Guðrøðr (who took as a concubine and later canonically
married Fionnghuala, probably the daughter of Niall Mac Lochlainn, king
of Cineál Eoghain (1170–76)),[33] is also said by Giraldus Cambrensis to
have contributed ships to the Hiberno-Norse counterattack on the English
in Dublin in May 1171; Giraldus observes that his motive was 'fear of the
threat of English domination, inspired by the successes of the English',[34]
illustrating that the English conquest of Ireland had repercussions that
extended beyond the shores of Ireland and reverberated around the Irish
Sea basin.[35] (Manx forces are, incidentally, also mentioned in the late
twelfth-century Anglo-Norman chronicle or *geste* (revised in the first half
of the thirteenth century) usually known as 'The Song of Dermot and the
Earl', as having participated in this attack, although no precise numbers of

29 *Chron. Man*, fos. 33r–v.   30 *AI*, p. 247; *Chron. Man*, fo. 33v.   31 For which see Seán Duffy,
'Irishmen and Islesmen in the kingdoms of Dublin and Man, 1052–1171', *Ériu*, 43 (1992),
93–133, and idem, *Ireland in the Middle Ages* (Dublin, 1997), pp 42–3.   32 *Chron. Man*, fos.
37r–v; the dating of the episode is problematic.   33 *Chron. Man*, fo. 40r; see also *NHI*, ii, p. 135.
34 *Expugnatio*, pp 78–9.   35 See R.A. McDonald, 'The English conquest of Ireland and
Hiberno-Manx relations', in Seán Duffy (ed.), *Medieval Dublin VIII. Proceedings of the Friends
of Medieval Dublin Symposium 2006* (2007); and Duffy, 'Irishmen and Islesmen', 132–3.

vessels is provided).[36] Guðrøðr II's son Rögnvaldr, who had an Irish mother (*not*, however, Fionnghuala) and succeeded his father in the kingship in 1187/88, also flexed his military muscle in Ireland. An Irish praise-poem composed in his honour, probably in the first half of his long reign, around 1200, depicts him as plundering and raiding round the shores of Ireland: raids or attacks on Colptha's Strait (Colp, the lower reaches of the Boyne Valley), Dublin, Tráigh Bhaile (Dundalk Strand), and Aran are mentioned. 'You'll seek harbour behind Aran', the poet sings, 'while probing Ireland's cold shores'.[37] The poet's claims are not inherently improbable, though the representation of Rögnvaldr as entertaining a claim to kingship in Ireland is surely wishful thinking in light of the English entrenchment there since the late 1160s. When next we hear of Rögnvaldr's involvement in Irish military affairs it is in a very different capacity, however, caught up in the Anglo-Irish baronial politics of the early thirteenth century and stemming from the marriage of his sister to John de Courcy, the English conqueror of Ulster. The Manx Chronicle relates, following de Courcy's expulsion from Ulster in 1204:

In the year 1205 John de Courcy regained his strength and collected a massive force, and he took Reginald [Rögnvaldr] king of the Isles with about a hundred ships to Ulster with him. When they landed at the port called Strangford they laid siege to the castle of Rath [Dundrum] in a dilatory manner. However Walter de Lacy suddenly arrived on the scene with a large army and put them to flight in great confusion.[38]

The episode is also recorded in the Annals of Loch Cé, which state that 'no good resulted from this expedition, however; but the country was destroyed and plundered; and they afterwards departed without obtaining power'.[39] While John de Courcy's career entered its nadir, his brother-in-law King Rögnvaldr prospered from newfound English connections. Far from falling foul of King John, he was courted and wooed and ultimately ended up with the grant of a knight's fee in Carlingford from King John in 1212, the fine harbour there, overlooked by the castle, undoubtedly providing an Irish base for Manx galleys.[40] From this point onward there

---

36 *The deeds of the Normans in Ireland. La geste des Engleis en Yrlande. A new edition of the chronicle formerly known as the song of Dermot and the earl*, ed. Evelyn Mullally (Dublin, 2002), ll. 2255–2492. *The deeds of the Normans* and Giraldus's *Expugnatio* are in considerable agreement on the assault on Dublin in 1171, but there are differences between them, the most significant of which is the relationship of the naval attack to the unsuccessful siege of Dublin by Ruaidhri and his allies: in Giraldus the sea-attack precedes Ruaidhri's assault, but the *geste* has it follow: see *Expugnatio*, pp 304–5, note 106, where the chronology of Giraldus is preferred. Whichever sequence of events is accepted there is no doubt of Manx support for the attack.   37 Clancy, *Triumph tree*, p. 239; Ó Cuív, 293.   38 *Chron. Man*, fo. 41r.   39 *ALC*, i, pp 234–5 (s.a. 1205).   40 *Rotuli chartarum in Turri Londinensi asservati ab anno MCXCIX ad annum MCCXVI*, ed.

is (perhaps predictably) a marked decline in Manx predatory activities in Ireland, though Manx galleys would certainly have been in evidence in Irish waters, since subsequent Manx kings were charged with guarding the English and Irish coasts (see below). The change from sea-rovers to guardians of the coast was no doubt due in large measure to the consolidation of the English conquest as well as the newfound status of the Manx kings as vassals of the English monarchs; just possibly it also serves as a barometer for the relative power of the Manx sea-kings from Guðrøðr Crovan to Rögnvaldr as compared to their thirteenth-century successors, who do not, perhaps, appear as great warlords on a scale to rival their forefathers.

Manx vessels and fleets also plied Welsh waters, particularly those of north Wales, around Anglesey, on several occasions in the eleventh and twelfth centuries. The twelfth-century text *Historia Gruffud vab Kenan*, which recounts, sometimes in confused fashion, the epic life of Gruffudd ap Cynan, prince of Gwynedd (d. 1137), relates how Gruffudd led a Welsh attack against the Normans in Gwynedd around 1094. Gruffudd is said by the author of the Historia to have sought assistance from king *Gothrei* (Guðrøðr Crovan), 'his ally', pleading his case for ships, equipment, and gear in the 'islands of Denmark' as the biographer puts it – a term used in the biography to describe Man and the Hebrides.[41] The Welsh ruler was not disappointed, and the next thing we are told is that Gruffudd voyaged with sixty ships to Anglesey, where battle was joined, but the Manx fleet departed soon thereafter.[42] At least one scholar thinks that aid from the Isles was invaluable to Gruffudd's cause.[43] Dating the episode is problematic, but it may be that the withdrawal of the Manx fleet was related to Guðrøðr's troubles in Dublin in 1094. In this particular instance military actions mirrored genealogical connections, since Guðrøðr Crovan and Gruffudd ap Cynan were distant kinsmen, both being members of the Hiberno-Norse dynasty of Dublin. About a century after Guðrøðr offered help to Gruffudd, another Manx king aided another north Welsh dynast. In 1193, the native Welsh chronicle known as the *Brut y tywysogyon*, or *Chronicle of the princes*, records:

T.D. Hardy (London, 1837), p. 186b; Oliver, *Monumenta*, ii, pp 35–6, misdated this to 1213. See further McDonald, *Rögnvaldr*, ch. 4.   41 See Colmán Etchingham, 'North Wales, Ireland and the Isles: the insular Viking zone', *Pertitia*, 15 (2001), 145–87, at 159.   42 For the *Historia Gruffud vab Kenan*, see *A mediaeval prince of Wales. The life of Gruffudd ap Cynan*, ed. and trans. D. Simon Evans (Lampeter, 1990), pp 40, 72; see also David Moore, 'Gruffudd ap Cynan and the mediaeval Welsh polity', in *Gruffudd ap Cynan. A collaborative biography*, ed. K.L. Maund (Woodbridge, 1996), pp 37–9 for discussion of the confused chronology of this period in Gruffudd's career.   43 B.G. Charles, *Old Norse relations with Wales* (Cardiff, 1934), p. 71.

That year Rhodri ab Owain subdued the island of Anglesey through the help of [the son of] Guðrøðr, king of Man; and before the end of the year he was expelled by the sons of Cynan ab Owain.[44]

Rhodri ap Owain (d. 1195) was one of several contenders for power in the north Welsh kingdom of Gwynedd following the death of his father, the mighty Owain Gwynedd, son of Gruffudd ap Cynan, in 1170;[45] Guðrøðr king of Man died in 1187, and the words 'the son of' have almost certainly been omitted, so that the Manx king in question must therefore be Rögnvaldr Guðrøðarsson.[46] A papal letter of 1199 reveals that Rögnvaldr's daughter had married Rhodri sometime before his death in 1195,[47] and there can be little doubt that the military aid from Rögnvaldr to Rhodri flowed by virtue of this matrimonial connection. The entry in the *Brut* makes it clear that Anglesey was successfully subdued, although it is also clear that Rhodri was soon expelled again. However, an entry in another Welsh text refers to the year 1193 as *Haf y gwydyl* or 'Summer of the Gael', which George Broderick has argued might refer to fairly substantial Gaelic-speaking forces brought by Rögnvaldr to Anglesey; the episode has, accordingly, interesting implications for the linguistic situation in Man and the Hebrides in the late twelfth-century, suggestive as it is of a bilingual environment, as well as the military situation, and is discussed at further length below.[48] Like Ireland, Manx military intervention in Wales seems to have followed other contacts, and to have mirrored a variety of diplomatic, political, and matrimonial contacts that existed into the middle of the thirteenth century.[49]

Compared to Ireland and Wales there is less evidence for Manx military activities in Scotland, though there is no doubt that Manx fleets were active in Scottish waters, particularly in the north and west. *Orkneyinga saga*, the saga-history of the Orkney jarls from the inception of the earldom down to the end of the twelfth century, contains an account of the assistance rendered by King Rögnvaldr to King William I of Scotland (1165–1214) in the latter's struggle against the formidable Haraldr Maddaðsson (d. 1206):

---

44 *Brut y tywysogyon or the chronicle of the princes: Red Book of Hergest version*, trans. Thomas Jones (Cardiff, 1955), p. 173 (s.a. 1193).   **45** R.R. Davies, *The age of conquest. Wales 1063–1415* (Oxford, 1987), pp 238–9; see also K.L. Maund, *The Welsh kings. The medieval rulers of Wales* (Stroud, 2000), pp 113–17.   **46** *Brut y tywysogyon*, p. 296, note.   **47** *Patrologiae Cursus Completus. Series Latina*, ed. J.P. Migne. 221 vols (Paris, 1844–64), pp 214, 791–2 (letter of 25 November 1199); calendared in *Cal. papal letters*, i, p. 8; see also pp 13, 19.   **48** *Gwrtheyrn Gwrtheneu to King John*, in *The Text of the Bruts from the Red Book of Hergest*, ed. J. Rhys and J.G. Evans (Oxford, 1890), ii, p. 405; see also Broderick, 'Irish and Welsh Strands', p. 36 and note 31.   **49** *Chron. Man*, fos. 45r–v; *Acts of the Welsh rulers, 1120–1283*, ed. Huw Pryce

56 R. Andrew McDonald

William, king of Scots, heard that ... Earl Haraldr Maddaðsson, without bothering to consult him, had taken over the whole of Caithness and sent messengers to Rögnvaldr Guðrøðarsson, king of the Hebrides ... At that time King Rögnvaldr was the greatest fighting man in all the western lands. For three whole years he had lived aboard longships and not spent a single night under a sooty roof. As soon as he got the message, Rögnvaldr started gathering men all through the Hebrides and from Kintyre, to add to a strong force he had with him from Ireland. Then he traveled north and stayed for a while in Caithness, taking over the whole territory.[50]

Roger of Howden's *Chronica*, begun in the 1190s and continued down to his death in 1201 or 1202, supports the saga account. Howden was well-informed on northern affairs, and John Gillingham has remarked that 'for students of later twelfth-century Ireland and Scotland, there is no English historian more important than Roger of Howden'.[51] Like the saga, Howden's *Chronica* relates the conflict between William, king of Scots, and Haraldr, jarl of Orkney. It tells how 'William, king of Scots, collected a large army and entered Moray to subdue Harald MacMadit [Haraldr Maddaðsson], who had occupied that land'. Haraldr retreated and promised the surrender of hostages, but failed to deliver them all as promised, and two rounds of negotiations with the Scots then fell through. At this point Howden says that 'Reginald, son of Somerled, king of Man, came to William king of Scots and bought Caithness from him, saving the king's yearly revenue'.[52] There has in the past been some confusion about which of the two Insular rulers whose name was Latinized as Reginald – Rögnvaldr of Man or the Rögnvaldr (d. *c*.1209) who is better-known as Raghnall, the son of Sumarliði – was involved, though the question appears to have been settled definitively by A.A.M. Duncan in favour of the Manx ruler.[53] The dating of the episode remains problematic, but probably belongs around 1200.[54] As with Ireland and Wales, Manx

(Cardiff, 2005), no. 317 (p. 490) where 'Godredo filio regis Mannie' witnesses a charter of Llywelyn ap Gruffudd of 1241; discussion in Broderick, 'Irish and Welsh Strands', 32–8. 50 *Orkneyinga saga* ch. 110. 51 John Gillingham, 'The travels of Roger of Howden and his views of the Irish, Scots and Welsh', *Anglo-Norman Studies* 20 (1997), pp 151–69 at 151. 52 For Howden, see *Chronica Magistri Rogeri de Houedene*, ed. Thomas Arnold (London, 1868–71), iv, pp 10–12; trans. in Anderson, *Scottish annals*, pp 316–18. 53 A.A.M. Duncan, 'Roger of Howden and Scotland, 1187–1201', in *Church, chronicle and learning in medieval and early Renaissance Scotland*, ed. Barbara Crawford (Edinburgh, 1999), p. 143 and notes 51, 55 on p. 155; but cf. W.D.H. Sellar, 'Hebridean sea kings: The successors of Somerled, 1164–1316' in *Alba: Celtic Scotland in the medieval era*, ed. E.J. Cowan and R.A. McDonald (East Linton, 2000), pp 193–9 who makes a case for Raghnall son of Sumarliði. 54 Duncan, 'Roger of Howden and the Scots', p. 143, suggests 1199; W.P.L. Thomson, *New history of Orkney* (2nd edn, Edinburgh, 2001), p. 126, suggests 1201. Evidence is collected in R.A. McDonald, *Outlaws of medieval Scotland: challenges to the Canmore kings, 1058–1266* (East Linton, 2003), pp 39–41. The episode is also discussed in Barbara Crawford, 'The earldom of Caithness and the kingdom of Scotland, 1150–1266', in *Essays on the nobility of medieval Scotland*, ed. K.J. Stringer

military activities in Scotland presumably flowed from earlier diplomatic and political contacts: Rögnvaldr's father, Guðrøðr, had sheltered for a while at the court of the Scottish king Maol Choluim (Malcolm) IV (1153–65) during his exile from Man between 1158 and 1164.[55]

Guðrøðr of Man and Maol Choluim of Scotland may have had much to discuss on the occasion of the Manx ruler's visit to Scotland in 1159 or 1160. That is because both kings shared a common adversary in the person of Sumarliði (Somhairle mac Giolla Bhrighde), the Hebridean chieftain whose rise to prominence by the 1150s posed a real threat to both. The Manx Chronicle records two sea-battles between Sumarliði and Guðrøðr of Man: one in 1156, resulting in the division of the Isles between the two rivals, and another in 1158, in which Sumarliði ravaged Man and chased Guðrøðr into ignominious exile; Guðrøðr only returned in 1164, following the demise of Sumarliði in an invasion of the Scottish mainland at Renfrew.[56] From 1156 the kingdom of the Isles was in fact a divided one, with the Manx kings controlling the Isle of Man itself as well as the Skye and Lewis groups of the Hebrides, while the descendants of Sumarliði controlled the Mull and Islay groups.[57] Enmity between the two rival lines is clear, though the sources only provide tantalizing hints and glimpses of outright warfare, as in the 1209 entry in the Annals of Ulster, which records, 'the sons of Raghnall, Somhairle's son, fought a battle against the men of Skye; and slaughter was made of them there'.[58] The context of this conflict is not entirely clear, and it may need to be considered in relation to a Norwegian expedition to the Isles in 1210, but whether that is the case or not, since Skye was under the control of the Manx kings at this time the entry may be indicative of ongoing conflict. Other clues to the relationship between the two rival kindreds of sea-kings may be provided by the Irish praise-poem in Rögnvaldr's honour. In several places the poem describes Rögnvaldr as the ruler of territories that seem to have been under the control of Clann Somhairle at the time. Thus, in one stanza Rögnvaldr is praised as 'bright-haired lord of Mull's harbour', and in another as 'king of Coll'.[59] Both islands fell under the jurisdiction of Clann Somhairle by the thirteenth century, and while it seems likely that these references may be discounted as poetic licence or else stock imagery,[60] a third reference in the praise-poem proves more puzzling and potentially more significant. Towards the end of the poem the bard

(Edinburgh, 1985), p. 31.   **55** *The acts of Malcolm IV, king of Scots 1153–1165*, ed. G.W.S. Barrow (Edinburgh, 1960), no. 131.   **56** *Chron. Man*, fos. 37v–38r, 39r–39v.   **57** *Chron. Man*, fo. 37v.   **58** *AU* ii, pp 248–9.   **59** Clancy, *Triumph tree*, pp 238, 239; Ó Cuív, 292, 294.   **60** A praise-poem for Aonghus Mór, great-grandson of Sumarliði, of *c.*1250, described him as 'lord of Coll': Clancy, *Triumph tree*, p. 289.

remarks that Rögnvaldr has 'brought a crushing defeat on Maelbheirn'.[61]
If, as W.M. Hennessy thought, this represents Morvern,[62] the rugged,
roughly triangular-shaped peninsula adjacent to the Isle of Mull and
bounded by Loch Sunart, Loch Linnhe and the Sound of Mull that fell
under the jurisdiction of Sumarliði's descendants by the turn of the
twelfth/thirteenth centuries, then a battle here between Manx and
Somerledian forces is not implausible.

Befitting the situation of Man as a small island in the midst of the Irish
Sea, within sight of surrounding lands, the tendrils of Manx foreign
relations under the Crovan kings extended to the shores of all of those
lands. It is scarcely surprising, then, that Manx fleets were active from
Anglesey to Caithness between the late eleventh and mid-thirteenth
centuries, or that military aid often flowed from the ties of the Manx kings
to rulers of surrounding regions. An intriguing aspect of the Manx galley-
fleet is therefore the extent to which it – or part of it – was placed at the
disposal of the allies and kinsmen of the Manx kings, something that is
considered in greater detail below; but first it is necessary to take a closer
look at the nature of the fleet, beginning with the galleys themselves.

* * *

The nature of the vessels that comprised the formidable Manx fleet must
be inferred from a variety of predominantly non-Manx evidence: the
Manx Chronicle fails to provide any detail about the nature of these
vessels, and the Isle of Man itself lacks the artistic and sculptural evidence
so abundant in the Hebrides and the neighbouring mainland of Argyll,
where the West Highland galley forms a common motif on monumental
sculpture of the later middle ages.[63] There is in fact only a single surviving
representation of a Viking or late Norse ship from a Manx context, a
rather elaborate one cut onto a memorial stone at Maughold discovered
during the excavation of a keeill (chapel) in the churchyard, which also
bears the runic inscription 'Hethin set up this cross after his daughter
Hlíf. Árni carved these runes'. This shows a vessel in outline with a long
narrow hull and high stems, a tall mast with the sail furled, and with some
rigging represented. Instead of a fixed rudder it has a steering oar (lightly

61 Clancy, *Triumph tree*, p. 241; Ó Cuív, 296.   62 'Baile Suthain Sith Eamhna', trans. W.M.
Hennessy in W.F. Skene, *Celtic Scotland*, 3 vols (Edinburgh, 1880), iii, Appendix II, pp 411–27
at p. 427 and note 12; cf. Ó Cuív, 301, note.   63 K.A. Steer and J.W.M. Bannerman, *Late
medieval monumental sculpture in the West Highlands* (Edinburgh, 1977), pp 180–4; see also D.
Rixson, *The West Highland galley* (Edinburgh, 1998).

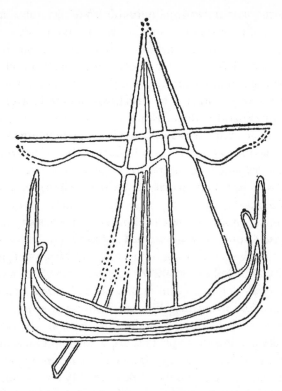

Detail of a ship on the Hedin cross, Kirk Maughold, Isle of Man
(image provided by kind permission of the Manx National Museum).

incised) near the stern (on what seems to be the port rather than the
starboard side), and there are no oars or oar-ports visible (fig. 1).[64] It could
be as early as the eleventh century, but it could also be as late as the
thirteenth century and it would appear that it cannot be more firmly dated
than belonging to the period of the kingdom of Man and the Isles.[65]

A vessel similar to that on the Hedin memorial stone was also utilized
on the waxen seals of the Manx kings from the twelfth and thirteenth
centuries. King Haraldr Óláfsson (d. 1248) possessed a seal that depicted a
lion on one side and a ship with furled sails on the other; the originals
were destroyed along with the documents to which they were attached in a

64 MM no. 142 is in the Kirk Maughold cross-shelter. See P.M.C. Kermode, 'First appearance
of a Viking ship on a Manx monument', *Mannin*, 2/3 (1914), 178–80; idem, 'The Hedin Cross,
Maughold, Isle of Man', *Saga Book of the Viking Society*, 9/2 (1914–18), 333–42; idem, 'A rune-
inscribed slab from Kirk Maughold; and the first figure of a Viking ship on a Manx monument',
IoMNHAS Proc., 2/1 (1923), 107–13; idem, *Manx crosses*, with an introduction by David M.
Wilson (Balgavies, 1994), Appendix C, pp 24–8.　65 D.M. Wilson, 'Manx memorial stones of
the Viking period', *Saga Book of the Viking Society*, 18 (1970), 15.

fire in the Cottonian Library in London in 1731, but the antiquarian Sir
Christopher Hatton had accurately preserved their likenesses about a
century earlier.[66] Despite the fragmentary nature of the seals at the time
they were illustrated, it is possible to discern ships with high stem-posts,
masts, and rigging. One shows a sail furled; no rudders, platforms, oars or
oar-ports are visible, although the vessels appear to be clinker-built. Other
Manx kings also possessed ship seals.[67]

These representations of vessels in a Manx context bear comparison
with a variety of other visual points of reference, from further away in time
and space: graffiti with ship-motifs from Dublin dating to the eleventh
century that show longships with long narrow hulls ending in high stems
and with masts;[68] sketches cut into wood or plaster from Scandinavia,
which often depict longships with high stems, masts and sails, and side-
rudders; or the famous and evocative thirteenth- or fourteenth-century
Bryggen rune-stick that shows some forty-four ships lined up, several of
which have figureheads and weather vanes.[69] Of this remarkable artifact
one scholar remarks: 'It is unlikely that we will ever find a more pertinent
visual impression of a traditional Norse fleet comprised of longships ...
The image has a quality that matches the best of the skaldic verses
describing similar fleets in words that are worthy to praise kings'.[70] Still
another visual parallel is the famous Bayeux Tapestry with its representations of the vessels used by Duke William of Normandy for his invasion
of England in September 1066.[71] Parallels for the Manx ship-seals are
found in the perhaps better-known examples of the Hebridean chieftains
descended from Sumarliði; a good example is that of Aonghus Mór of
Islay of 1292, which shows four men seated in a galley with a furled sail.[72]

Archaeology offers little help in understanding the nature of Manx
medieval galleys. Although the Isle of Man has yielded two Viking-Age

66 Northamptonshire Record Office/ FH 170: 'Sir Christopher Hatton's Book of Seals', nos.
428 and 432, ff. 91 and 92; the images of the seals are not reproduced in Lewis and Stenton's
edition but the story of the documents and their destruction is traced. H.R. Oswald, *Vestigia
Insulae Manniae antiquiora, or a dissertation on the armorial bearings of the Isle of Man* (Douglas,
1860) reproduces the seals (from Hatton's Book of Seals) as a frontispiece. 67 See B.R.S.
Megaw, 'The ship seals of the kings of Man', *JMM*, 6:76 (1959–60), 78–80; also J.A. Goodall,
'Manx arms and seals revisited', *IoMNHAS Proc.*, 11:3 (2001–3), 441–52. 68 A.E.
Christensen, 'Ship graffiti and models', in *Medieval Dublin: excavations 1962–81. Miscellanea 1*,
ed. P.F. Wallace (Dublin, 1988), pp 13–26. 69 M. Blindheim, *Graffiti in Norwegian stave
churches c.1150–c.1350* (Oslo, 1985), passim; L. leBon, 'The Bryggen "ship stick": a challenge in
art and ship technology', in *Ships and commodities* (The Bryggen Papers Supp. Series 7. Oslo
2001), pp 9–34; A.E. Christensen, 'Boat finds from Bryggen', *The Bryggen Papers* (Main Series
1. Oslo, 1985), pp 47–278. 70 *The Skuldelev ships I. Topography, archaeology, history,
conservation and display*, ed. O. Crumlin-Pedersen and O. Olsen (Roskilde, 2002), p. 193.
71 *The Bayeux tapestry*, intro. D.M. Wilson (London, 1985), pp 35–6, 40–4, 226–7. 72 W. de

ship-burials, in the north at Knock y Doonee and in the south at Balladoole, both belong to the early settlement period,[73] while hardly a single plank survives from a West Highland galley of medieval date.[74] A vessel raised from Roskilde Fjord in Denmark in 1962 and now housed in the Vikingeskibsmuseet at Roskilde brings us closer to the Manx sea-kings, however. The ship known as Skuldelev 2, reconstructed from very partial and fragmented remains originally thought to belong to several vessels, proved to be a magnificent sleek longship, about 30m in length and 4m wide, capable of carrying 65 warriors across the sea under oars and sail. Scientific analysis of the planks used to build and patch the ship showed that it was built of oak that had been felled *c.*1042 in eastern Ireland, likely around Dublin; it had been constructed by highly-skilled craftsmen who worked within Norse traditions of shipbuilding. The vessel had a long working life in the Irish Sea region, since it had been patched in the 1060s, about twenty to twenty-five years after it was initially launched. It was probably scuttled in the 1070s.[75] Clearly built for some great lord with the resources to construct, maintain, and man it, the dating of Skuldelev 2 means that, at least in its later life, it was contemporary with Guðrøðr Crovan, though of course it cannot be known whether it ever sought harbour in the Isle of Man.

Finally, literary sources like the Icelandic sagas reveal something of the famous ships of the era and their significance to Norse rulers.[76] Many examples exist, but several from Sturla Þórðarson's (d. 1284) *Hákonar saga Hákonarsonar*, a chronicle of King Hákon IV Hákonsson of Norway (1217–63), are of particular interest because they describe thirteenth-century vessels of a type that had plied the seas between Britain and Ireland in the days of the Manx sea-kings. Sturla lavished considerable attention upon the fleets and flagships of King Hákon, including the *Kross-súðin* ('The Cross'), *Máriu-súðin* ('The Mary') and *Krist-súðin* ('The Christ'). Here, for example, is Sturla's vivid portrait of 'The Mary':

Gray Birch, *Catalogue of seals in the Department of Manuscripts of the British Museum*, 6 vols (London, 1887–1900), iv, p. 437; Rixson, *West Highland galley*, plate 3a.   73 G. Bersu and D.M. Wilson, *Three Viking graves in the Isle of Man* (London, 1966), pp 1–44, 91–2; P.M.C. Kermode, 'Ship-burial in the Isle of Man', *Antiquaries Journal*, 10 (1930), 126–33.   74 D.H. Caldwell, 'The Scandinavian heritage of the lordship of the Isles', in *Scandinavia and Europe, 800–1350: contact, conflict and coexistence*, ed. J. Adams and K. Holman (Turnhout, 2004), p. 75, mentions two unfinished end-posts found in peat on the island of Eigg in the Hebrides, dated to 885–1035; see also B.E. Crawford, *Scandinavian Scotland* (Leicester, 1987), pp 15–16.   75 *The Skuldelev ships I*, pp 141–94 for Skuldelev 2.   76 A.W. Brøgger and H. Shetelig, *The Viking ships: their ancestry and evolution* (Oslo, 1951) remains a seminal work.

After that King Hákon began his journey from Tunsberg, and he had with him 'The Mary'. She was a dragon-ship [warship] of thirty rooms, and was the most handsome of all the ships made in Norway. The head and the necks were covered with gold, and the sail was set with beautiful figures. King Hákon had many other great ships, excellently outfitted. And it seemed as if, in the sunshine, fire burned on the heads and weather-vanes and gilded shields that were ranged from stem to stern.

Of 'The Cross', Sturla wrote:

When 'The Cross' came into her berth beside the other ships her planking sat as high in the water as the awning-poles on those ships and on 'The Óláfr'. The sides of the ship were nine ells above the water on 'The Cross'. That ship was of all those that were there the greatest; and it was the talk of old men that they had not seen so many great ships in one levy.[77]

Snorri Sturluson's *Skáldskaparmál* ('The language of poetry') included dozens of kennings for ships, and the Irish praise-poem in Rögnvaldr's honour characterizes them in terms of swans; 'the Swan' may in fact have been the name of King Rögnvaldr Guðrøðarsson's galley.[78]

All of this would suggest that the vessels comprising the fleets of the Manx sea-kings were of a type well-known in the contemporary Scandinavian and North Atlantic world: clinker-built, high stemmed, propelled by oars and sails, these were potent symbols of power, wealth, and prestige, something evidenced by their utilization on the seals of the Manx kings, as well as the carving on the Hedin cross-slab.

* * *

A further consideration is the size of the fleets in question. Moving beyond the stock references in the Manx Chronicle and the various other sources noted above to the 'large fleets' mustered by the Manx kings, it is possible to ascertain something of the size of Manx fleets. The Manx Chronicle contains several statements relating to specific numbers of vessels: in 1205, when Rögnvaldr provided one hundred vessels to his brother-in-law, John de Courcy; in 1223/4 when Rögnvaldr's brother Óláfr came to Man with thirty-two ships to seize a share in the kingdom;

77 *Hakonar saga*, p. 293 (ch. 291), p. 274 (ch. 278). P.G. Foote and D.M. Wilson, *The Viking achievement* (London, 1970; rpr. 1980), p. 237, suggest that the *drekar* or dragon-ships were the biggest warships of the Norse era, named because of their ornate prows. J. Jesch, *Ships and men in the late Viking Age. The vocabulary of runic inscriptions and skaldic verse* (Woodbridge, 2001) offers valuable insights into the technical terms utilized in descriptions of ships: see esp. pp 137–66.   78 Snorri Sturluson, *Edda: skáldskaparmál*, ed. A. Faulkes, 2 vols (London, 1998), i (Introduction, text and notes), pp 74–6 (ch. 51), pp 127–9 (ch. 75); Ó Cuiv, passim.

and in winter 1229, when Rögnvaldr came to Man with five ships in a final bid for restoration. It is worth bearing in mind that as it now exists the Manx Chronicle is a mid-thirteenth-century work, and the difficulties associated with extrapolating accurate numbers of armies and fleets from medieval chronicles are well known. So if these figures given in the Chronicle are treated with a grain of salt, it is also worthwhile observing that the overall scale is reasonable and in fact fits remarkably well with other evidence. Thus, for example, the *Historia Gruffud Vab Kenan* suggests that Guðrøðr Crovan provided his kinsman Gruffudd ap Cynan with 60 ships in the 1090s,[79] while an entry in the Annals of the Four Masters suggests that Guðrøðr could command 90 vessels.[80] In May 1171, King Guðrøðr II sent thirty Manx vessels to support the Hiberno-Norse assault on English-held Dublin. Nearly a century later, when the last Manx king, Magnus Óláfsson, was subjugated by the Scots king Alexander III (1249–86) in 1264, one of the terms of Magnus's submission was that he should provide 'ten pirate-type galleys' for the Scottish navy – five of 24 oars and five of 12 oars respectively. These ten vessels undoubtedly represent only a fraction of the strength available to the ruler of Man at the time.[81]

Undoubtedly the size and composition of the Manx fleet will have varied from time to time and according to a variety of political and military circumstances. Thus, for example, the massive fleet of one hundred galleys that Rögnvaldr took to the aid of his brother-in-law John de Courcy in 1205 – if even a remotely accurate figure – must represent a very large proportion of the entire Manx fleet. By contrast, the thirty-two galleys that Rögnvaldr's brother Óláfr brought to Man in 1224 undoubtedly represented only the vessels that could be mustered by Óláfr and his supporters, perhaps augmented by some Scottish vessels since Óláfr was allied to the powerful Scottish up-and-comer Fearchar Mac-an-tSagairt of Ross.[82] The 60 and 90 galleys said to have been under the command of Guðrøðr Crovan must also represent a significant proportion of the Manx fleet; significantly, Guðrøðr was in control of Dublin as well as the Isle of Man between 1091 and 1094/5, so ships from Dublin presumably augmented the Manx fleet. On the other hand, reversals in Manx fortunes may have impacted both the size of the fleet and its availability for mercenary ventures: as noted above, Guðrøðr Crovan's expulsion from Dublin may have resulted in the withdrawal of the Manx fleet from Welsh operations around 1094, justifying the observation that 'Godfrey

79 *Historia Gruffud vab Kenan*, ed. Evans, pp 40, 72.   80 *AFM*, ii, pp 946–7 (s.a. 1094).
81 *Scotichronicon*, ed. Watt, v, pp 348–9.   82 *Chron. Man*, fo. 43r.

[Guðrøðr] could only afford to dispense men and ships when his own position was secure'.[83] This would apply with equal measure to Guðrøðr's successors as Manx kings. Similarly, the division of the insular kingdom between Guðrøðr II and his rival, the upstart Sumarliði of Argyll, in the mid-1150s, must have reduced somewhat the naval capacity of the Manx kings as the Mull and Islay groups of the isles were wrested from their grasp. Is it possible that the 30 vessels sent by Guðrøðr II in support of the Hiberno-Norse assault on Dublin contrasts with the 60 vessels provided by Guðrøðr Crovan to Gruffudd ap Cynan 80 years earlier precisely because Guðrøðr II ruled a more truncated kingdom?

Some appreciation of the scale of Manx fleets may be obtained by comparison with the fleets of surrounding powers. It would hardly be fair to compare the fleets at the disposal of the Manx kings with those at the beck and call of the Norwegian kings: the formidable Hákon IV Hákonsson commanded a massive fleet of between one and two hundred large and well-manned ships that cruised through the Hebrides in 1263 and fought the Scots at Largs on the Ayrshire coast for possession of the Western Isles, while for an expedition against Denmark in 1257 Hákon is said to have taken 320 ships – an astonishing number, if true.[84] On the other side of the coin, however, the Scottish kings came late to the maritime arena of the western seas and it was not until the 1220s that they were able to muster sufficient naval resources to contemplate engaging Hebridean chieftains on their own terms.[85] Better comparisons for the Manx fleet in fact lie closer to home, with the aforementioned Hebridean chieftains or the powerful rulers of Galloway in southwest Scotland. Thus, for his naval engagements with King Guðrøðr II, Sumarliði is said to have mustered 80 and 53 ships respectively in 1156 and 1158, and for his ill-fated invasion of the Scottish mainland in 1164 he is said to have commanded 160 galleys – a very impressive figure, if even remotely accurate, and one that squares rather well with the figures for the sizes of Manx fleets given in the Chronicle and elsewhere.[86] Another comparison is with the lords of Galloway in southwest Scotland, great sea-captains and active participants in the tempestuous politics of the Irish Sea, with whom the Manx sea-kings were connected by marriage.[87] An Icelandic author described Alan

83 Charles, *Old Norse relations with Wales*, p. 70.   84 See *Hakonar saga*, in *Icelandic sagas and other historical documents relating to the settlements and descents of the Northmen on the British Isles*, ed. G. Vigfusson and G.W. Dasent, 4 vols (London 1887–94), ii, p. 335 (ch. 319); 295–6 (ch. 293); Dasent's translation in volume iv of this edition has been found wanting, and all translations are accordingly my own unless otherwise indicated.   85 John MacInnes, 'West Highland sea power in the Middle Ages', *TGSI*, 48 (1972–4), 518–56, at p. 525; see also McDonald, *Kingdom*, chs 3, 4.   86 *Chron. Man*, fos. 37v, 39r.   87 Óláfr I married a daughter of Fergus of Galloway in the early twelfth century, and Rögnvaldr Guðrøðarsson married a

of Galloway (d.1234), Rögnvaldr's ally in his struggle with his brother
Óláfr, as 'the greatest warrior at that time. He had a great army, and many
ships' – perhaps 100–200, in fact.[88] Keith Stringer has remarked of the
military forces at Alan's disposal that 'few magnates in Britain ... could
command such resources'.[89] Stringer's remark is equally applicable to the
Manx kings, who commanded fleets on a par with the lords of Galloway
and who proved themselves to be, for nearly two centuries, a power to be
reckoned with in the Irish Sea.

* * *

Two important and related questions that have never, to the best of my
knowledge, been systematically explored in the Manx context relate to the
construction of these vessels: where were they built, and where was the
timber for their construction and maintenance acquired? The obvious
answer – the Isle of Man – in fact appears unlikely because it was probably
largely deforested by the late Norse period.[90] It has been suggested that
some 50 to 58 cubic metres of timber (oak was preferred when it was
available but ash, beech, alder, willow and pine were also utilized) were
required to construct a longship 20 to 25 metres in length.[91] Both literary
and archaeological evidence suggests that such timber was in short supply
on the Isle of Man, though the matter is contentious. An entry in the
native Welsh chronicle, the *Brut y tywysogyon*, for example, states that the
Norse king Magnus *berrfott* (Barelegs) took timber from Anglesey to
construct forts in the Isle of Man around 1100 – suggesting a shortage in
Man itself.[92] Riveted wooden coffins of Norse date uncovered in the Peel
Castle excavations of 1982–88 have been interpreted as showing that by
this period trees capable of providing broad planks were no longer found
on the island; some later burials showed no detectable coffin at all,

daughter to the son of Alan of Galloway in 1225: *Chron. Man*, fos. 35v, 43v.   **88** *Hakonar saga*,
ed. Vigfusson and Dasent, p. 144 (ch. 163); see also K.J. Stringer, 'Periphery and core in
thirteenth-century Scotland: Alan son of Roland, lord of Galloway and constable of Scotland',
in Alexander Grant and K.J. Stringer (eds), *Medieval Scotland: crown, lordship and community*
(Edinburgh, 1993), pp 82–113, at p. 84.   **89** Stringer, 'Periphery and core', p. 84.   **90** D.E.
Allen, 'The vanished forests', *The Peregrine*, 2/4 (May 1956), 7–9; L. Garrad, 'Some thoughts
on Manx woodland', *IoMNHAS Proc.*, 7:4 (1970–2), 666–86; see now R. Chiverrell and G.
Thomas (eds), *A new history of the Isle of Man. Volume 1: the evolution of the natural landscape*
(Liverpool, 2006), pp 300–26.   **91** James Graham-Campbell, *The Viking world* (London, 1980),
pp 50–1; see also A. Forte, R. Oram and F. Pedersen, *Viking empires* (Cambridge, 2005), ch. 5,
esp. pp 138–9, for discussion of components and types of preferred wood; see also E. Harris, J.
Harris and N.D.G. James, *Oak: a British history* (Macclesfield, 2003), pp 105–6.   **92** *Brut y
tywysogyon*, p. 45 (s.a. 1100–2).

suggesting an even greater shortage of wood.[93] On the other hand, the Manx Chronicle and the abbeyland boundaries appended to it indicate the presence of at least some native woodlands (perhaps scrubby in nature), particularly in the northern part of the island: Guðrøðr Crovan won his famous victory at Sky Hill by hiding three hundred of his warriors in a wood (*silva*) on the north side of the hill overlooking Ramsey, for example.[94] Whatever the case may be, the large, straight timbers required for keels, strakes, crossbeams and masts were almost certainly not to be found on the island by the era of the Crovan kings.[95] As Barbara Crawford has put it in the context of the Orkney earldom: 'For a society whose way of life was based on control of the seas … access to timber must have been a prime requirement'.[96] Where, then, did the Manx rulers gain access to such timber to build and maintain the fleets of galleys essential for their control of the seas?

Norway was one obvious possibility. Some of the contemporary Orkney jarls seem to have acquired ships from here, as indeed, Guðrøðr Óláfsson seems to have done in 1153/4 when he returned from Norway to take the kingship following the assassination of his father.[97] But a papal letter of 1244 described the voyage from Man to Trondheim as being 'long and dangerous',[98] and Norway can never have been a particularly significant source of ships or timber – especially when other, closer, options existed. Wales, which, as noted above, provided timber for Magnus *berrføtt* to build forts on the Isle of Man, and with which the Manx rulers had close links, was one such option.[99] Even closer at hand, however, was Ireland, the native woodlands of which were commented upon by Giraldus Cambrensis and remained significant into the early modern period.[1] The Skuldelev 2 longship was built here, on the east coast, probably around Dublin, and it is worth noting that the Manx kings enjoyed connections with Dublin until its conquest by the English in 1170 and with both native Irish and English thereafter: Rögnvaldr Guðrøðarsson patronized Gaelic

---

93 Freke, *Peel Castle dig*, p. 16; idem, *Excavations on St Patrick's Isle*, pp 79–82, 441.   94 *Chron. Man*, fos. 33r, 47v, 54r.   95 But see L. Garrad, with T.A. Bawden, J.K. Qualtrough, and W.J. Scatchard, *Industrial archaeology in the Isle of Man* (Newton Abbot, 1972), p. 21 for the suggestion that ships may have been built on the island throughout the Norse period. 96 Barbara Crawford, *Earl and mormaer. Norse-Pictish relationships in northern Scotland* (Rosemarkie, 1995), p. 11.   97 *Orkneyinga saga*, ch. 85; *Chron. Man*, fo. 36v.   98 *Cal. papal letters*, i, p. 206.   99 Anglesey may have been largely deforested by the end of the twelfth century: A.D. Carr, *Medieval Anglesey* (Llangefni, 1982), pp 19–21.   1 Giraldus, *Opera*, v, p. 26 (*Topographia Hib.*); trans. O'Meara, p. 34; see also Rixson, *West Highland galley*, 109–10; V.A. Hall, 'The development of the landscape of Ireland over the last two thousand years; fresh evidence from historical and pollen analytical studies', *Chronica: An electronic history journal*, 1 (1997), 1: 11–12 <http://www.ucc.ie/chronicon/hall.htm>.

bards, was the brother-in-law of John de Courcy, conqueror of Ulster, and, in 1212, received a knight's fee in Carlingford from King John. Still another potential source of timber and vessels was the Hebrides and West Highlands of Scotland; it is worth noting that the Manx kings controlled parts of it by virtue of their possession of the Skye and Lewis groups of the Hebrides (as well as other parts intermittently) throughout the late Norse period. Timber may have been scarce in some islands in the windswept Outer Hebrides but it was apparently abundant in Skye into the sixteenth and seventeenth centuries; in 1463 John, lord of the Isles and earl of Ross, granted Sleat with its oakwoods (specifically mentioned in the charter recording the grant) for the service of a ship with eighteen oars.[2] Wood was also plentiful in the adjacent mainland region of Glenelg, which like Skye was controlled by the Manx rulers, although in circumstances that remain obscure.[3] Finally, there was Galloway – easily visible from the Isle of Man across a mere 30km of the Irish Sea on a clear day. The medieval lords of Galloway, kinsmen by marriage of the Manx rulers, possessed formidable fleets of galleys as well as the natural resources to construct and maintain them: the woods of Galloway were still providing timber for Scottish vessels and other military requirements as late as the fifteenth and sixteenth centuries.[4] Thus, even if the Isle of Man itself was not able to provide the large timbers vital to the construction and maintenance of galleys, the Hebridean possessions of the Manx kings almost certainly allowed access to such resources, while political connections with Wales, Ireland and Galloway may have also provided recourse to the timber of these regions as well. It remains difficult to discern where such ships were built, but lacking direct evidence on the matter it seems possible that vessels may have been constructed at various times in Norway, Ireland, the Hebrides, the West Highlands and Galloway, if not in the Isle of Man itself.[5]

* * *

2 *The acts of the lords of the Isles, 1336–1493*, ed. Jean Munro and R.W. Munro (Edinburgh, 1986), pp 126–8; *Monro's Western Isles of Scotland and genealogies of the clans 1549*, ed. R.W. Munro (Edinburgh, 1961), p. 68. See also T.C. Smout, A.R. Macdonald, and F.J. Watson, *A history of the native woodlands of Scotland, 1500–1920* (Edinburgh, 2005), ch. 14, on Skye in particular; see also Hugh Cheape, 'Woodlands on the Clanranald estate: a case study', in *Scotland since prehistory: natural change and human impact*, ed. T.C. Smout (Aberdeen, 1993), pp 50–63. 3 *The acts of the parliaments of Scotland*, ed. T. Thomson and C. Innes (Edinburgh, 1814–75), i, p. 110. 4 J.M. Gilbert, *Hunting and hunting reserves in medieval Scotland* (Edinburgh, 1979), pp 238–9; see also Smout et al., *Native woodlands*, p. 153. 5 See McDonald, *Rögnvaldr*, forthcoming, for further discussion.

Another important question regarding the ships under the command of the Manx kings is the means by which they were obtained. The answer sheds light upon not only the role of the king as war-leader but also upon the powers and prerogatives of the Manx rulers of the period, and is of significance for an understanding of the degree of administrative sophistication that existed within the late Norse kingdom of Man and the Isles. Niels Lund, who has written extensively on the subject, argues that 'Viking fleets and armies as well as the fleets and armies raised by Scandinavian kings in the two centuries immediately following the age of the Vikings were *ad hoc* phenomena and consisted of whatever forces a king or chieftain could persuade to follow him'.[6] The same is probably true of the Isle of Man, and there can be little doubt that the Manx fleets comprised galleys provided by the potentates frequently described by the Manx Chronicle as the 'chieftains of the Isles',[7] as well as the Manx kings themselves. But the twelfth century saw the development in the Scandinavian world of the system known as *leidang* (ON *leiðangr*), a naval militia, the essence of which was 'the provision of a fleet of longships adequately manned and equipped; and as the king himself had no revenues available for such a project, the obligation was imposed on his subjects'.[8] Such a system seems to have come into being in the Scandinavian countries in the twelfth and thirteenth centuries, and it is also quite likely that it also existed in the late Norse Isle of Man under the Crovan kings. Although the matter is contentious, and the minutiae of the debates need not concern us here, it has been argued that the Manx *leidang* (based upon the land divisions in the Isle of Man of sheadings and treens) provided the rulers of the island with between six vessels of twenty-six oars and up to four times that number.[9] The former is surely a small estimate, given the substantial size of the Manx fleets attested in the folios of the Manx Chronicle, but in what is probably a late Norse reference to the system, when the king of Scots subjugated the Isle of Man and Magnus, its last native ruler, in the 1260s, the terms of Magnus's submission included the provision of 'ten pirate-type galleys ... five of

6 Niels Lund, 'Naval force in the Viking age and in high medieval Denmark', in J.B. Hattendorf and R.W. Unger (eds), *War at sea in the middle ages and the Renaissance* (Woodbridge, 2003), pp 25–34, at p. 34; see also idem, 'The armies of Swein Forkbeard and Cnut: *leding* or *lið*', *Anglo-Saxon England*, 15 (1986), pp 105–18.   7 e.g., *Chron. Man*, fos. 33v, 34r, 35r, and passim.   8 H. Marwick, 'Leidang in the West or the Norse fleets of Orkney and the Isle of Man', *Proceedings of the Orkney Antiquarian Society*, 13 (1934–5), 15; see also idem, 'Naval defence in Norse Scotland', *SHR*, 28/105 (1949), 1–11.   9 C.J.S. Marstrander, 'Det Norske Landnåm på Man', *Norsk Tidsskrift for Sprogvidenskap*, 6 (1932), pp 40–386 [with full English summary at pp 333–55]; cf. Marwick, 'Leidang', 17, 28–9; land divisions discussed in E. Davies, 'Treens and quarterlands: a study of the land system of the Isle of Man', *Transactions and Papers of the Institute of British Geographers*, 22 (1956), 97–116.

which should have twenty-four oars and the other five twelve'.[10] These would probably have been provided by the *leidang*, and some of the fourteenth-century Scottish charters for ship-service pertaining to the Isle of Man (such as that for Thomas Randolph in 1326) have been interpreted as preserving this inheritance as well, though there is little agreement among scholars as to whether this is actually the case or not.[11]

Whatever the case may be with regard to the precise size of the fleets, it is important to place the origins of the *leidang* system within the broader context of the development of administrative structures required to support it. Thus, in a Scandinavian context, the origins of the *leidang* have been shown by Niels Lund to date, not from the ninth or tenth century, but rather to the twelfth, when the requisite degree of royal control and bureaucratic sophistication to administer it seems to have come into being.[12] The same may hold true for the Isle of Man, and although no precise date for the introduction of the *leidang* system can be suggested in a Manx context, its operation under the kings of the Crovan dynasty is not seriously in doubt. If Lund's arguments about the organizational sophistication required to sustain such a system in Scandinavia can be applied to the Manx context as well, then it may prove possible to discern, through the *leidang* system, something of the administrative capacity of the Manx kings:[13] as has been remarked in the broader Scandinavian context, 'the formation of the kingdoms involved the development of a more elaborate and formalized military organization'.[14] Indeed, it may be significant that P.S. Andersen thinks the land-valuated assessment-units known as treens in the Isle of Man were established in the twelfth century, by the Crovan kings;[15] since the treens are thought to have been part of the Manx leidang system,[16] this might provide one clue as to the date of the system in a Manx setting. It is also worth noting in the present context that there existed, in the late Norse period, a fairly sophisticated coast-guard system within the Isle of Man known as 'watch and ward'.[17]

* * *

10 *Scotichronicon*, ed. Watt, v, pp 348–9.   11 *Registrum magni sigilli regum Scotorum*, ed. J.M. Thomson et al. (11 vols, Edinburgh, 1882–1914), i, app. I, no. 32; Marstrander, 'Norske Landnåm', 312, 350; cf. Marwick, 'Leidang', 29; McDonald, *Kingdom*, pp 144–5.   12 Lund, 'Naval force', pp 25–34; idem, 'Armies', pp 105–18.   13 I discuss the subject at greater length in *Rögnvaldr*, forthcoming, ch. 5.   14 T. Lindkvist, 'Early political organization: (a) introductory survey', in K. Helle (ed.), *Cambridge history of Scandinavia. Volume 1: prehistory to 1520* (Cambridge, 2003), p. 164.   15 P.S. Andersen, 'When was regular, annual taxation introduced in the Norse islands of Britain? A comparative study of assessment systems in north-western Europe', *Scandinavian Journal of History*, 16 (1991), 73–83, at p. 79.   16 Marstrander, 'Norske Landnåm', 312–13, 350–1; Marwick, 'Leidang', 17.   17 The first documented reference to

Manx fleets were clearly valued by rulers around the shores of the Irish Sea, who often benefited from access to them, thus demonstrating one of the ways in which the Manx kings and their fleets fit into the world of the galloglass. Sometimes it is difficult to disentangle mercenary aspects from obligations imposed by kinship or marriage, however. It seems equally possible that the fleets put at the disposal of Welsh rulers in the 1090s and 1190s were the result of kinship connections between Manx and Welsh rulers, or else represented fleets for hire. Similarly, it is not beyond the bounds of possibility that the thirty Manx vessels that participated in the attack on English-held Dublin in May 1171 represented vessels hired for the purpose: Giraldus Cambrensis significantly has the archbishop of Dublin promise generous financial rewards to the Manx king in return for his support.[18] On the other hand, Guðrøðr II had other pressing reasons of his own to support the effort, namely, fear of the threat of English domination in the Irish Sea.[19] So the episode of 1171 seems to show how the rulers of the Isles could be motivated by both mercenary opportunities as well as political considerations.[20] (Ironically, only six years earlier, in 1165, Welsh sources reveal that King Henry II of England [1154–89] hired the Ostman fleet to support his Welsh campaign.[21]) Another possible case of the Manx fleet being hired out by a foreign power is represented by King Rögnvaldr's aid to the Scots king William I around 1200. It may be significant that according to the account in *Orkneyinga saga* it was the Scottish king who approached Rögnvaldr for assistance. The statement by the fifteenth-century chronicler Walter Bower in his *Scotichronicon* to the effect that King William I prepared a naval expedition against Jarl Haraldr Maddaðsson of Orkney in 1202 may also need to be taken into account; this is the first reference to a Scottish king utilizing ships in a domestic campaign, and the Manx king, who had already rendered military assistance to William, may have provided them.[22] It is also interesting that Roger of Howden's account of northern Scottish events around 1200 includes the information that Haraldr Maddaðsson himself travelled to Man and 'there collected a fleet and many men' for use in his struggle with his Norwegian-appointed rival, Haraldr the younger; this force could

watch and ward occurs in 1417: *The statutes of the Isle of Man. Volume 1*, ed. J.F. Gill (London, 1883; rpr. 1992), p. 4; see also W.C. Cubbon, 'Watch and ward in AD 1627', *IoMNHAS Proc.*, 3:3 (1928), 258–65; B.R.S. Megaw, 'A thousand years of watch and ward: from Viking beacon to home guard', *JMM*, 5:64 (1941), 8–13; Andrew Johnson, 'Watch and ward on the Isle of Man: the medieval re-occupation of iron-age promontory forts', in Davey and Finalayson (eds), *Mannin revisited*, pp 63–80. 18 *Expugnatio*, pp 78–9. 19 Ibid. 20 Duffy, 'Irishmen and Islesmen', 132. 21 *Brut y tywysogyon*, pp 146–7 (s.a. 1163–5). 22 *Scotichronicon*, ed. Watt, iv, pp 426–7 and p. 597 note; I am grateful to Mandy Bateman for this reference.

represent a mercenary one, but Rögnvaldr and Haraldr were also kinsmen.[23] Whatever the case may be with the ambiguous examples cited above, an entry from the Annals of the Four Masters seems to clinch the matter. Under the year 1154 we read that 'The Cinel-Eoghain and Muircheartach, son of Niall, sent persons over sea to hire (and who did hire) the fleets of the Gall-Gaedhil, of Ara, of Ceann-tire, of Manainn, and the borders of Alba in general, over which Mac Scelling was in command'.[24] The mercenary fleet subsequently engaged, and was defeated by, the Connacht fleet: 'The foreign host was however defeated and slaughtered; they left their ships behind, and the teeth of Mac Scelling were knocked out'. This would seem to offer clear proof that while Manx fleets served the interests of their masters in the Isle of Man, they were also a commodity available to the highest bidder and as such played an important military role in the maritime environment of the Irish Sea world. This is also suggested by the fact that by the early thirteenth century the Manx kings and their fleets had been co-opted into English service to guard the coasts of Ireland and England – a development that is considered at greater detail below.

Roger of Howden's passing reference to Earl Haraldr Maddaðsson's recruitment of not just a fleet but also warriors in the Isle of Man in the course of his struggle against the Scottish king serves as a reminder that it was not just Manx fleets that were a desirable commodity: a great fleet also denoted a great army. Precisely how great is difficult to assess, but an entry in the Annals of Ulster for the year 1098 provides a useful starting point. It records the defeat of three ships of the 'Foreigners of the Isles', by the Ulstermen, resulting in 120 casualties.[25] Though it is difficult to know whether Manx, Hebridean, or Norwegian vessels are meant, the implication is that a warship of the late eleventh century carried a crew of about forty men. Using this as a point of reference, and assuming some degree of similarity between these vessels and those commanded by the Manx kings, the hundred galleys that Rögnvaldr sent to Ulster in 1205 could, for example, have borne an army of some 4000 warriors. Multipliers for the capacity of longships are diverse,[26] of course, but even if halved, this remains a formidable fighting force by the standards of the day, comparable to that commanded by Alan of Galloway (d. 1234), whose fleet of

23 Howden, *Chronica*, ed. Arnold, iv, pp 10–12. A daughter of Hákon Paulsson was wedded to King Óláfr Guðrøðrsson (d. 1153): *Ágrip ap Nóregskonunga Sögum. Fagrskinna – Nóregs Konunga Tal*, ed. B. Einarsson (Reykjavík, 1985), p. 373; see also Anderson, *Early sources*, ii, p. 139, note 2. 24 *AFM*, ii, pp 1112–13 (s.a. 1154). 25 *AU* ii, pp 58–9 (s.a. 1098). 26 Multipliers are diverse: Else Roesdahl, *The Vikings*, trans. S.M. Margeson and K. Williams, 2nd ed. (London, 1998), p. 192 estimates 50 warriors per ship; Stringer's calculations in 'Periphery and core', p. 84, would allow only about 15 warriors per vessel.

150 to 200 ships and army of 2000–3000 fighting men made him one of the most formidable magnates of his time.[27] If rough estimates are the best that can be accomplished based on the nature of the evidence, there is little doubt that contemporaries stood in awe of the armies as well as the fleets commanded by Manx kings. The praise-poem in Rögnvaldr's honour describes his warriors as the 'the hounds of the fine pack of Gofraidh'.[28] And if George Broderick is correct in his belief that an entry in the Welsh text *Gwrtheyrn Gwrtheneu*, which describes the year 1193 as *Haf y gwydyl* or 'Summer of the Gael', refers to substantial Gaelic-speaking forces brought by Rögnvaldr to Anglesey, then Manx military muscle may have been impressive indeed.[29]

The 'Summer of the Gael', by virtue of its allusion to Gaelic-speaking forces under the command of a Manx ruler, raises another significant point about the character of Manx military might in the Irish Sea, namely, its multiethnic dimension – something that mirrors the multiethnic nature of the kingdom itself.[30] The far-flung insular nature of the kingdom of the Isles, with its tentacles extending from Lewis and Skye to the shores of Ireland, meant that the Manx sea-kings, like other twelfth- and thirteenth-century Irish Sea warlords including Sumarliði of Argyll and Alan of Galloway, were able to maximize their military potential by utilizing forces from around the Irish Sea basin and the Hebrides. The best evidence of this is found in *Orkneyinga saga*, where it is stated that the army taken by King Rögnvaldr to Caithness around 1200 included forces recruited from 'all through the Hebrides and from Kintyre, to add to a strong force he had with him from Ireland'.[31] This is entirely plausible. Rögnvaldr's sea-girt kingdom embraced the northern Hebrides, while his familial connections extended to both Ireland and Kintyre. Manx connections with Dublin were as old as the dynasty of Guðröðr Crovan itself, and it would scarcely be surprising if some of the Ostman refugees who are said by Giraldus Cambrensis to have fled the town for the northern islands at the time of its conquest by the English ended up in the Isle of Man;[32] certainly Rögnvaldr's father had supported a Hiberno-Norse assault in 1171, and aid may have flowed both ways. Giraldus provided a famous pen portrait of the fierce warriors from the Isles that attacked Dublin in 1171, and it seems quite likely that his description is not out of place in the present context:

27 Stringer, 'Periphery and core', p. 84.   28 Clancy, *Triumph tree*, p. 240; Ó Cuív, 294.   29 *Text of the Bruts*, ed. Rhys & Evans, ii, p. 405; Broderick, 'Irish and Welsh Strands', 36.   30 See B.R.S. Megaw, 'Norseman and native in the kingdom of the Isles: a re-assessment of the Manx evidence', in P.J. Davey (ed.), *Man and environment in the Isle of Man* (Oxford, 1978), pp 265–314.   31 *Orkneyinga saga*, ch. 110.   32 *Expugnatio*, pp 68–9.

They were warlike figures, clad in mail in every part of their body after the Danish manner. Some wore long coats of mail, others iron plates skilfully knitted together, and they had round, red shields protected by iron round the edge. These men, whose iron will matched their armour, drew up their ranks and made an attack on the walls at the eastern gate.[33]

Rögnvaldr's forces also included Gaelic troops from the Hebrides and Ireland, however, and there must be a strong suspicion that these may have included the predecessors of the famous galloglass. The term is often translated 'foreign warrior' and was applied to mercenary troops of Gaelic and Gaelic-Norse extraction from the Hebrides; by the fourteenth century many of the Clann Somhairle kindreds were engaged in the business of supplying galloglass to the Irish. But the origins of the galloglass lie in the thirteenth century: they are first mentioned by name in Irish annals in 1290 in terms that suggest they were already a well-established feature of the contemporary military landscape and it is possible that such mercenaries were already an important part of the military scene from the middle of the century, if not earlier.[34] It may not, therefore, be too fanciful to suggest that Rögnvaldr in particular and the Manx kings of his dynasty in general were already tapping into the military potential offered by mercenary warriors of mixed Gaelic and Norse extraction in the Hebrides and the Irish Sea by the end of the twelfth century, something that was undoubtedly facilitated by the wide-ranging diplomatic, political and matrimonial connections of the Manx rulers. In the case of Rögnvaldr, his ability to recruit foreign troops may have been facilitated by his kinship by marriage with the Clann Somhairle lords of Kintyre,[35] and the possibility must also be entertained that troops were mustered from Ulster, since Rögnvaldr's sister had married John de Courcy, perhaps around 1180. Whatever the case, the forces at Rögnvaldr's disposal display that multi-ethnic composition that has been seen as characteristic of armies within the Irish Sea basin in the twelfth and thirteenth centuries, and it is also interesting to note that as late as 1251 Magnus Óláfsson was attempting to recruit forces in Ireland in his bid for the Manx kingship.[36]

* * *

33 Ibid., pp 76–7.   34 See the essays by Duffy, Nicholls, Simms, and Woolf in this volume; McDonald, *Kingdom*, pp 154–6; G.A. Hayes-McCoy, *Scots mercenary forces in Ireland (1565–1603)* (Dublin and London, 1937).   35 *Chron. Man*, fo. 42r says that Rögnvaldr's wife was the 'daughter of a certain nobleman from Kintyre', which means she was most likely a member of the Clann Somhairle kindred.   36 Magnus recruiting in Ireland: *CDI*, i, no. 3206; mixed forces: Stringer, 'Periphery and core', p. 87; Seán Duffy, 'The Bruce brothers and the Irish Sea world, 1306–29' *Cambridge* [now *Cambrian*] *Medieval Celtic Studies*, 21 (Summer 1991),

Perhaps the best barometer for Manx military power in the era of the Crovan dynasty is its harnessing by thirteenth-century English kings to guard the English and Irish coasts and patrol the waters of the north Irish Sea basin. Although there is some evidence for sporadic political and diplomatic contacts between the English kings and their Manx counterparts in the twelfth century,[37] it was not really until the years around 1200 that relations intensified. No doubt the Isle of Man acquired a new significance in the eyes of English rulers following the English invasion of Ireland in the late 1160s, and possibly also as a result of Manx aid to the Hiberno-Norse assault of English-held Dublin in 1171. The Manx ruler who had the most to gain – or to lose – from the newfound English interest in the Isle of Man was Rögnvaldr Guðrøðarsson, whose association with John de Courcy in the latter's struggle to recover his Ulster lordship in 1204–5 probably also managed to bring him to the attention of the English king, John. But whereas de Courcy slips into obscurity following the events of 1204–5, Rögnvaldr was catapulted into the limelight, being wooed and courted by John, who took considerable interest in his Manx protégé from early 1205 when Rögnvaldr was taken under the English king's protection.[38] Rögnvaldr of course had his own motives for welcoming an association with the English king (prime among them being support in a simmering dispute with his brother over the kingship), but there is evidence that John hoped to harness the forces at Rögnvaldr's disposal for the purpose of patrolling the Irish Sea. English interest in Man is certainly evident from the events of 1210, when an English fleet ravaged the island, presumably to teach King Rögnvaldr a lesson for wavering in his allegiance; further evidence of Man's strategic value to the English kings is to be found in English financial documents for August 1210, which show payment to Richard de Muroil for guarding the king's supply in the Isle of Man.[39] By 1212, when Rögnvaldr became John's liegeman, the two rulers promised each other mutual assistance: King John ordered his seneschals, governors, and bailiffs in Ireland 'that if any Wikini [Vikings], or others, should offend in the territory of Reginald, king of Man, you shall assist him in the destruction of his and our

55–86: 63; R.A. McDonald, '"Treachery in the remotest territories of Scotland": northern resistance to the Canmore dynasty, 1130–1230', *Canadian Journal of History*, 33 (August 1999), 161–92, at p. 184.   37 *Chron. Man*, fo. 35r says that Óláfr I was raised at the court of Henry I prior to his accession to the kingship in *c.*1113, while *The great rolls of the pipe for the second, third, and fourth years of the reign of King Henry II, A.D. 1155, 1156, 1157, 1158*, ed. J. Hunter (London, 1844), pp 155, 168 show his son Guðrøðr II received some aid from Henry II in the late 1150s.   38 Rymer, *Foedera*, i, pt i, p. 44; Oliver, *Monumenta*, ii, p. 25.   39 *Chron. Man*, fos. 41r–41v; *Rotuli de liberate ac de misis et praestitis, regnante Johanne*, ed. T.D. Hardy (London, 1844), p. 209; *CDI*, i, no. 407.

enemies, since he is bound to us by fealty and oath, to perform the same for us against those who offend in our territory'.[40] King Rögnvaldr may have been active in this newfound capacity in combined Anglo-Scottish operations between 1212 and 1215 against troublemakers based in Ulster.[41] Whether that is the case or not, the grant by King John of a knight's fee in Carlingford to Rögnvaldr, also in 1212,[42] must be regarded as significant in this context: Carlingford, with its fine harbour, no doubt helped facilitate Manx patrols in the Irish Sea by giving the Manx ruler a base in Ireland as well as in Man, and the grant highlights once again the strategic location of the Isle of Man within the Irish Sea basin as well as the value of Manx galleys to the English rulers. By the time of Óláfr II, Rögnvaldr's brother, rival, and eventual successor in the Manx kingship, the obligations of the Manx rulers with regard to their coast-guard duties were clearly defined. Thus, in 1235, Óláfr was charged by Henry III with 'guarding, at his own cost, the coast of the sea of England towards Ireland, and towards the Isle of Man, and likewise the coast of the sea of Ireland towards England, and towards the aforesaid Isle of Man, lest injury might happen to the aforesaid our lands of England and Ireland, by sea, upon these coasts'.[43] Access to Manx sea power was no doubt one of the primary reasons why the English kings entered into diplomatic relations with the Manx rulers from about 1205, and the co-opting of the Manx galley-fleets for coast-guard duty serves as a suitable reminder of the formidable nature of Manx sea power.

* * *

'You are the man of the brindled barques, the shore you will reach is cursed', the Irish poet sang of King Rögnvaldr Guðrøðarsson[44] – and the words would also apply to most of the members of his dynasty. For these Manx kings descended from Guðrøðr Crovan, the rulers of a far-reaching water-world between Britain and Ireland, survival depended above all else upon the substantial fleets of galleys under their command, galleys that were manned by warriors from the shores of their diffuse maritime

---

40 *Rotuli litterarum patentium in Turri Londinensi asservanti*, ed. T.D. Hardy (2 vols, London, 1835), i, p. 92b; Oliver, *Monumenta*, ii, p. 34. The reference to 'Wikini' is probably an allusion to Norwegian sea-rovers who had descended upon the Isles in 1210.   41 Stringer, 'Periphery and core', pp 85–7 on Anglo-Scottish campaigns; Daphne Brooke, *Wild men and holy places: St Ninian, Whithorn and the medieval realm of Galloway* (Edinburgh, 1994), p. 130 for Rögnvaldr's potential involvement.   42 *Rotuli chartarum*, ed. Hardy, p. 186b. Oliver, *Monumenta*, ii, pp 35–6, misdated this to 1213.   43 See note 6 above.   44 Clancy, *Triumph tree*, p. 239; Ó Cuív, 292.

kingdom. In fact, on almost any view, it is time that the Manx sea-kings were given their due as Irish Sea strongmen with a considerable amount of weight to throw around, something that was done with regularity from the late eleventh to the early thirteenth century when dealing death from smooth-plained Man proved an integral part of Manx kingship, in terms of mercenary, political, and undoubtedly economic considerations. The fact that Manx galleys were sought by the rulers of surrounding lands, from Wales to Ireland to Scotland to Orkney to England, demonstrates the integral place occupied by the Manx kings in the world of the galloglass.

A dead man at Ballyshannon

ALEX WOOLF

In 1247 Henry III's justiciar for Ireland, Maurice fitz Gerald, led an invasion of Tír Chonaill in which the king of that region, Maoilsheachlainn Ó Domhnaill, and his allies An Cammhuinealach ('Wry-neck') Ó Baoighill and Mac Somhairle were slain at Ballyshannon. The Annals of Loch Cé, the Annals of Connacht and the Annals of the Four Masters identify Mac Somhairle as *rí* (or in the latter case *tigerna*) *Airer Goidel* while the Annals of Ulster give him no title.[1] None of the chronicles supply a forename for Mac Somhairle and modern scholars have failed to reach a consensus as to his identity, other than to concede that he must be a member of the dynasty descended from Sumarliði (Somerled or Somhairle mac Giolla Bhrighde) (†1164) from whom so many of the great families of the West Highlands and Islands of Scotland have claimed descent.

In their groundbreaking article of 1957, which, in many ways, initiated modern historical research into the kingdom of the Isles, Archie Duncan and Al Brown failed to notice the death at Ballyshannon, perhaps because this particular annal had not found its way into Alan Orr Anderson's *Early sources of Scottish history* upon which they relied for their knowledge of Irish and Scandinavian sources.[2] In 1934, however, Osborn Bergin, in the preface to his edition of a Gaelic poem addressed to Aonghus of Islay, published in *Scottish Gaelic Studies*, had put forward the suggestion that the Mac Somhairle in question was Domhnall mac Raghnaill, the eponym of Clann Domhnaill (the Clan Donald).[3] Bergin argued that the poem appeared to be the first work of the father's poet for the son and that since Aonghus himself died in 1296 his father must have lived into the middle of the thirteenth century. Almost sixty years later Seán Duffy, in his paper on 'The Bruce brothers and the Irish Sea world' concurred with Bergin drawing attention to the claims made in the seventeenth-century *Book of Clanranald* that messengers had been sent to Domhnall from Ireland inviting him to take the leadership of the Gael.[4] Duffy linked this claim, frequently viewed as rhetorical flourish, to Maoilsheachlainn Ó Domhnaill's

---

1 *ALC; AC; AFM, AU* s.a. 1247.   2 A.A.M. Duncan and A.L. Brown, 'Argyll and the Isles in the earlier middle ages', *PSAS*, 90 (1956–7), 192–220; Anderson, *Early sources*.   3 Osborn Bergin, 'An address to Aonghus of Islay', *Scottish Gaelic Studies*, 4 (1934–5), 57–69; reprinted in idem, *Irish bardic poetry*, ed. David Greene and Fergus Kelly (Dublin, 1970), pp 169–74, trs. at pp 291–4.   4 Seán Duffy, 'The Bruce brothers and the Irish Sea World, 1306–29', *CMCS*, 21

war against the Geraldines which ended so abruptly at Ballyshannon in 1247.

The problem with accepting this identification is that there is little or no explicit contemporary evidence that Domhnall was a significant figure in his own right during his lifetime. One short or fragmentary praise poem addressed to him survives in the National Library of Scotland but it remains, as yet, unedited and unpublished.[5] This poem, and the allusions to Domhnall in the poem to his son edited by Bergin, in no way demand that he was a ruler in his own right rather than simply a significant aristocrat, something of which we can be assured on the basis of his pedigree alone. There is also one charter in the Paisley Register which purports to be issued by Domhnall but it is suspiciously similar to that of his son Aonghus in both the wording of the main text and the identical witness-list.[6] The one possible substantial account of Domhnall, if it is of our Domhnall, is that found in the *Chronicle of the kings of Man and the Isles*, fos. 47v. and 48r.[7] Here in a narrative related as a miracle performed in 1249 by St Mary of Rushen (which was the house in which the chronicle was kept), we are told that an aged and noble *princeps*, Dofnaldus by name, whom King Haraldr Óláfsson, who had just been drowned returning from Norway, had considered worthier than the rest (*pre ceteris specialis extitit*), was freed, along with his young son, from the clutches of the new regime headed by Haraldr Guðrøðarsson. Haraldr Óláfsson certainly depended upon forces raised in the Isles for his success in Man and it is quite likely that the nobles he considered worthier than the rest were Islesmen rather than Manxmen.

The difficulty with identifying this Domhnall with the eponym has been the fact that Aonghus is considered to have succeeded his father by 1249 but this dating is far from secure. In a grant to Paisley abbey, otherwise undated, Aonghus refers to King Alexander and his son Alexander and scholars have tended to recognize in these allusions Alexander II and the future Alexander III, and thus to date the document to the period 1241 to 1249 when these two were both alive.[8] It is far from impossible, however, that it refers to Alexander III and *his* son Alexander who was born in January 1264 and predeceased his father in 1284. Indeed if the

(1991), 55–86.   5 NLS Adv. MS 72.2.2, f. 16. I am grateful to Wilson MacLeod and Ronnie Black for drawing my attention to this poem and making a transcript available. Dr MacLeod is currently preparing an edition and translation of the poem to be included in *Duanaire na sracaire / The song-book of the pillagers: anthology of Scotland's Gaelic verse to 1600*, ed. Wilson McLeod and Meg Bateman (Edinburgh, 2007).   6 *Registrum monasterii de Passelet: carta privilegia conventiones aliaque munimenta complectens a domo fundata A.D. MCLXIII usque ad A.D. MDXXIX*, ed. C.N. Innes (Edinburgh, 1832), p. 126.   7 *Chron. Man*.   8 *Registrum monasterii de Passelet*, p. 128.

evidence of this grant of Kilkerran to Paisley is discounted there is no notice of activity by Aonghus before February 1256.[9] He might even be the child mentioned in the St Mary's story, whose author claims that he heard the narrative from Domhnall himself. His continued active career into the 1290s might make a later rather than an earlier starting-point for his career more likely, as indeed might the *floruunt* of his sons whose careers extend well into the fourteenth century and who do not look, like the present Prince of Wales, to be æthelings who have aged in waiting. If the aged Domhnall with the infant son who told his story to the author of the *Chronicle of the Kings of Man and the Isles* was Domhnall mac Raghnaill then he was most certainly not the man killed at Ballyshannon, unless miracles befell him as a matter of course.

R. Andrew McDonald, in his 1997 book on *The kingdom of the Isles* noted Duffy's identification of the dead man at Ballyshannon with Domhnall but considered that the fact that the Annals of Loch Cé described Mac Somhairle as *rí Airer Gaoidel* as significant and probably pointing towards Donnchadh mac Dubhghaill, Domhnall's cousin, as the most likely candidate.[10] This identification relies upon McDonald's assumption that the Gaelic title refers primarily to the Mac Dubhghaill lordship of Lorne. Gaelic scholars such as Wilson McLeod might be less happy to treat the titles applied by Irish chroniclers and poets to West Highland magnates with such precision.[11]

David Sellar has produced what is probably the most scholarly and useful account for the long thirteenth century in the kingdom of the Isles in his contribution to the *Alba* volume edited by Ted Cowan and Andrew McDonald.[12] Here he points out that Donnchadh mac Dubhghaill had visited Durham with his father in 1175, some seventy-one years before the battle of Ballyshannon and that he was probably a little too old to be fighting overseas in 1247.[13] The emphasis must be on the 'probably', however. Donnchadh was certainly still alive in 1244 when his name was appended to a letter from Alexander II and his nobles to the pope.[14]

Sellar himself favoured Domhnall's brother Ruaidhri as a candidate for death at Ballyshannon.[15] Ruaidhri certainly seems to have been the senior son of Rögnvaldr (Raghnall) son of Sumarliði. He first appears by name in

9 *CDI*, ii, no. 490, p. 80.   10 R. Andrew McDonald, *The kingdom of the Isles: Scotland's western seaboard, c.1100–c.1336* (East Linton, 1997), p. 94.   11 Wilson McLeod, '*Rí Innsi Gall, Rí Fionnghall, Ceannas nan Gàidheal*: sovereignty and rhetoric in the late medieval Hebrides', *CMCS*, 43 (2002), 25–49, esp. 30–32.   12 W.D.H. Sellar, 'Hebridean sea kings: the successors of Somerled, 1164–1316', in E.J. Cowan and R. Andrew McDonald (eds), *Alba: Celtic Scotland in the medieval era* (East Linton, 2000), pp 187–218.   13 Ibid., p. 201.   14 Matthew Paris, *Chronica majora*, ed. H. Richards Luard (7 vols, London, 1872–83), vol. iv, s.a. 1244, pp 381ff.   15 Sellar, 'Hebridean sea kings', p. 201.

1214 when, in alliance with Thomas of Atholl, the brother of Alan, lord of Galloway, he raided Derry, and we can probably infer with some safety that he was one of the unnamed sons of Rögnvaldr who had raided Derry with the same Thomas, and a fleet of seventy-six ships, two years previously.[16] The appearance of the sons of Rögnvaldr follows the notice in 1210 of the killing of their uncle Aonghus son of Sumarliði in Skye along with his sons, noticed by the *Chronicle of the Kings of Man and the Isles.*[17] Indeed one can produce a tentative succession of Mac Somhairle claimants to the kingship of the Isles from Rögnvaldr son of Sumarliði to his brother Aonghus and thence to Ruaidhri. Whether Rögnvaldr was preceded by his brother Dubhghall, whom the *Chronicle of the Kings of Man and the Isles* claims had been proclaimed King of the Isles by Þorfinnr Óttarsson (Thorfinn mac Ottair) in 1155 is less clear.[18] The scribe of the Durham *Liber vitae* who wrote in the names of Dubhghall, his sons and his chaplain, in 1175 did not think that he warranted any title. Dubhghall may have been supplanted by his brother on Sumarliði's death or indeed his place in the *Chronicle* account may owe as much to late thirteenth-century Mac Dubhghaill claims as twelfth-century facts.

Andrew McDonald has made the attractive suggestion that the 'Roderick' who assisted MacWilliam rebellions in the North of Scotland between 1223 and 1230 was in fact Ruaidhri mac Raghnaill.[19] None of this, however, has got us any nearer to identifying the dead man at Ballyshannon in 1247. Why is this?

The truth is that there is precious little evidence for Mac Somhairle activity between the second raid on Derry and the battle of Ballyshannon. From about 1225 Donnchadh mac Dubhghaill turns up witnessing various Scottish charters and Ruaidhri may possibly be engaged in aiding the MacWilliams, but they are otherwise apparently silent. In *Hákonar Saga*, in its accounts of the events of 1229–31, the installation of Óláfr II (Olaf the Black) as king of the Isles after the death of his half-brother, Rögnvaldr, we read only of the MacDougalls.[20]

The key to these events probably lies in the narrative found in fos. 42 and 43 of the *Chronicle of the Kings of Man and the Isles*. Here we are told that the two sons of Guðrøðr Óláfsson, Sumarliði's brother-in-law and rival for the kingship of the Isles, disputed their father's inheritance, and that Rögnvaldr, getting the upper hand, captured his half-brother Óláfr and handed him into the custody of King William of Scotland. This took place in about 1208. On William's death in 1214 Óláfr was released as part

16 *AU*, 1214 and 1212.   17 *Chron. Man*, fo. 41r.   18 Ibid., fo. 37v.   19 McDonald, *Kingdom of the Isles*, p. 82.   20 *Hákonar saga Hákonarsonar*, ed. M. Mundt (Oslo, 1977), pp 84–5.

of a general amnesty and, returning briefly to his brother's court to make peace with him, set out with other nobles of the kingdom on pilgrimage to Santiago de Compostella. Upon his return from Santiago, Óláfr was persuaded by his brother to take as his wife 'Lauon', the daughter of a certain nobleman in Kintyre. This woman was the sister of Rögnvaldr's own wife. The wedding complete, Óláfr was sent to Lewis as viceroy or sub-king. Whilst there, however, he separated from Lauon and married instead Christina the daughter of Ferchar, earl of Ross. As a result of this Guðrøðr, Rögnvaldr's son, who was based on Skye, urged on by the *Regina insularum* (his mother according to the *Chronicle*), drove Óláfr out of Lewis and returned home. Óláfr fled to Ross and with the help of Ferchar and Pál, the vicecomes of Skye, attacked Guðrøðr and maimed him. This we are told happened in the year 1223.

Rögnvaldr's queen is never named but she and her sister are clearly important parts of this story and it is also clear that the chronicler wished to lay some of the responsibility for this kin strife at their door. All we are told of their origin is that they emanate from Kintyre. The second marriage, that of Óláfr and Lauon, must have taken place in about 1216 and, if Guðrøðr was truly Lauon's nephew, as the *Chronicle* tells us, the first marriage is likely to have taken place some time before 1210. It is extremely likely that these women were daughters of a Clann Somhairle dynast, for the charter evidence and the contemporary chronicles link Clann Somhairle more closely with Kintyre than with any other territory in the early period,[21] and that these marriages reflected a rapprochement between the two branches of the royal dynasty that had been in conflict since 1155. The alliance noted between Ruaidhri and Thomas of Galloway may also be significant here for Rögnvaldr son of Guðrøðr was consistently allied to Thomas's brother, Alan.[22]

Such a rapprochement may explain the disappearance of Clann Somhairle from the chronicle record for this period. Rögnvaldr's marriage may well have been part of a deal by which his kingship in the Isles was recognized by the leading Clann Somhairle dynast, presumably Ruaidhri, who was perhaps the girls' father or brother, in return for his recognition of Ruaidhri's position as a major magnate within the kingdom. A reunification of the kingdom of the Isles, perhaps as early as the death of Aonghus son of Sumarliði in 1210, might also explain both King William's decision to free Óláfr on his deathbed and his son Alexander's

---

21 See, for example, *Registrum monasterii de Passelet*, pp 125ff.   22 K.J. Stringer, 'Periphery and core in thirteenth-century Scotland: Alan son of Roland, lord of Galloway and constable of Scotland', in Alexander Grant and K.J. Stringer (eds), *Medieval Scotland: crown, lordship and community. Essays presented to G.W.S. Barrow*, pp 82–113 at pp 94–5.

expedition or expeditions to Argyll in 1221 or 1222 or both. David Sellar has suggested, persuasively, that Alexander's expedition or expeditions resulted in the establishment of the Mac Dubhghaill lordship of Argyll, evidence for which begins with Donnchadh's appearance as a witness to a charter of Maoldhomhnaidh, earl of Lennox, in about 1225.[23] If the MacDougalls did operate as agents for the Scottish crown it may well have been the reunification of the kingdom under Rögnvaldr that led to their establishment as a rival focus for west-coast factions. The timing of Óláfr's divorce from Lauon in or shortly before 1223 may also have resulted from a Scots desire to destabilize the kingdom, and Earl Ferchar's involvement in his struggles may have been the opening of a northern front in the war. Óláfr may thus have played a similar role in the North to that of Mac Dubhghaill in the South.

Such an interpretation of these events would certainly create a motive for Ruaidhri's involvement in the MacWilliam risings of 1228 to 1230 if he is indeed the 'Roderick' of the chronicles, as McDonald suggests.[24] It would also explain the absence of the descendants of Sumarliði's son Rögnvaldr in the Norwegian accounts of conflict in this period in which the sons of Guðrøðr and the MacDougalls are presented as the only players.

If Ruaidhri and/or Domhnall were firm adherents of King Rögnvaldr it is odd that we hear no more of them in the period following Rögnvaldr's death. Should they not have remained firm opponents of his brother Óláfr who had repudiated their kinswoman Lauon, and who now strove to take over the kingdom? A great deal may depend on the maternity of Óláf's son and heir Haraldr, who did indeed rely upon Islesmen for support. Unfortunately although we are told his age at his father's death in May 1237 it is fourteen years,[25] which places his birth in 1222 to 1223 almost exactly the point at which Óláfr was replacing Lauon with Christina and either could be his mother. If he were Lauon's son and if the Domhnall of the St Mary's miracle story were the eponymous Domhnall then this would make them uncle and nephew or perhaps even grandfather and grandson but there is a great dependence upon 'ifs' in this argument.

The 1230s and early 1240s are extremely difficult to fathom. The *Chronicle of the Kings of Man and the Isles* presents this period as a largely peaceful era in which rule passed from Óláfr to his son Haraldr with a minimal fuss by the standards of the kingdom of the Isles.[26] *Hákonar Saga* leaves the Isles in the beginning of the 1230s with Donnchadh mac Dubhghaill and his brother Dubhghall *Screech*, known only from this

23 Sellar, 'Hebridean sea kings', p. 201. The charter is to be found in *Registrum monasterii de Passelet*, pp 216–17.   24 McDonald, *Kingdom of the Isles*, p. 82.   25 *Chron. Man*, fo. 44v. 26 Ibid.

source, still alive.[27] If the 'Roderick' associated with the MacWilliams is Ruaidhri, he may also have gone on living into the 1230s, though perhaps still aligned to Óláfr and Haraldr. This might incline us to accept Andrew McDonald's view that the Mac Somhairle who died at Ballyshannon was most likely a Mac Dubhghaill, even if we modify this position with David Sellar's *caveat* that Donnchadh would not have been up to it. Our knowledge of these families is so dependent upon fragmentary chronicle and saga evidence that it is not beyond the realms of possibility that Donnchadh died between 1244 and 1247 and was succeeded by a brother, Dubhghall *Screech* (?), or son who was himself slain at Ballyshannon, leaving the lordship open to Donnchadh's best-known son Eoghan Mac Dubhghaill (the famous Ewen MacDougall).

Approaching the problem from the aftermath of Ballyshannon may be fruitful (but don't hold your breathe). Sellar noted that 'the death of Mac Somhairle in 1247 is likely to be connected with the appearance in Bergen the following year of Eoghan son of Donnchadh and Dubhghall son of Ruaidhri, each seeking the kingship of the isles'.[28] This seems on the face of it a fair assessment, although if both men thought themselves the heir of Ó Domhnaill's ally it does not help us to decide which was the closer kinsman to the dead man. Were this the case, however, it would underline the fact that the kingship was seen as a single prize worth grasping. The idea put forward in the seventeenth-century *Book of Clanranald* and still largely accepted by Scottish historians that the lordship of Sumarliði was divided between his sons on his death has no place here.[29]

Unfortunately there may be other explanations for why Eoghan and Dubhghall went to Norway in 1248. The year 1247 had seen not only the death of Mac Somhairle but also the coronation of Hákon IV and it may be that the new king wished simply to assert his lordship in the Isles. There is, however, something slightly suspicious about this interpretation. Islesmen do not seem to have been noted for their ready acquiescence to the whims of distant kings. Eoghan and Dubhghall will have travelled to Bergen hoping that there was something in it for them, and yet when they got there they found Haraldr Óláfsson already on hand and engaged to be married to Hákon's daughter Cecilia.[30]

Haraldr Óláfsson's relationship with Hákon may well hold the key to these events. According to the *Chronicle of the Kings of Man and the Isles*, in 1247 Haraldr had gone to England to be knighted and be given great

27 *Hákonar saga*, p. 85.   28 Sellar, 'Hebridean sea kings', p. 204, following *Hákon's saga*, p. 146.
29 See, for example, the maps on pp 183–6, in *The atlas of Scottish history to 1707*, ed. P.G.B. McNeill and H.L. MacQueen (Edinburgh, 1996).   30 *Hákonar saga*, p. 146.

gifts and friendship by Henry III. It is hard to imagine that this did not involve some kind of act of submission and that Henry, concerned as he was with Irish affairs, in something of a mess since he had 'let down the pilot' in the form of the de Burghs, and the de Lacys and various native kindreds had popped out of their boxes, may have seen the kingdom of the Isles as the key to secure police action in the difficult territories stretching from the de Lacy lordship in Down to the justiciar's own little empire growing up in Sligo.[31] In these conditions Hákon of Norway may well have sought an alternative candidate to Haraldr. As things seem to have turned out, the threat of switching support to one of Sumarliði's descendants appears to have been enough to bring Haraldr back into the Norwegian orbit, but was it?

English court records show that Haraldr's trip to England did not occur, as the *Chronicle of the Kings of Man and the Isles* would have it, in 1247 but in the first quarter of 1246.[32] The missing piece of our narrative may well fit into this lost year with the Mac Somhairle who fell fighting Maurice fitz Gerald being a rival king of the Isles set up in response to Haraldr's submission to Henry III, a solution to the problem which might also explain why he was engaged against the English interest in Ireland. Looking at the problem from an Anglo-Irish perspective lends us one further clue. According to Henry's financial records in 1248, Walter Bisset, engaged by the crown in Antrim, entered Scotland and fortified a castle at, it can be inferred, Dunaverty at the south end of Kintyre.[33] Interpreting this action in detail is difficult. The topography of the region is such that the capture of Dunaverty might have been aimed at the Mac Somhairle heartland in Kintyre or it may simply have been Bisset's task to 'close the gate' of the North Channel and to cut off Man from the rest of the kingdom of the Isles.

In the event Hákon's attempt to patch things up with Haraldr came to nought, as the Islesman and his bride drowned on their way home.[34] The sequel to these events perhaps gives us our final clue as to the identity of the dead man at Ballyshannon. Hákon awarded the kingship to Eoghan Mac Dubhghaill,[35] but within a year it had passed to his kinsman Dubhghall mac Ruaidhri,[36] even though Eoghan had twenty years of

---

31 Michael Dolley, *Anglo-Norman Ireland* (Dublin, 1972), pp 131ff.   32 *Calendar of patent rolls preserved in the Public Records Office: Henry III, A.D.1232–1247*, ed. J.G. Black (London, 1906), p. 469, entry for 9 January 1246, giving Haraldr protection until Whitsunday.   33 *Calendar of patent rolls preserved in the Public Record Office: Henry III, A.D.1247–1258*, ed. J.G. Black (London, 1908), p. 11, noting Walter's fortification of a castle in Scotland on 26 March; and p. 127, noting John Bisset's defence of Dunaverty on 30 January 1252.   34 *Chron. Man*, f.46v. *Hákonar saga*, p. 147.   35 *Hákonar saga*, p. 148.   36 *Islamdske Annaler indtil 1578*, ed. G. Storm

active career ahead of him. Eoghan's assumption of the kingship of the Isles alienated Alexander II of Scotland who responded by leading an armed expedition into Eoghan's patrimony of Lorne forcing him into submission.[37] It is clear that just as Henry II of England had not been prepared to see his earl of Pembroke make himself king of Leinster, so Alexander II of Scotland was not prepared to see one of his barons make himself king of the Isles. His swift and unequivocal reaction to Eoghan's kingship makes it almost certain that no previous Mac Dubhghaill lord of Lorne had held the kingship of the Isles or made so serious a bid for it.

Dubhghall mac Ruaidhri, however, had no such qualms about offending the king of Scots and he, it seems, established dominion in the Isles for his dynasty and their descendants. Like his predecessor, who died at Ballyshannon, he engaged fully with Irish affairs, in 1258 killing Jordan d'Exeter off the coast of Connacht and in the following year marrying his daughter to Aodh Ó Conchobhair at Derry and, according to some accounts, giving her a dowry of young warriors of the Isles.[38] But that is another story.

(Christiania, 1888), version C, s.a. 1249.   **37** *Hákonar saga*, pp 148–9.   **38** *AC*; *ALC*, 1258 and 1259; cf. Sellar, 'Hebridean sea kings', p. 206.

Scottish mercenary kindreds in
Ireland, 1250–1600

KENNETH NICHOLLS

The late G.A. Hayes-McCoy, in his book, *Scots mercenary forces in Ireland (1565–1603)*[1] went far beyond the scope of his title to discuss in detail the *gallóglaigh*, and in this respect his work was indeed a pioneering one. He noted the distinction between the sixteenth-century 'New Scots' (often referred to as 'Redshanks' by contemporary Englishmen, a term which seems to have been resented as derogatory by those to whom it was applied),[2] and the *gallóglaigh*, although to the end the latter, of only remotely Scottish ancestry, continued to be called in Latin *Scotici*. The 'gallogle Chlene Suene' – the MacSweeney galloglass serving the MacCarthys – are styled *Scotici* in 1519, as are Ormond's MacSweeney galloglass in 1538, and in 1553 Alexander (mac Toirdhealbhaigh) Mac Domhnaill was captain of the King's '*Scotici* otherwise galloglass'.[3] Hayes-McCoy also pointed out that the bulk of the rank-and-file 'galloglass' were recruited from the general Irish population, only their captains coming of the recognized galloglass stock, and he noticed also that even some of the captains were of native Irish lineage: the first galloglass recruited by the earls of Kildare were a band of twenty-four led by one of the Barrett lineage of County Mayo.[4] Given the strength of the Mac Domhnaill presence there by that date it is probable that he had learned his galloglass skills from them, and quite possible that his mother had been a Mac Domhnaill. The genealogy of the O'Beirns of Roscommon, too, notes a Ruaidhri of the chiefly line 'who was a galloglass on the borders' (mid-fifteenth century).[5] At the end of his book, Hayes-McCoy lists what he calls 'two peculiar usages' of the term galloglass regarding which he could only make wild guesses, one to a 'galloglass' in Lord Deputy FitzWilliam's household, and the other to 'the lord's galloglass (*gallóglach tighearna*)' in the proclamation by Aodh

---

1 Dublin and London, 1937: rpr. Dublin, 1996.   2 In 1596, Denis Campbell, dean of Limerick, reacted angrily when his bishop, the abrasive Englishman John Thornburgh, described his chief, Argyll, and the whole Campbell clan as 'Redshanks' (*CSPS*, xii, *1595–1597*, p. 198).   3 NLI, MS D. 1999 (i); *SP Henry VIII*, iii/2, p. 91n; *Irish fiants, Edward VI*, p. 1195 – 'O'Donell' (*sic*); cf. *Irish fiants Philip & Mary*, 369.   4 Hayes-McCoy, *Scots mercenary forces*, p. 36.   5 Séamus Pender (ed.), 'The O'Clery book of genealogies', *Analecta Hibernica*, 18 (1951), 92.

Ó Néill (Hugh O'Neill) regarding the *buannadha* or mercenaries.[6] In fact the two instances cited refer to the same office, and I can add two more: a witness in a lawsuit in 1605 gives, as the reason for his knowledge of the matters in question, that 'he was galliglasse to Connor O Brien [3rd earl of Thomond, died 1580] and waited on him in his chamber',[7] and Fynes Moryson speaks of Lord Mountjoy having his galloglass, who on the occasion referred to was carrying Mountjoy's helmet.[8] The 'lord's galloglass', then, is an attendant on an Irish lord – or, by cultural borrowing, a high English official in Ireland – presumably his personal bodyguard, and the figure holding a galloglass axe who stands beside the Irish lord in Derricke's picture must be his 'galloglass'.[9] His connection with the true *gallóglaigh* – from whom the bodyguard would, presumably, have been originally recruited – is shown by the fact that he was entitled to one dead pay ('black man') in every company of a hundred mercenaries.[10]

Nevertheless, when it comes to matters of detail regarding the galloglass, Hayes-McCoy is a very unreliable guide. Quite apart from his strange schematic ideas regarding the nature of native Irish society,[11] he was ill-informed regarding the lineages and their genealogy and seems not to have understood the practice of employing patronymics instead of surnames. Thus he says:

Hebrideans, or men of Hebridean extraction … had drifted southwards into various parts of Ireland by the 1560–1600 period. In some cases they can quite definitely be linked up with the gallóglaigh, and the inference is that their dispersal was due to the gallóglach movement. Two MacColls occur in Sligo in 1590; three MacColls with a MacAlistran, a MacAline and two MacKeys in O Flaherty country in Galway in the same year. MacAlistran is of course MacAllister of the Loup clan, and of this name there is a further occurrence in Galway in 1593 and two in Munster in 1601. MacAline is likely MacLean …[12]

In fact the three MacColls [*recte* macCollys] in County Galway were members of the Joyce clan, sons of a Colla Joyce; the MacAlistran (the same man in 1590 and 1593) and the MacAline were also Joyces,[13] while

6 Hayes-McCoy, *Scots mercenary forces*, pp 359–60.   7 Petworth House Archives, Bundle I.C.3, Deposition of Donoghe O'Connell of Lissofin.   8 Fynes Moryson, *An itinerary containing his ten yeeres travel through the twelve dominions of Germany, Bohmerland, Sweitzerland, Netherland, Denmarke, Poland, Italy, Turkey, France, England, Scotland and Ireland* (2nd edn, 4 vols, Glasgow, 1907/8), ii, p. 269.   9 John Derricke, *The image of Irelande, with a discourse of woodcarne* (London, 1581: rpr. Edinburgh, 1883 and Belfast, 1985).   10 John O'Donovan, 'Military proclamation, in the Irish language, issued by Hugh O'Neill, earl of Tyrone, in 1601', *UJA*, 1st ser., 6 (1858), 61.   11 Hayes-McCoy, *Scots mercenary forces*, pp 46 ff; they are expounded at length in 'Gaelic society in Ireland in the late sixteenth century' in G.A. Hayes-McCoy (ed.), *Historical Studies IV* (London, 1963), pp 45–61.   12 Hayes-McCoy, *Scots mercenary forces*, p. 68.   13 *LMG*, iii, (168) 832.6, (170) 832, 13.25. Some of the persons in question recur in 1593, this time with the surname Joy (*Irish fiants, Elizabeth*, 5800).

there is no reason to think that the MacKeys and the two Munster MacAllistrums were not also natives. A little further on, he seems to think that the well-known Mayo clan of MacAndrew – a branch of the Barretts – were also of Scottish origin. Given these weaknesses, it is clear that his account of the *gallóglaigh* must be used with considerable caution.

In this paper, in listing the lineages of Scottish origin who served as mercenaries in Ireland, I will commence with one which, although mercenaries, were never classed as *gallóglaigh*. These were the MacQuillans (Mac Uibhilín, Mac Uidhilín, Mac Uighilín: in its Anglo-Norman form, MacHoulyn) who traditionally claimed a Welsh origin. The question which must be posed is whether they were not in fact Strathclyde Welsh. The main indication that they were is that they were named as collaterals in an early Campbell genealogy,[14] although the strange name Corcaruo (Corc Ruadh?), given in it to their ancestor, does not occur in the Gaelic genealogies of the lineage. In this context it may be noted that W.W. Scott has suggested that the Dundonald family, prominent in Anglo-Norman Ireland and who survived in Mayo under the adopted Gaelic surname of Mac Roibeird, took their name from Dundonald in Kyle.[15] What is interesting is that the Dundonalds/Mac Roibeirds also claimed Welsh extraction;[16] were they also Strathclyde Welsh? Whatever the original home of the MacQuillans, there was nothing Gaelic about them when they first make their appearance in history; they were definitely Anglo-Norman in culture. The name Stephen which recurs in their genealogy in the thirteenth and fourteenth centuries was used by them in its Norman-French form, Estevene, as is shown by its appearance in the Gaelic genealogy (as in that of the MacJordan Dexters) as Sleimhne, while the mercenary force which they led was known by the French term *route*, which (in its Gaelicized form, *an Rúta*) was eventually transferred to the territory in north Antrim of which they ended up as lords. As late as 1470, however, as T.E. McNeill has pointed out, *an Rúta* still seems to be used in a non-territorial sense, to denote the force led by MacQuillan.[17]

The earliest genealogy of the MacQuillans is that found in a manuscript dating from *c.*1500 in the Benchers' Library in King's Inns, Dublin.[18] It

---

14 W.D.H. Sellar, 'The earliest Campbells – Norman, Briton or Gael?', *Scottish Studies*, 17 (1973), 121.   15 In a review of T.B. Barry, Robin Frame and Katharine Simms (eds), *Colony and frontier in medieval Ireland*, in *SHR*, 76/1 (1997), p. 125.   16 *LMG*, iii, (164) 830.6, (186) 842–3.   17 T.E. McNeill, *Anglo-Norman Ulster: the history and archaeology of an Irish barony, 1177–1400* (Edinburgh, 1980), pp 120–1, citing *AU*, iii, pp 270–1. The same sense seems to occur in an entry of 1454 in the Mac Fhirbhisigh Annals ('The annals of Ireland from the year 1443 to 14687, by Duald MacFirbis', ed. John O'Donovan, in *Miscellany of the Irish Archaeological Society*, i (1846), p. 236) and *AFM* (iv, pp 986–7, where O'Donovan's translation unjustifiably inserts the words 'the territory of' before the term *an Rúta*.)   18 MS G.11, fo. 4.

differs from all the other versions[19] in inserting a Niocol Ruadh as son and grandson of two Stephens (Sleimhne), the elder of whom was son of the eponym Houlyn. Niocol was the father of William MacHoulyn, presumably the constable of Ulster who had ceased to occupy that post (died?) by 1323,[20] and would have been contemporary with the Seonach Mac Uidhilín who appears as a leader of mercenaries in the service of Aodh Ó Conchobhair, king of Connacht, whom he treacherously killed in 1310 before transferring his services to Ó Conchobhair's enemy, Sir William de Burgh. He was killed himself in the following year.[21] William's son Stephen (Esteuene MacHoulyn) paid £200 to the earl of Ulster in 1331 for the office of constable of Ulster, the former holder, Henry de Mandeville (who had succeeded William MacHoulyn in 1323) having been arrested for his alleged involvement in the conspiracy of the earl of Desmond.[22] Stephen is styled constable of Ulster at his death in 1368, but in 1346 the office had been restored to Henry de Mandeville's son Richard, which may be the reason why Stephen transferred his allegiance to Aodh Ó Néill of Tír Eoghain, in whose company 'McHolyn' was warring against the English in 1350.[23] Stephen's son Alexander does not occur in contemporary records, but Alexander's son Jenkin (Seinicín: 'Synnich') was serving the then seneschal of the Ulster earldom, Edmond Savage, in 1395 and was still chieftain in 1427 and 1448.[24]

Before turning to the great *gallóglaigh* stocks who continued to play a prominent role in Ireland through the later medieval period, I will touch on some lineages that occur as captains of *gallóglaigh* in the early phase of activity but subsequently disappear, at least from the written record. The MacRuaidhris of Garmoran and Kintyre, a branch of Clann Somhairle, turn up in Ireland as leaders of *gallóglaigh* at the time of the Scottish wars of independence, but the last reference to them in Ireland which I can discover is that to Mac Ruaidhri, captain of *gallóglaigh* to Toirdhealbhach Ó Conchobhair, king of Connacht, slain in 1342.[25] It is possible, as Professor Lydon has suggested, that this was the Gregory MacRyry who with his following had been serving in the earl of Desmond's 'rout' in 1328.[26] The probability is that the lineage, in Ireland as in Scotland,

19 Printed by Edmund Curtis in his very misguided article, 'The MacQuillan or Mandeville lords of the Route', *RIA Proc.*, 44 C (1937–8), 99–113: see also *LMG*, iii (166–9) 831.9–832.1. 20 McNeill, *Anglo-Norman Ulster*, p. 70. 21 *AC*, 1310.5, 6; 1311.13. 22 McNeill, *Anglo-Norman Ulster*, p. 70. 23 K.W. Nicholls, 'Anglo-French Ireland and after', *Peritia*, i (1982), 384; McNeill, *Anglo-Norman Ulster*, p. 70; Philomena Connolly (ed.), *Irish exchequer payments, 1270–1446* (IMC, Dublin, 1998), p. 435. 24 Nicholls, 'Anglo-French Ireland', 386n; W.G.H. Quigley and E.F.D. Roberts (eds), *Registrum Johannis Mey* (Belfast, 1972), p. 172; D.A. Chart, *The register of John Swayne* (Belfast, 1935), p. 28. 25 *AC*, 1342.3. 26 J.F. Lydon, 'The Scottish soldier abroad: the Bruce invasion and the galloglass', rpr. in Seán Duffy (ed.), *Robert the Bruce's*

petered out in the fourteenth century. In 1305 Mag Buirrche, 'chief of the *gallóglaigh*', fell in a battle in Bréifne, along with 'the heir (*oighre*) of the Clann Suibhne',[27] and in 1346, again in Bréifne, the two leaders of Ó Ruairc's galloglass who were slain in battle were Mag Buirrche and Mac Néill Caim.[28] That this latter was a surname, not a mere patronymic, would seem to be indicated by the fact that a later Mac Néill Caim, a captain of galloglass, was slain in Connacht in 1377.[29] The genealogy of 'Mag Buirrche' found in the Irish collections, as David Sellar has pointed out and as was indeed known to Mac Fhirbhisigh,[30] is that of the Lamonts: it is hard to resist the conclusion that these two galloglass captains were the chiefs of the Lamont line, perhaps Maol Choluim (Malcolm) son of the eponymous Ladhmann and his son Eoin. Sellar has argued for the descent of the MacNeills of Barra (and perhaps those of Taynish, geographically much closer) from the same stock as the Lamonts and MacSweeneys:[31] could the surname of the Taynish clan have been originally MacNéill Caim? In any case, the surname does not recur in Ireland.

There seems to be a general assumption that the immigrants to Ireland from the Western Highlands and Islands who made permanent settlements ended about 1400, and that the later wave of Scottish mercenaries, who did not make such settlements, did not commence until the mid-sixteenth century. These assumptions, however, may not be true. Colla, son of MacDougal of Lorne (Mac Dubhghaill na hAlban) was slain in an internecine feud among the Burkes of Mayo in 1480:[32] he was presumably there as a mercenary, rather than on a friendly visit. And an unnamed son of another of the Lorne MacDougals was slain at the Castle of Cúl mhic an Treoin (Castleforward, County Donegal) in 1529.[33] Two MacLeans, Alan (Alún) and Ruaidhri, were slain in 1486 while serving, alongside the MacCabe *gallóglaigh*, in west Bréifne.[34] That this has been overlooked by the MacLean historians is no doubt due to the fact that in the index to the Annals of Ulster they appear as MacCabes! The party of *Albanaigh* who were defeated and slaughtered in Armagh by the O'Neills of the Fews on St Patrick's Day, 1501, may have been raiders rather than mercenaries, as we are not told of their being in anyone's service: their leaders who fell, among sixty in all, were the son of the Laird of Eigg (Allan mac Ruaidhri of Clanranald?) and the three sons of Colla mac Alexandair Mhic Dhomhnaill, whom I cannot identify.[35] Somhairle Aneloigh (*an Eloigh*: of

Irish wars (Stroud, 2002), pp 89–106.   **27** *Misc. Ir. annals*, p. 131; *AU*, ii, pp 402–3; *AC*, 1305.3. **28** *AU*, ii, pp 482–3; *AC*, 1346.2.   **29** *AC*, 1377.9.   **30** W.D.H. Sellar, 'Family origins in Cowal and Knapdale', *Scottish Studies*, 15 (1971), 21–38, at 28; *LMG*, i (304) 125.2.   **31** Sellar, 'Family origins', 32.   **32** *AU*, iii, pp 272–3.   **33** *AFM*, v, pp 1396–7.   **34** *AU*, iv, pp 304–5.   **35** *AU*, iii,

Islay?) son of Aonghus Mac Domhnaill, who was leading a band of Scots in the service of Mag Uidhir in 1504 (when he was captured by Aodh Mac Mathghamhna of Dartry) and was in the service of another Mag Uidhir in 1506,[36] may – from his epithet – have been a collateral of Clann Eoin Mhóir of Kintyre and Islay. In any case, these *Albanaigh* have nothing to do with the established Mac Domhnaill galloglass of Ulster. As for more permanent settlements of West Highlanders, there is the mysterious Eoin Odhar Mac Néill (called Owen Ower in English records, showing that the confusion between Eoin (Ian, John) and Eoghan (Ewen, Eugene) did not originate with the Gaelic Revival of the twentieth century) who in 1577 was installed by Sir Nicholas Malby, governor of Connacht, at Cavetown (Baile na hUamha) in north Roscommon 'to oppose the Scots'.[37] This was the great raiding party from the Isles, led by a Sleat Mac Domhnaill (Eoin mac Aonghusa mhic Ghiolla Easpaig Bháin) and two MacFies, who had been plundering northern Connacht for two months and had now moved down into Roscommon. Eoin Odhar succeeded in slaying one of the MacFies, Feardorcha. On 4 March 1577/8 a formal pardon was granted to him and to Gyllecollom and Donell McNeille.[38] However, in 1579 he was slain by some MacDermots and on the same day some of his followers were killed by the English garrison of Roscommon, suggesting a concerted attack.[39] Who was Eoin Odhar? Since the annalist distinguishes him from the *Albanaigh*, he was not a new arrival from Scotland nor, I suggest, would the English administration have trusted him if he were. Were he and his kinsmen second-generation immigrants, the Irish-born sons of a Taynish or Barra MacNeill?

CLANN SUIBHNE

It is difficult to discover the exact circumstances in which the Clann Suibhne were deprived of their ancestral territory of Knapdale in Argyll,[40] in which they had erected the fortress of Castle Sween, or to reconcile the contemporary (Scottish) evidence with the largely legendary family history written after 1514.[41] The difficulties in doing so are not lessened by the fact that the legendary history, as is shown by the earliest

p. 456. The three sons were Toirdhealbhach, Donnchadh and Ludar, a name which recurs as that of one of the sons of Somhairle Buidhe Mac Domhnaill. **36** *AU*, iii, pp 466–8, 480–2. In O'Ferrall's *Linea Antiqua* of 1706 Somhairle Mac Alexandair, ancestor of the Connacht MacDonnells (see below), is called Sorley an Eloi (NLI, G.O. MS 155, p. 153). **37** 'in aghaidh cogaidh Albanach', *ALC*, ii, pp 418–19. **38** *Irish fiants, Elizabeth*, 3211. **39** *ALC*, ii, pp 424–5. **40** For the background see Sellar, 'Family origins'. **41** Edited by Paul Walsh as *Leabhar Chlainne Suibhne* [*LCS*] (Dublin, 1920). For the date, see n. 67 below.

written genealogy, in the late fourteenth-century Book of Ballymote,[42] has omitted two generations and has merged the Murchadh who, after being captured in the west of Ireland, perhaps on a piratical expedition, died as a prisoner of the earl of Ulster in 1267,[43] with his grandson, Murchadh Mear ('the mad') from whom the Irish MacSweeneys were to descend. It would therefore follow that the husband of Beanmhidhe (died 1269), daughter of Toirdhealbhach (mac Ruaidhri) Ó Conchobhair (king of Connacht, deposed 1228, died 1239) was not Maolmhuire, father of the first Murchadh, but the latter's son of the same name, to whom therefore the epithet *an Sparáin* would properly belong.[44] Murchadh Mear and his brother Suibhne would therefore have been the sons of Beanmhidhe, and Suibhne almost certainly the elder, since it was his descendants who claimed the Knapdale lands. According to the legendary history, this Suibhne's sons were John (Eoin), of whom a whole series of heroic feats are related, and who was the first to conquer the territory of Fanad in Donegal, and Toirdhealbhach: are these not the John and Toirdhealbhach, sons of 'Swiene of Argyll', to whom with their third brother Murchadh, King Edward II in July 1310 granted the whole land of Knapdale which their ancestors had held, if they could recover it from the then occupiers?[45] John was with Hugh Bisset of the Glens and the fleet which he was commanding in the English cause when he (John 'son of Suffne') wrote to the English king pointing out that Knapdale was in the hands of the latter's enemy, John of Menteith.[46] This letter, with two others (from Hugh Bisset and from Aonhgus Óg of Islay) which accompanied it, has been dated in 1301, but John of Menteith was then a trusted servant of Edward I, and in fact the letter refers to the king's grant of Knapdale to John MacSuibhne, who had gone there and viewed it (*adivi et visitavi*) but had been unable to gain possession. (Does this imply that John had no previous acquaintance with Knapdale?) The true date of these letters, therefore, was in September 1310, after Menteith had gone over to the side of King Robert Bruce.[47] Could John's father have been the 'Suny Magurke' (Suibhne Mag Bhuirrche) whose lands in Knapdale and Glendaruel were granted by Edward II to Dungal of Gyveleston in 1314?[48]

42 *Book of Ballymote*, 77, printed in *LCS*, pp 78–80.   43 *AC*, 1267.3.   44 For Beanmhidhe see *AC*, 1269.6; *AU*, ii, p. 338. She is called 'wife of Maolmhuire Mac Suibhne', which to me suggests that the latter was still alive. The purse (*Sparán*) which gave Maolmhuire his epithet was, according to *LCS*, a magical one, bestowed on him by his fairy lover!   45 *Rot. Scot.*, i, p. 90b, printed again in Niall D. Campbell (aft. 10th duke of Argyll), 'MacEwens and MacSweens', *Celtic Review*, 7 (1911–2), 272–84, at 279.   46 *CDS*, ii, no. 1255.   47 I had come to this conclusion before reading the article by B.W. MacEwen, 'The English fleet of 1301', *WHN & Q*, 1st ser., 24 (Aug. 1984), 3–7, in which the case for the later date is conclusively put. I am grateful to David Sellar for drawing my attention to this article.   48 Campbell, 'MacEwens

But the Irish annals, as we have seen, distinguish Mag Buirrche from Clann Suibhne. In any case, the statement in the legendary history that John son of Suibhne was the father of the Mac Suibhne daughter who was the mother of Aodh Ó Domhnaill, king of Tír Chonaill (with intervals) from 1281 to 1333, is chronologically impossible.[49]

All the Irish lines of MacSweeneys descended from the two sons of Murchadh Mear: Murchadh Óg, from whom descended the two ruling lines of Mac Suibhne Fanad and Mac Suibhne na dTuath in Tír Chonaill, and Maolmhuire, from whom descended all the early galloglass lines. A branch of Maolmhuire's descendants returned to Tír Boghaine (Banagh) in Tír Chonaill to become the third line of Mac Suibhne local rulers, generally known as MacSweeney Banagh. The return may well have been in the first case as *gallóglaigh*, if Maolmhuire, ancestor of the Banagh line, is (as Walsh thought) the same man who died as constable of Tír Chonaill (or, to Ó Domhnaill) in 1424.[50] All the settled families of Clann Suibhne *gallóglaigh* whom we find in the fifteenth and sixteenth centuries in Connacht, Thomond and the Butler territories came of this stock; only the three lines who settled in the service of the MacCarthys of South Munster in the late fifteenth and early sixteenth centuries came from those settled in Tír Chonaill.

As early as 1367, at the battle of Tráigh Eochaille near Sligo, we find the beginnings of the factional adherence which saw Clann Suibhne providing the galloglass arm of that great alliance in Connacht headed by one line of Burkes, Mac Uilliam Uachtar of Clann Riocaird, and which supported, for the (increasingly nominal) kingship of Connacht, the branch of the O'Connors that acquired the name Ó Conchobhair *Donn*, while the galloglass of the opposing faction, led by another Burke line, Mac Uilliam Íochtar (of Mayo), and supporting Ó Conchobhair *Ruadh*, were provided by branches of Clann Somhairle.[51] The account of the battle in the surviving annals would lead one to assume that the members of Clann Suibhne who fell[52] were among the 150 *gallóglaigh* who fell on the losing side, that of Tadhg son of Maghnus Ó Conchobhair, around the Clann

and MacSweens', 280.   **49** In the O'Donnell genealogies she is called simply daughter of Mac Suibhne. Even if Aodh was a teenager when he was first inaugurated as king in 1281 his mother could hardly have been born much later than 1250.   **50** *AFM*, iv, p. 858 (where he is called Mac Suibhne Connachtach), p. 862; cf. p. 806. The obit is not in the other surviving annals. According to the genealogies, he was the eldest son of Eoin na Lathaighe, mentioned below. **51** For these factions see Kenneth Nicholls, *Gaelic and Gaelicised Ireland in the middle ages*, 1st ed. (Dublin, 1972), 2nd ed. (Dublin, 2003), pp 170–7.   **52** Their names, according to a note from the lost O'Mulconry annals not printed by O'Donovan, were Suibhne mac Domhnaill Connachtaig Mic Suibhne and two sons of Eoghan Mac Suibhne (*AFM*, new ed., de Burca Rare Books, Dublin, 1990), App. to Introduction s.a. 1367.

Somhairle captains, Domhnall (mac Somhairle) Mac Domhnaill, his son
Domhnall Óg and William Mac Síthigh, and indeed the Annals of
Ulster say precisely that.[53] However, the account of the battle in the lost
Mac Fhirbhisigh Annals, printed by O'Donovan in a footnote to the
Four Masters, shows that the Clann Suibhne under Toirdhealbhach
Mac Suibhne were on the victorious side, that of Domhnall (mac
Muircheartaigh) Ó Conchobhair.[54] Now it is far from impossible that the
Clann Suibhne were divided, one section being with Tadhg mac
Maghnusa, but it is also possible that the annalists, as on other occasions,
lumped together the names of the slain on both sides. The Toirdhealbhach
of 1367 must be the Toirdhealbhach, high-constable of Connacht, who
died in 1378,[55] and the unnamed Mac Suibhne, high-constable of
Connacht 'north of the mountains', who fell with his two brothers in
the great defeat of the *Donn* faction at the Curragh of Kinnitty near
Roscommon on 14 August 1397,[56] must be Toirdhealbhach's brother Eoin
'na Lathaighe'.[57] The surviving *gallóglaigh* of his party under his son
Domhnall fled north, to participate in the victory at Lissadell near
Sligo on 7 September, by which the descendants of Domhnall (mac
Muircheartaigh) Ó Conchobhair consolidated their hold on Sligo against
their factional enemies, the sons of Cathal Óg, close kinsmen of Tadhg
mac Maghnusa of 1367 and allies of Ó Conchobhair Ruadh. At this battle
fell Marcus Mac Domhnaill, Eoin Mac Síthigh and many of the Clann
Domhnaill galloglass.[58] Domhnall – called in the genealogies Domhnall na
Madhmann ('of the defeats') – was the commander of the galloglass of the
victorious side at the battle of Athlighean (Ballyline) in Clanrickard in
1419, when all the galloglass of the invading force led by Mac Uilliam
Íochtar and Ó Ceallaigh (O'Kelly) were killed, along with one of their
commanders.[59] He was the ancestor of the later galloglass lines settled in

53 *AU*, ii, p. 530; *AC*, 1367.7; *AFM*, iii, pp 637–9.   54 *AFM*, ii, pp 637–8n.   55 *AC*, 1378–1;
AClon, p. 306. Another source calls him Mac Suibhne Connachtach (Gearóid MacNiocaill (ed.),
'Annála gearra, 1360–1402', *Galvia*, 5 (1958), 39: misdated 1375).   56 *AU*, iii, pp 32–4; *AClon*,
pp 317–18; *AFM*, iv, pp 750–53; *Misc. Ir. annals*, pp 156–8. No source actually names the Mac
Suibhne constable.   57 The genealogy of Toirdhealbhach, Eoin and their four brothers
(including Donnchadh and Donnshléibhe, who both fell at Kinnitty) occurs in the Book of
Ballymote under the heading 'Mac Suibhne Connachtach' (*LCS*, p. 80). Fr Walsh thought that
the eldest brother Toirdhealbhach was the constable slain in 1397, and does not hazard a guess at
the identity of the man of 1378. In this he was moved by a late list of the MacSweeney lords of
Tír Boghaine (Banagh) in the O'Clery Book; this list, however, as he himself noted, is defective
(*LCS*, p. 80n, pp 110–11nn). The O'Clery Book is confused regarding Eoin 'na Lathaighe',
whom it consistently turns into Eoghan (like his father). Identification of these persons is made
difficult by the contemporary existence of an Eoghan 'Connachtach' and his son Toirdhealbhach
Óg in the MacSweeney na dTuath (Doe) line (*LCS*, p. 79).   58 *AU*, iii, pp 34–6; *AClon*, pp
318–19; *AFM*, iv, pp 753–6.   59 *AU*, iii, p. 80; *ALC*, ii, pp 148–50; *AC*, 1419.17, 18.

Clanrickard and Thomond, as well as of the numerous kindred who settled in the Ó Dubhda territory of Tireragh in County Sligo, where they took over much of the land of the declining Ó Dubhda sept of Ardnaglass.[60] A descendant of this line, Eugene (Eoghan), an exile serving in the Spanish Cavalry in 1659, Hispanicized his name into the very aristocratic Spanish one of Zuñiga![61] The branch which served the Butlers of Ormond claimed descent from Domhnall's brother Donnshléibhe.[62] From their other brother Donnchadh, killed (like Donnshléibhe) at the Curragh of Kinnitty in 1397, came the sept which remained in the service of Ó Conchobhair Donn.[63]

The factional allegiances of the galloglass lineages established in Connacht carried over into the rest of southern Ireland, where the Clann Suibhne provided the galloglass arm of the O'Briens of Thomond, the Butlers of Ormond and the MacCarthys of south Munster, all enemies of the Geraldine earls of Desmond, whose own galloglass were the Clann Síthigh (MacSheehys), who claimed to be a branch of Clann Somhairle. When the Geraldine earls of Kildare recruited galloglass at the end of the fifteenth century they recruited MacDonnells from Connacht. It was no doubt because of this factional allegiance of the MacSweeneys that the remarkable marriage treaty (1513) of Lady Eleanor FitzGerald, daughter of the Great Earl of Kildare with Domhnall Mac Carthaigh Riabhach (MacCarthy Reagh) of Carbery, by which he conceded to her, among other things, equal authority with himself within his lordship, provided that if those *Scotici* whom he then employed, namely *Gallogle Chlene Suene*, were not conformable to her will he would dismiss them and replace them with other *Scotici* acceptable to her.[64] In the event, however, the Clann Suibhne must have made their peace with her, since they remained in Carbery. When in 1568 Lord FitzMaurice of Kerry hired galloglass against his enemy, the earl of Desmond, it was a MacSweeney from Thomond who provided them, leading to the well-known anecdote related by the Four Masters.[65] The attacking force, led by the earl's cousin James fitz Maurice,

60 NAI, Salved Chancery Pleadings, Box X, no. 21. 61 Micheline Walsh (ed.), *Spanish knights of Irish origin: documents from continental archives*, 2 vols (Dublin, IMC, 1960–78), ii, pp 1–2. For his genealogy, see *LMG*, i (300) 123.2 (=*LCS*, p. 84). For his immediate ancestors, *Irish patent rolls of James I* (rpr. IMC, Dublin, 1966), pp 22, 322. 62 The number of generations seems, however, too few. For these MacSweeneys in Butler service, see *SP Henry VIII*, iii/2, p. 91n; *AFM*, v, p. 1784. 63 Mac Fhirbhisigh makes them descend (like those in Thomond) from Donnchadh, son of Domhnall, but all other sources (including Bodleian Library, Oxford, University College MS 103, fo. 12r, as *Clann Suibhne Baile in Tobair*) derive them from the latter's brother. Again the number of generations seems too few. 64 K.W. Nicholls, 'The development of lordship in County Cork, 1300–1600' in Patrick O'Flanagan and C.G. Buttimer (eds), *Cork: history and society* (Dublin, 1993), p. 193. 65 *AFM*, v, pp 1624–8.

knew that the term of service of FitzMaurice's galloglass had expired – galloglass were hired for a quarter of a year at a time – and had planned their attack accordingly, but the hired *gallóglaigh* did not think it right to leave their employer in his hour of need, and participated in inflicting a catastrophic defeat on James and his MacSheehy galloglass. The Four Masters' account implies a deep-rooted animosity between the two galloglass lineages, Clann Suibhne and Clann Síthigh. However, such animosities could exist, as will be seen, between different branches of the same lineage.

The three MacSweeney septs which served the MacCarthys differed from those already referred to in deriving their origin from the lords of Fanad and of the Trí Tuatha (Mac Suibhne na dTuath, or 'Doe') in Tír Chonaill. Brian mac Toirdhealbhaigh of the house of Fanad was invited to Munster by Finghin, son of the ruling MacCarthy Reagh, and was with him at the defeat of their cousin and rival Cormac at Knocknalurgan in 1477,[66] and his son Maolmhuire ('Bacach') with the allied MacCarthys in their defeat of the earl of Desmond at Mourne abbey in 1519.[67] Another MacSweeney, this time from the Doe territory, Donnchadh mac Toirdhealbhaigh, also came to serve Finghin Mac Carthaigh Riabhach, and although his son Maolmhuire, then a child, returned to the north on his father's death, he subsequently returned, this time to serve Mac Carthaigh Mór as constable.[68] Between these two lines there existed 'mortal malice, so much as whensoever any of them did meet they did assuredly fight'.[69] The third MacSweeney sept in Munster was that in Muskerry, descended from the house of Fanad:[70] Éamonn mac Dubhdara was invited to Munster by Cormac son of Tadhg Mac Carthaigh of Muskerry, and was slain there with his brother in 1498.[71] They became

66 Nicholls, 'Development of lordship', p. 192. The later genealogy of this sept (*Sliocht Mhaolmhuire Bhacaigh*) is to be found in Lambeth MS 635, fos. 13v–14; *AFM*, v, p. 1712, omits a generation. 67 *LCS*, pp 56–7, showing that the final compilation of that text was later than that year. Note that the date 1524, given for the battle of Mourne abbey in Nicholls, *Gaelic and Gaelicized Ireland*, is an (inexplicable!) error. 68 The genealogy of this sept (*Sliocht Dhonnchaidh Mhóir*) is given quite differently in different sources. See *LCS*, pp 89, 112–13; Bodleian Library, University College MS 103, fo. 11v (a Munster source and perhaps to be preferred: it agrees with *AFM*, v, p. 1712); RIA MS 23.M.17, p. 133 (= NLI MS G. 177, p. 65). In this last-named source there also appears a related line of MacSweeneys, down to *Murchadh mac Gofraigh mic Bhriain Dhorcha mic Émuinn Bhuidhe*, for which I cannot give a location. 69 Nicholls, 'Development of lordship', p. 193; *UJA*, 1st ser. 5 (1855), 319. Cf. *AFM*, v, p. 1712; Lambeth MS 635, fos. 12v–13. 70 *Éamonn* is miscalled *Eoin* in the genealogy given by O'Clery (*LCS*, p. 113). That in MS 23.M.17 (p. 133) agrees with this (except in the error). University College MS 103 (fo. 11v) gives a somewhat different version, inserting another Éamonn as father of Dubhdara, omitting (by accident?) Toirdhealbhach and inserting (as suggested by Walsh, in *LCS*, p. 113n) Murchadh Óg. 71 Nicholls, 'Development of lordship', p. 174.

extremely numerous in Muskerry,[72] and probably the majority of the present MacSweeneys (or MacSwineys, as it is sometimes archaically spelt) in County Cork come of this line.

CLANN SOMHAIRLE

There is no doubt that all the major stocks of Mac Domhnaill *gallóglaigh* in Ireland were descended from the younger Alexander, son and heir[73] of Aonghus Mór of the Isles.[74] The one exception might be the obscure line of MacDonnells of Roslee in Tireragh, County Sligo, whose genealogy as given by Mac Fhirbhisigh derives them from a Giolla Adhamhnáin son of Alexander Óg son of Alexander Mór, brother of Aonghus Mór.[75] The whole line as given, however, looks unconvincing and is probably a late construct. The oldest written genealogy of the Mac Donnells[76] – one which, incidentally, replaces the strange name *Meirgi* of later versions with the much more credible *Inneirge* – is that by Ádhamh Ó Cianáin, written down no later than 1346, which brings the line down to Eoin Dubh and Toirdhealbhach, sons of Alexander, and their nephew Domhnall son of Somhairle. Eoin Dubh was killed in 1349 by Maghnus Mac Mathghamhna.[77] He had been in Ireland long enough to have married the daughter of a Mac Mathghamhna (Murchadh, died 1331) belonging to a rival branch. His son Somhairle is described as 'constable of the province of Ulster' and one eligible to the kingship of Innse Gall when in 1365 he was atrociously murdered by yet another Mac Mathghamhna, Brian, who had persuaded Somhairle to divorce his Ó Raghallaigh wife and to marry his (Mac Mathghamhna's) daughter. In revenge Niall Ó Néill (probably Somhairle's employer), Somhairle's uncle Toirdhealbhach, and the latter's son Alexander Óg, accompanied by Somhairle's maternal uncle (and Brian's rival for the lordship of Oirghialla) Niall Mac Mathghamhna and by Somairle's son Eoin Óg, attacked Brian, plundering him and driving him temporarily from his territory. A further attack by them in 1368 led to Brian agreeing to pay an *éraic* (blood-price) for the murdered man. This,

72 Both University College MS 103 and Lambeth MS 635 (fo. 163v) give many branches, all descended from Éamonn. 73 *Registrum monasterii de Passelet* ed. Cosmo Innes, Maitland Club (Edinburgh, 1832; rpr. 1877), pp 128–9. 74 Nicholls, 'Anglo-French Ireland', 387n. For Alexander and his sons, see W.D.H. Sellar, 'MacDonald and MacRuairi pedigrees in MS 1467', *WHN & Q*, 1st ser., 28 (Mar., 1986), 7–8. 75 *LMG*, ii, (96) 345.11–17. For this elder Alexander and his offspring, see Sellar, 'MacDonald 'MacDonald and MacRuairi pedigrees', 5–6. 76 NLI MS G.2, fo. 26v. 77 *AU*, ii, p. 488, misprinted as '408' in Nicholls, 'Anglo-French Ireland', 387n.

however, did not satisfy either Niall Mac Mathghamhna or Alexander Mac Domhnaill, who agreed among themselves to launch a surprise attack on Brian, but were themselves defeated and killed.[78] In 1366 Toirdhealbhach and Alexander Óg had joined Ó Néill's brother Domhnall in his revolt against Ó Néill, and another son of Alexander, Raghnall, had come to Ireland from the Isles to help Ó Néill. In the ensuing conflict Raghnall's son – another Alexander? – was killed and Alexander Óg taken prisoner. Raghnall's men wished to kill him in revenge for his cousin, but the father forbade it, saying that he did not want to lose a second near kinsman.[79] It is tempting to suspect that this Raghnall, who had until then been in the Isles and who is described as 'heir (*oighre*) of Clann Alaxandair', was confused in tradition with Raghnall mac Ruaidhri of Garmoran (died 1346) to produce the 'Reginald' who, according to the Sleat historian, usurped the government of the Isles for nine years, especially as the historian seems to have been aware of the connection between him and 'John surnamed the Bald', Eoin Maol.[80] Sellar's suggestion[81] that the MacAllisters of Loup in Kintyre also descended from Alexander the younger rather than, as had been previously assumed, from his uncle and namesake, is certainly correct: Alexander's grandson Gofraidh 'Angusii' (found in the genealogies) is given the alternative surname MacAlasandair in a papal indult of 1395, as is his son John 'Goffredi', a cleric and eventually abbot of Iona.[82] It would seem therefore that in this Gofraidh we have the first recognizable MacAllister.

Raghnall's son Eoin Maol may have been the 'Mac Donndyll (*recte* MacDounayll) captain of the Scots dwelling in Ulster' who made peace with the English of Louth on 15 July 1373,[83] or this could have been another descendant of Alexander. But the reference shows that there was already a Mac Domhnaill community established in Ulster. But Eoin Maol, the ancestor of the later Mac Domhnaill Gallóglach of Tír Eoghain, is certainly the John or Schan MacDonyld, 'chief of his name and

78 *AU*, ii, pp 520–2, 532–4; Mac Niocaill (ed.), 'Annála gearra, 1360–1402', 36, 37 (misdated at 1362 and 1365 respectively); *AC*, 1365.8, 1368.13; *AClon*, p. 302. Eoin Óg's genealogy is in the early collections: see Nicholls, 'Anglo-French Ireland', 387n. 79 *AU*, ii, pp 524–6; *AC*, 1366.11; *AClon*, p. 303. See Nicholls, 'Anglo-French Ireland', 387n. 80 J.R.N. MacPhail (ed.), *Highland papers*, i, Scot. Hist. Soc., 2nd ser., no. 5 (Edinburgh, 1914), pp 17–19. 81 Sellar, 'MacDonald and MacRuairi pedigrees', 6, 8. The Sleat historian derives the MacAllisters from an Alexander Durach ('of Jura'), illegitimate son of Aonghus Mór (*Highland papers*, i, p. 16); he otherwise ignores the younger Alexander. 82 Francis McGurk (ed.), *Calendar of papal letters to Scotland of Benedict XIII of Avignon, 1394–1419*, Scot. Hist. Soc., 4th ser., no. 13 (Edinburgh, 1976), pp 51, 56, 144; E.A. Lindsay and A.I. Cameron (eds), *Calendar of Scottish supplications to Rome, 1418–1422*, Scot. Hist. Soc., 3rd ser., no. 23 (Edinburgh, 1934), p. 264. 83 Brendan Smith (ed.), *The register of Milo Sweteman, Archbishop of Armagh 1361–1380* (Dublin, IMC, 1996), no. 10.

constable of the Irish of Ulster', who wrote in 1394 to King Richard II
offering his services and complaining of his kinsman (or cousin:
consanguineus) Donald Macdonyld, lord of the Isles, who had expelled
him to Ireland from his homeland (*patria*).[84] Unhappily, Curtis's misiden-
tification of the constable with Donald's brother John of Duniveg has
proved – like so many historical errors – very difficult to kill.[85] On the face
of it, it is hard to see how anyone could accept that John of Duniveg
would have called his own full-brother (*germanus*) his *consanguineus*, or that
he would have styled himself 'chief of his name' – a title that would easily
be claimed by the head of the senior line, the Clann Alaxandair – quite
apart from the fact that all the other holders of the office of constable,
both before and after this John, were of Clann Alaxandair. Eoin Maol
was the ancestor of the later line of Mac Domhnaill Gallóglach of
Tír Eoghain.[86] These possessed an extensive territory around Ballygawley
in County Tyrone: a survey of Tyrone in 1567 recorded that 'this
Ballyngawle is the land of the MacDonells who are a sept of Galoglas and
MaccDonnell is always cheffe Capten of the Same', naming other small
territories which were under his overlordship.[87] By the late sixteenth
century they had also acquired the territory of Clancarney, corresponding
to the parish of Kilclooney in County Armagh: there is no evidence of an
earlier settlement by them there, although one is possible.[88]

With one of the three MacDonnells whose genealogy is given by Ó
Cianáin, Domhnall son of Somhairle son of Alexander, begins that
factional allegiance of Clann Somairle *gallóglaigh* which I have referred to

84 Edmund Curtis, *Richard II in Ireland* (Oxford, 1927), pp 87–8, rpr. in Jean and R.W. Munro,
Acts of the Lords of the Isles, 1336–1493, Scot. Hist. Soc, 4th ser. 22 (Edinburgh, 1986), pp 20–1;
Nicholls, 'Anglo-French Ireland', 386–7. 85 It has been accepted blindly by Donald M.
Schlegel, 'The MacDonalds of Tyrone and Armagh', *Seanchas Ardmhacha* 10/1 (1980–1), 198;
by the Munros (*Acts of the Lords of the Isles*, lxxvi, though a doubt is recognized on p. 21); and by
John Marsden, *Galloglas: Hebridean and West Highland warrior kindreds in medieval Ireland* (East
Linton, 2003), pp 48–9. It has been rejected by Simon Kingston in his *Ulster and the Isles in the
fifteenth century* (Dublin, 2004), p. 50n. 86 For whom see Schlegel, 'The MacDonalds of
Tyrone and Armagh'. In 'Anglo-French Ireland and after', 387, I misidentified Toirdhealbhach
mac Giolla Easpaig, grandson of Eoin Maol, with the Toirdhealbhach MacDomhnaill who died
in 1435: he must rather be the Toirdhealbhach, constable to Ó Néill, who was slain in the latter's
defeat by the Clann Aodha Buidhe in 1444 (*AFM*, iii, pp 932–4: O'Donovan (ed.), 'The annals
of Ireland by Duald MacFirbis', *Ir. Arch. Soc. Misc.*, i (1846), pp 203–4 (the source of the *AFM*
entry): *AU*, iii, p. 152). The Toirdhealbhach of 1435 must be Toirdhealbhach Mór (mac
Marcuis) of Connacht (see below). 87 Bodleian Library, Oxford, MS Carte 55, fo. 593. The
other territories named as being 'underneath' Mac Domhnaill were Ballyreagh and Clan Enys
(both in Killeshill Parish), Cosse One (in Clonfeakle Parish) and Clan Erte (Donaghmore
Parish). All these are in Dungannon Lower Barony: Ballygawley is in Clogher Barony. I cannot
locate 'Cnocke-Conight' which the Sleat historian says was given to the MacDonnells (*Highland
Papers*, i, p. 19). 88 Clancarney was known to the Sleat historian (*Highland Papers*, i, p. 18).

in writing of Clann Suibhne, as he was killed along with his son Domhnall Óg while serving Tadhg son of Maghnus Ó Conchobhair in the battle of Tráigh Eochaille in 1367, where the Clann Suibhne *gallóglaigh* appear on the opposing side.[89] Domhnall's brother Marcus, whose name is inserted by a later hand in the Book of Ballymote genealogy of his brother,[90] was slain in 1397 fighting for the sons of Cathal Óg Ó Conchobhair (Tadhg's cousin) against Domhnall mac Muircheartaigh's sons. His son Dubhghall, who also fell, had been in the service of Cathal Óg's sons.[91] Two of Marcus's sons, Somhairle Buidhe (killed in 1398) and Donnchadh (died after 1413) were successively constables to Mac Diarmada, a principal leader of the Ó Conchobhair Ruadh faction.[92] It was from a third son of Marcus, Toirdhealbhach Mór (died 1435), that the later Mac Domhnaill *gallóglaigh* of Connacht and Leinster were descended. Toirdhealbhach Mac Domhnaill and Alexander Mac Dubhghaill (MacDowell) were constables to the *Ruadh* faction when the latter suffered their great defeat at Ballyline in 1419, when all their galloglass fell along with Mac Dubhghaill himself and two of his sons, although Toirdhealbhach escaped.[93] One of his sons, Aodh Buidhe, was constable to Mac Uilliam Íochtar (Burke of Mayo, the leader of the *Ruadh* faction) and was killed, with two of his sons, three of his brothers and five or six others of the Clann Domhnaill, along with 160 galloglass at the great defeat inflicted on Mac Uilliam by the other Burke, Mac Uilliam Uachtar of Clann Riocaird, at Crossmacrin in 1467.[94] He was the ancestor of the sept called Sliocht Aodha Buidhe, the most powerful branch of the lineage in Mayo. Mac Fhirbhisigh gives detailed genealogies of the descendants of Aodh Buidhe's brother Fearadhach, but is strangely ignorant of those of Aodh Buidhe, being unaware even of the ancestry of Aonghus the abbot (of Cong), whose son Marcus *Mac an Ab* of Togher was their chief in the 1590s.[95] Only from Roger O'Ferrall's *Linea Antiqua* of 1706 do we learn that Abbot Aonghus

---

89 See above n. 51. Another Domhnall Óg, 'son of Mac Domhnaill', a constable of *gallóglaigh*, was slain in the service of the *Ruadh* faction in 1388 (*AFM*, iv, p. 712; *AU*, iii, p. 20). Was he perhaps a son of Marcus?   90 *Book of Ballymote*, 116c.   91 *AFM*, iv, pp 752–6; *AU*, iii, p. 36; *AClon*, pp 318–19; *Misc. Ir. annals*, p. 159. I have assumed that the Dubhghall, son of Marcus, who is recorded as being killed with his father is identical with the Dubhghall, 'son of MacDomhnaill Gallda', who was in the service of Cathal Óg's sons, but it is possible that they were different persons, and the latter a new arrival from Scotland.   92 *AC*, 1398.24, 1413.10; *AFM* (new ed., Dublin, 1990), Appendix to Introduction, s.a. 1403.   93 *AU*, iii, p. 80; *ALC*, ii, p. 148–50; *AC*, 1419, 17, 18. *AC* says that Toirdhealbhach's son was killed: the others that he escaped with his father. Toirdhealbhach must be the man, *Sai gallglach*, who died 1435 (*AU*, iii, p. 149; *AC*, 1435.14).   94 *AC*, 1467.9; O'Donovan (ed.), 'The annals of Ireland by Duald MacFirbis', *Ir. Arch. Soc. Misc.*, i (1846), p. 261; *AU*, iii, pp 216–18; *AFM*, iv, p. 1048.   95 *LMG* ii, (94–6) 344, 345.1–10. The ancestry there ascribed to the founder Marcus is entirely spurious.

was the son of Aodh Buidhe's son Feidhlim.[96] MacDonnells remained prominent in Mayo long after the end of the Gaelic order; Patrick Randal Mac Donnell, was a local populist politician whose murder on the orders of his enemy George Robert FitzGerald led to the latter's execution in 1786.

From Donnchadh, nephew of Aodh Buidhe through his brother Toirdhealbhach Óg, descended the Clann Domhnaill of Leinster, constables first to the earls of Kildare and then, after the fall of the Kildares, they provided the galloglass forces of the English administration in Ireland. Donnchadh himself is probably 'the son of Toirdhealbhach Óg, constable to the earl [of Kildare]', who was slain by the O'Mores of Laois in 1514.[97] Three great-grandsons of Donnchadh[98] received grants of land in the Laois–Offaly plantation, not that this secured their loyalty to the crown: two of these lines were forfeited, their heads having fallen on the rebel side in the Nine Years War. The third and most important, the house of Tinnakill, lasted down to the Cromwellian period and after.[99] A fourth sept, that of Boystown or Baltyboys in west Wicklow, also called *Clann Domhnaill an tSléibhe Ruaidh*,[1] may not have been descended from Toirdhealbhach Óg. Their founder, Alexander mac Toirdhealbhaigh 'O'Donnell', described in 1553 as 'captain of the king's *Scotici* otherwise galloglass', was perhaps the Alexander 'son of Terence son of Melmory MacDonell' who was resident and in possession of lands in the O'Byrnes Country (in east Wicklow) by 1524.[2] Had he taken them as a pledge for unpaid *buannacht*?

It was no doubt factional allegiance which led the earls of Kildare to recruit Mac Domhnaill *gallóglaigh* from Connacht. Another stock claiming to descend from Sumarliði (Somairle) had already been serving the other great Geraldine house, the earls of Desmond. These were the Mac Síthigh (MacSheehy) *gallóglaigh* who claimed to descend from the elder Alexander, brother of Aonghus Mór, through his son Eachann.[3] Sítheach *an Dornáin*, according to the genealogy, was the father of Uilliam Fionn, presumably the Uilliam Mac Síthigh who fell along with Domhnall Mac Domhnaill at

---

96 NLI, G.O. MS 155, p. 153. For Abbot Aonghus, see *Cal. papal letters*, xviii, pp 78–9. 97 *AC*, 1514.5; *AU*, iii, p. 512.　98 For the genealogical connection between these septs, see the pedigree in Lambeth MS 635, fo. 146. It however miscalls Eoin Carrach, son of Donnchadh, 'Farriagh' (*Fearadhach*).　99 Lord Walter FitzGerald, 'The MacDonnells of Tinnakill Castle', *Kildare Arch. Soc. Jn.*, iv (1903–4), 205–15; Anne O'Sullivan, 'The Tinnakill Duanaire', *Celtica*, 11 (1976), 214–28; and the still valuable disquisition by John O'Donovan (*AFM*, v, pp 1641–4, nn.)　1 *ALC*, ii, p. 408.　2 *Irish Fiants, Edward VI*, 1195; *AFM*, v, p. 1642n.　3 Sellar, 'MacDonald and MacRuairi pedigrees', 6. For the Gaelic genealogy see *LMG* ii, (98), 360.2.

the battle of Tráigh Eochaille in 1367. An Eoin Mac Síthigh was slain beside Domhnall's brother Marcus in 1397.[4] But the lineage thereafter moved out of Connacht into Munster, traditionally accompanying the daughter of Mac Uilliam who married James, earl of Desmond, in the year 1420, thereafter spreading in many branches throughout the Desmond territories in Munster as constables to the Desmond earls,[5] and playing a very prominent role in the Desmond Risings of the Elizabethan period.

The last branch of Sumarliði's descendants who served as *gallóglaigh* in Ireland were the Mic Dubhghaill or, in the Anglicized form used in Ireland, MacDowells. David Sellar has discussed the ancestry and genealogy of the galloglass branch in Connacht,[6] who, like the MacDonnells served the *Ruadh* faction. The Mac Dubhghaill Gallóglach slain in 1377, while serving Mac Uilliam Burke and Ó Ceallaigh,[7] was probably the Eoghan (Ewen) mac Giolla Pheadair of the genealogies, whose son Eoin was slain in Connacht in 1381. Another son, Alexander, was one of the leaders of the *Ruadh* galloglass in 1419 at Ballyline, where – as has already been noted – he fell with two of his sons and all their force. His first wife, the mother of his three eldest sons, was a member of the rival house, the Clann Suibhne, perhaps even a sister of the Eoin who fell in 1397.[8] His descendants continued in the service of the same faction, as constables to the O'Connors *Ruadh*, to the MacDermots and to the O'Kellys. Alexander's son Toirdhealbhach occurs in a rather humiliating context in 1445, when he and his band, who had been serving in Leinster under Gerald Mac Murchadha Caomhánach (McMurrough Kavanagh), acting as king during the captivity of his brother Donnchadh, were captured on their way home by Mac Eochagáin (Mageoghegan) and stripped of their weapons, armour, money and clothes, Toirdhealbhach and some others being held to ransom.[9] Perhaps they were taken unawares while sleeping off the effects of carousing! In 1469 the then-chief, Eoghan, was treacherously killed in his own house by his cousins, the sons of Alexander's son

4 See nn. 53, 58.   5 Hubert Gallwey, 'The MacSheehys of Connello in County Limerick', *Irish Genealogist*, 4/6 (1973), 564–77. I no longer incline to the view, there quoted, that the MacSheehys may have been MacFies (*Mac Dhuibhshíthe*). Since the Y-chromosome of Somerled has been identified, DNA analysis might solve the question of their origin.   6 W.D.H. Sellar, 'MacDougall pedigrees in MS 1467', *WHN & Q*, 1st ser. 29 (1986), 14–15. Working from a microfilm, Sellar did not know that the account in the *Leabhar Donn* is incomplete owing to a chasm in the MS: the missing portion would presumably have included the Duibhgenn son of Eoghan of *AC*, 1469.14.   7 *AC*, 1377.9.   8 *LMG* ii, (100), 361.1. She was Mór, daughter of Eoghan Connachtach Mac Suibhne, but there were two with that epithet (see n. 57), whence the doubt.   9 O'Donovan (ed.), 'The annals of Ireland by Duald MacFirbis', *Ir. Arch. Soc. Misc.*, i (1846), p. 210.

Colla.[10] The later genealogies of the lineage, brought down to the 1630s,[11] are extraordinarily confused in the earlier portion, inserting as ancestors of Giolla Pheadair a number of names which give the impression that another (late) genealogy has been accidentally combined with that of Mac Dubhghaill.

The only other major mercenary lineage which remains to be considered is that of Mac Cába (MacCabe), although their sphere of operations was confined to southern Ulster and the north midlands. Maoilsheachlainn Mac Cába (died 1424) is described as constable of the two parts of Bréifne (West Bréifne, ruled by Ó Ruairc, and East Bréifne, by Ó Raghallaigh), of Fir Manach and of Oirghialla,[12] a multiplicity of employers which must have involved conflicts of interest, and which raises the question of whether a galloglass captain would simultaneously provide mercenaries for two opposing sides. If so, would they actually fight each other? It seems unlikely, but the alternative – that each of these four lords would retain a captain of mercenaries who stood a three-to-one chance of deserting him – is even more improbable! The MacCabes, unlike the lineages we have considered, claimed a Scandinavian origin: according to the genealogies – and there is no reason to doubt it – the strange patronymic Mac Cába was originally an epithet of their ancestor Tormód (ON Þormóðr), the earliest genuine name in their genealogy.[13] Mac Fhirbhisigh identifies this Tormód with the earlier of the two Tormóds in his version of the MacLeod genealogy – which bears no resemblance to that found in earlier, Scottish sources[14] – but the preceding generations (beginning with a 'Constantine of the island of Britain') are nonsense and the connection is certainly a genealogical fiction. There is no reason to assume – as some have done – that Tormód's son Alexander *na hArainne* derived his epithet from Harris in the Out-Isles rather than from Arran in the Firth of Clyde: it may be noted that in Ireland the MacCabes operated in a region where, as has been discussed above, another lineage from the Clyde region – Mag Buirrche – were operating *c*.1300–46. Alexander certainly lived in the thirteenth century: his grandson, Flaithbheartach (son of Giolla Chríost *Coirrshleagach*) may have been given his rare name after the second Mag Uidhir lord of Fir Manach, who acceded in 1301 and died in 1327. The

10 *AC*, 1469.14.   11 To Brian MacDowell of Kiltrustan or Mullaghcreigh (NLI, G.O. MS 157, fo. 19) and to Toirdhealbhach Óg Mac Dubhghaill (TCD MS 1337 (H.3.18) and G.O. MS 155: a truncated version in *Analecta Hibernica*, no. 18, 126).   12 *AU*, iii, p. 96.   13 *LMG* iii, (50) 776.3.   14 As that in W.F. Skene, *Celtic Scotland* (Edinburgh, 1890), iii, 460–1. I suspect the erased final six generations of this genealogy may have been the final six given by Mac Fhirbhisigh (776.2), ending with Alexander (fl. *c*.1370), rather than those suggested by Skene.

genealogy given by Mac Fhirbhisigh is chronologically consistent: it gives three generations subsequent to Henry, who succeeded his brother Cormac as constable of (East) Bréifne in 1447 and died in 1460.[15] We are told that there were fourteen score of galloglass axes in his funeral procession. Another (eldest?) brother Mathghamhain was slain in 1413.[16] The Maoilsheachlainn already referred to may have been another brother. Henry was succeeded as constable of East Bréifne by his son Mathghamhain, who died in 1464.[17] The earliest members of the lineage to figure in the Irish annals are Aodh, constable of Fir Manach, slain in 1358 and Brian, constable of Oirghialla, who died in 1394.[18] Neither is in the genealogies. The genealogies of the later Oirghialla MacCabes are in the earlier portion totally confused,[19] while those of the Fir Manach MacCabes go back to a late fourteenth-century Somhairle who appears to have been a collateral of the line given by Mac Fhirbhisigh, but seem also confused in detail.[20]

It is to be noted that the establishment in Ireland of the galloglass lineages, coming from the Western Highlands and Islands, occurred in a particular period, the late thirteenth and the first half of the fourteenth centuries, and that there is no evidence that any later arrivals established permanent settlements – if we discount the possible case of the MacNeills mentioned above. The factional allegiances of the galloglass, established soon after their arrival, remained largely intact throughout the period, although by the sixteenth century they were beginning to break down, no doubt aided by lineage proliferation and the emergence of internal feuds, such as those of the MacSweeney septs mentioned above. At the bloody but indecisive battle of Shrule in 1570, the Leinster Clann Domhnaill who served as the Queen's galloglass were joined on the government side not only by five battalions (420 'axes') of Clann Suibhne *gallóglaigh* of Clann Riocard, serving under their earl, but also by a battalion of Clann Dubhghaill, presumably from Roscommon and serving purely as mercenaries. Their opponents, the *gallóglaigh* of Seán Mac Uilliam Íochtar, were the Clann Domhnaill of Mayo.[21]

The proliferation of both Clann Suibhne and the various branches of Clann Somhairle parallels, of course, that of the native Irish and 'Anglo-Norman' dynasties. Apart from the case of the MacDonnells of Roslee,

15 *AU*, iii, pp 160, 200; *AC* 1460.3; O'Donovan (ed.), 'The annals of Ireland by Duald MacFirbis', *Ir. Arch. Soc. Misc.*, i (1846), p. 241.   16 *AU*, iii, p. 64; cf. *AC*, 1403.11.   17 *AU*, iii, p. 210. This Mathghamhain ends a (defective) genealogy in a number of MSS, including RIA D.1.3 fo. 78v. It includes the mythical names before Tormód.   18 *AU*, ii, p. 506, iii, p. 28; *AFM* (new ed., Dublin, 1990), Appendix to Introduction s.a.1357; *AClon*, pp 300, 316.   19 TCD MSS 1366 (H.4.25) 1658, 1372 (H.4.31), fo. 36–7. The later, genuine, portions go back to a Maine son of Connla.   20 *Analecta Hibernica*, 3 (1931), 113–15.   21 *AFM*, v, pp 1640–8; *ALC*, ii, p. 408.

cited above, and the doubt as to the affiliation of Clann Síthigh, there is no reason to doubt the genuineness of the descents, allowing of course, for the children of hidden adulteries and those affiliated to the lineage falsely or on slender grounds.[22] In the case of Clann Somhairle, we must note the existence of a numerous native lineage of Mac Domhnaill, sometimes wrongly assumed to be of galloglass origin, in Fir Manach and Oirghialla – the Clann Domhnaill of Clann Ceallaigh and of Coininis respectively (assuming that these two close neighbours were branches of the same stock) – while in more recent times some of the MacDaniels of County Kerry (descendants of a, probably Welsh, thirteenth-century settler) have become Mac Donnell, just as genuine Mac Domhnaills have become MacDaniel. In the galloglass lineages, then, we have another, and a particularly unchallengeable, example of the patrilineage expansion so typical of the Celtic nations, as of Asia and Africa, but so little to be found, so far as evidence goes, elsewhere in Western Europe.

---

22 For the practice of affiliation, see K.W. Nicholls, *Gaelic and Gaelicized Ireland in the middle ages* (2nd ed., Dublin, 2003), pp 88–9. On the whole process of lineage proliferation see Kenneth Nicholls, 'Genealogy', in N. Buttimer, C. Rynne and H. Guerin (eds), *The heritage of Ireland* (Cork, 2000), p. 157.

Images of the galloglass in poems
to the MacSweeneys

KATHARINE SIMMS

My inspiration for this essay came from an incidental remark by Wilson McLeod, to the effect that he did not regard galloglass families who had been resident for generations in Ireland, and had long intermarried with the Irish nobility, as still Scottish in any meaningful sense, so that poems addressed to them by Irish bards did not come within the ambit of his enquiries.[1] The MacSweeney family are a classic example of galloglass who became integrated into Irish society, and I thought it might be interesting to see how the leaders of this kindred regarded themselves.

To answer this question I have been looking at bardic poems addressed to the MacSweeneys. As I have argued elsewhere,[2] bardic poems were expensive works, commissioned by the patron for recital in his presence at ceremonial banquets, and reflect the patron's own desired self-image more accurately than the individual poet's opinions. Through my ongoing work on an electronic catalogue of the extant corpus of bardic poems (thirteenth to seventeenth centuries), I tracked down thirty-two MacSweeney poems,[3] of which only seven have so far been published, a surprisingly low proportion, since the average publication-rate for the bardic corpus as a whole is nearer 70% (in absolute terms 1,291 poems out of 1,967 listed entries). Sixteen of the MacSweeney poems are pre-served in the sixteenth-century manuscript RIA 475, the Book of the MacSweeneys of Fanad.[4] This manuscript started as an anthology of religious tracts and saints' lives compiled for the pious Máire daughter of Ó Máille, wife of Ruaidhri Mac Suibhne, chief of Fanad. She died in 1523, in the Carmelite friary she herself had founded in Rathmullan, on the peninsula of Fanad, Co. Donegal. Between 1532 and 1544 a prose genealogical tract on the history of the MacSweeney family was freshly composed and written into the same manuscript by Tadhg mac Fíthil, and

---

1 See Wilson McLeod, *Divided Gaels: Gaelic cultural identities in Scotland and Ireland* c.*1200*–c.*1650* (Oxford, 2004), pp 225, 227.   2 Katharine Simms, 'Bardic poetry as a historical source', in *The writer as witness*, ed. Tom Dunne (*Historical Studies XVI*, Cork, 1987), pp 58–75 at pp 60–7.   3 See Appendix at the end of this article.   4 Dublin, RIA MS 475 (24/P/25). The history and contents of this manuscript are described in detail in *LCS*.

thereafter sixteen bardic poems to the MacSweeneys of Fanad were added at various times in the sixteenth century, four of which have been edited with a translation in an unpublished thesis by Seán Ó Foghlú.[5] Of these 16 poems, some 11 or 12[6] are addressed to Domhnall son of Toirdhealbhach Mac Suibhne, chief of Fanad from 1570 to his death in 1619 and to his wife and kinswoman Gráinne, the daughter of Maolmhuire Mac Suibhne. Of the poems occurring in other sources two address Eoghan Óg Mac Suibhne na dTuath, chief of the Trí Tuatha (the north-west portion of the barony of Kilmacrenan, Co. Donegal) and constable of Tír Chonaill from 1570 to his death in 1596, the main foster-father to the young Aodh Ruadh Ó Domhnaill (Red Hugh O'Donnell).[7]

Members of the MacSweeney family, or Clann Suibhne, are first mentioned in the annals in 1265/7 with reference to the capture of Murchadh Mac Suibhne by Domhnall (mac Maghnusa) Ó Conchobhair, lord of the Owles of Mayo, and his subsequent death in the prison of Walter de Burgh, earl of Ulster and lord of Connacht.[8] Prior to this, a poem attributed to the mid-thirteenth-century Giolla Bhrighde Mac Con Midhe tells us that until 1258 Domhnall Óg Ó Domhnaill, subsequently king of Tír Chonaill, was fostered in Scotland with Clann Suibhne,[9] and in 1269 a death-notice in the annals implies that some time earlier Murchadh's father Maolmhuire Mac Suibhne had married the daughter of Toirdhealbhach son of the highking Ruaidhri Ó Conchobhair (d. 1198), who reigned briefly as king of Connacht in the late 1220s.[10] The next mention of Clann Suibhne in the annals is a notice of the death of Mac Buirrche, and the heir of Clann Suibhne, who fell fighting for Pilib Ó Raghallaigh (Philip O'Reilly), chief of East Bréifne, along with 140 galloglass in 1305.[11]

---

5 Appendix, entries 13, 20, 21, 26. Seán Ó Foghlú, 'Four bardic poems from *Leabhar Chlainne Suibhne*' (M.Litt. thesis, Trinity College Dublin [1992] 1993), catalogued as Thesis no. 2732. I am most grateful to Mr Ó Foghlú who gave me a copy of his thesis immediately after its completion. 6 In one poem (Appendix no. 23) the patron is identified only as Domhnall Mac Suibhne. However its association in the anthology with other poems explicitly addressed to Domhnall son of Toirdhealbhach, chief of Fanad, suggests that he is the person intended here also. 7 *AFM*, v, pp 1862–3. See Appendix, nos. 17, 25. 8 *AC*, pp 148–9; *ALC*, i, pp 452–3, 456–7; *AFM*, iii, pp 402–3. For the cooperative relations between Domhnall mac Maghnusa and the Anglo-Normans, see Katharine Simms, 'A lost tribe – the Clan Murtagh O'Conors' in *Galway Arch. Soc. Jn.*, 53 (2001), pp 1–22, at p. 6. 9 N.J.A. Williams (ed.), *The poems of Giolla Brighde Mac Con Midhe* (Irish Texts Society, Dublin, 1980), pp 80–1. 10 *AC*, pp 152–3, §6. 11 *AC*, pp 206–7; *ALC*, i, pp 530–33; *AFM*, iii, pp 480–81; *Misc. Ir. Ann.*, pp 130–1. The annal-entries clearly distinguish between 'Mac Buirrche' and the 'heir of Clann Suibhne', but the name 'Mag Buirche' appears in the Clann Suibhne pedigree in the late fourteenth-century Book of Uí Mhaine, fo. 1v, col. b, line 20 (facsimile ed. by R.A.S. Macalister, IMC, Dublin 1942), and subsequent genealogies. See W.D.H. Sellar, 'Family origins in Cowal and Knapdale', in *Scottish Studies*, 15 (1971), pp 21–37, at pp 25–7.

Tadhg mac Fíthil in his genealogical tract on the MacSweeneys would have us believe that in the late thirteenth century a certain Eoghan Mac Suibhne, stated to be the father-in-law of Domhnall Óg Ó Domhnaill, had defeated the O'Breslin (Ó Breasláin) chief of Fanad, Co. Donegal, massacred the whole O'Breslin family, and taken possession of the peninsula of Fanad.[12] There are, however, a number of problems with this story. In the first place, the O'Breslin chiefs of Fanad were dispossessed before 1281 by a branch of the O'Donnells. In the battle of Desertcreat in that year the annals record the death of Cormac son of the Lector Ó Domhnaill, chief of Fanad.[13] Secondly, the same genealogical history of the MacSweeneys records a series of named estates on the peninsula of Fanad being granted in the mid-fourteenth century to Maolmhuire Mac Suibhne by the O'Donnell family in reward for his services during a prolonged succession struggle among the O'Donnells themselves for the kingship of Tír Chonaill.[14] If the Mac Suibhne chief already ruled the whole peninsula of Fanad, why would sections of it be granted to him piecemeal at this late date? Thirdly, this allegedly catastrophic massacre of the O'Breslin family goes unrecorded in the annals. The historian Tadhg mac Fíthil ends his tract with a colophon 'if there be a mistake in it, the writer is not responsible for it, but the fact that he did not compose the book beforehand, and that it was mainly out of his head that he set it down'.[15] In general his facts and dates, as one might expect, seem to get progressively more reliable as the story nears his own time.

Another problematical tradition alleges that the MacSweeney family descended from a branch of the O'Neill kings of Tír Eoghain. This first appears in the genealogies in the Book of Uí Mhaine from the end of the fourteenth century, where the genealogy of Toirdhealbhach Mac Suibhne (d. 1399), the first recorded Mac Suibhne lord of Fanad, is placed imme-diately after that of Niall Mór Ó Néill, who reigned from 1364 to 1397, and his chief vassal Ó Catháin (O'Kane) of Derry.[16] This genealogy does not appear in the mid-fourteenth century collection NLI G 2, compiled 1344–5.[17] Two pieces of evidence suggest why the Clann Suibhne may have originally wished to associate themselves with Ó Néill of Tír Eoghain, an association that became an embarrassment for their poets in the later sixteenth century, when the MacSweeneys were conducting a feud against Toirdhealbhach Luineach Ó Néill. The first is a throwaway statement in the late genealogical tract on the O'Neill family, first

---

12 *LCS*, pp 16–17. 13 *AU*, ii, p. 361, s.a. 1281. Later entries indicate that Cormac was ancestor of the Macmenamin O'Donnells, who became a clerical dynasty in Tír Chonaill. 14 *LCS*, pp 30–3. 15 Ibid., p. 75. 16 *Bk Uí Maine*, fo. 1v, col. b, line 9. 17 Nessa Ní Shéaghdha (ed.), *Catalogue of Irish manuscripts in the National Library of Ireland*, fasc. 1 (Dublin, 1967), p. 13.

compiled under Toirdhealbhach Luineach himself, that Domhnall O Néill, the king of Tír Eoghain who instigated the Bruce invasion and died in 1325, was the first lord to grant an estate of land in Ireland to galloglass, and that the recipient was Mac Buirrche, of the Clann Suibhne,[18] presumably the leader who died in 1305, and that Domhnall did this to maintain his war of succession against the O'Neills of Clann Aodha Buidhe (Clandeboye). The second piece of evidence is the entry in the Annals of Connacht for 1343 which says: 'Niall O Domnaill [king of Tír Chonaill] was deposed by Aengus O Domnaill, Domnall Dub O Baigill and O Dochurtaig [of the nobility of Tír Chonaill], supported by Aed Remor O Neill [king of Tír Eoghain] and by the Clann Suibne [galloglass] at large. These all made Aengus king.'[19] The most natural way of reading the order in which these names are given is to interpret the Clann Suibne's role in the succession struggle as arising from their association with Aodh Ó Néill, the king of Tír Eoghain who died in 1364. Tadhg mac Fíthil's genealogical history of the MacSweeneys dates the first named grants of land on Fanad, received by Maolmhuire Mac Suibhne, to the time of the death of Niall Garbh Ó Domhnaill in 1348, five years after the 1343 incident, and tells us that the formal contract of vassalage by which Maolmhuire's son, Toirdhealbhach Caoch, became hereditary constable to the O'Donnell kings, in return for the service of two galloglass for every quarter of land he held, took place in the reign of Toirdhealbhach-an-Fhíona Ó Domhnaill, that is, from 1380 onwards. Mac Fíthil adds that until that date Clann Suibhne had been freelance mercenaries: 'It was the Scottish habit [of military service] they had observed until that time, namely each man according as he was employed'.[20]

From about 1380 onwards, therefore, the MacSweeneys of Fanad, and somewhat later the MacSweeneys of the Trí Tuatha, had a dual role. They ruled as lord of their own territory, in effect as a *rí tuaithe* or petty king, and the term *rí* is applied to the head of the family in the bardic poems I have been examining. Yet on the other hand they held an official position as commander of a professional army under the O'Donnell kings of Tír Chonaill, and the poems also term their patrons *consabal*, 'constable', which like the title 'constable of France' meant 'supreme military commander'. Even more interestingly the poets also use the term *buanna*, 'billeted mercenary' or 'professional soldier', as an honorific title. In deliberately celebrating this professional service the poems to the MacSweeneys are unique. This aspect is most noticeable in poems to the

18 Tadhg Ó Donnchadha (ed.), *Leabhar Cloinne Aodha Buidhe* (Dublin, 1931), p. 31. 19 *AC*, p. 295, s.a. 1343. Additions in square brackets are mine. 20 *LCS*, p. 45.

late sixteenth-century Eoghan Og Mac Suibhne na dTuath, and Domhnall
Mac Suibhne of Fanad, who reigned or held office under Aodh son of
Maghnus Ó Domhnaill and his son, the notoriously arrogant and
overbearing Aodh Ruadh (Red Hugh) Ó Domhnaill, when the reliance of
the ruler of Tír Chonaill on his mercenary armies was at its height.

POEMS REFERRING TO THE FAMILY'S SCOTTISH ORIGINS

When I came to survey all thirty-two of the MacSweeney poems, I found
that only two of them referred to the Scottish origins of the family, and
these two may be the earliest surviving compositions. One is the famous
'*Dál chabhlaigh ar Chaistéal Suibhne*' ('An assembling of a fleet to go
against Castle Sween'). This is an address to an Eoghan Mac Suibhne,
preserved in the Book of the Dean of Lismore, and recently re-edited by
Donald Meek.[21] In the accompanying commentary Meek suggested two
possible dates for its composition – either very early in the fourteenth
century, if this was the Eoghan Mac Suibhne traditionally credited with
massacring the O'Breslin dynasty and first taking possession of Fanad, or
in the fifteenth century, if a possible place-name identification in the poem
was understood as linking the patron Eoghan to Tír Boghaine in south
Donegal, which was not acquired by a MacSweeney dynast until the
fifteenth century.[22]

In favour of an early date for the poem is its reference to the Clann
Suibhne as *Lochlannaigh* or Hebridean Norsemen, and *ármuinn*, a Norse
loanword into Gaelic, signifying 'stewards', royal officials. There is no hint
of the later fourteenth-century claim that Mac Suibhne descended from
an Ó Néill of Tír Eoghain. Also the poet's emphasis on Mac Suibhne's
fleet of ships is not typical of the later period. On the other hand, as Meek
has pointed out, the Eoghan Mac Suibhne of the poem is clearly identified
as a resident of Ireland, all the place-names associated with him are Irish,
and his fleet sails from an Irish port. The expedition itself seems merely a
visionary one, a projected vindication of Mac Suibhne's ancestral rights to
a Scottish castle and lordship, since the galleys that set sail are described as
encumbered with pavilions and beds for the accommodation of women
and stately maidens, and the expedition is to be met at Castle Sween by a
welcoming party of poets, rather than by military resistance from the
castle's present occupants.

---

21 Donald Meek, '"Norsemen and Noble Stewards": the MacSween poem in the Book of the
Dean of Lismore', in *CMCS*, 34 (Winter 1997), pp 1–49. 22 Ibid., pp 8–12, 18.

Given the indications that Castle Sween has been so long out of the family's possession that its military recapture is no longer a realistic goal, together with the other signs of a comparatively early date for the poem, perhaps one could suggest a compromise date of 1340s–1380s and point to Eoghan Mac Suibhne, brother of Toirdhealbhach, first lord of Fanad as a possible patron. In that case one could argue that the poet's dreaming up an expedition to recapture Castle Sween enabled him to compliment his patron without challenging the territorial claims in Ireland of Eoghan's brother Toirdhealbhach, just as the thirteenth-century poet Giolla Bhrighde MacCon Midhe dreamed up a vision on a May morning of his patron Roalbh Mac Mathghamhna (MacMahon) being crowned king at Eamhain Macha by the poets of Ireland,[23] an acceptable compliment that did not challenge in any way his brother Brian Mac Mathghamhna's position as the reigning king of Oirghialla. But the reality is that we will probably never reach certainty on the true context of this imaginative poem, putting the MacSweeneys of Ireland back in touch with their Scottish roots.

The other poem to mention Mac Suibhne's followers as Scotsmen is '*Uaisle cinidh Clann Suibhne*' perhaps to be interpreted 'Nobles of lineage are Clann Suibhne'. This text is unpublished, preserved in a single manuscript, the miscellaneous seventeenth-century anthology, the Book of O'Conor Don. At this point I should explain that where the poems are still unedited and unpublished I am not in a position to supply full and trustworthy translations. I can only give brief glimpses of their contents based on those lines that I feel reasonably sure I understand. I am most grateful to the project director Professor Damian McManus for making available to me the first drafts of electronic transcripts from unpublished manuscripts made as part of the work of comprehensive scanning and transcription of the corpus of bardic poetry being undertaken by the Irish Department in Trinity College Dublin under the auspices of the Irish-Scottish Academic Initiative. I am even more grateful to him for casting an eye over my suggested interpretations and emending them in places, though the blame for any remaining inaccuracies is of course mine. The poem '*Uaisle cinidh*' is addressed to a Toirdhealbhach son of Maolmhuire Mac Suibhne, head of his kindred, and to his wife Gráinne, the daughter of Ó Domhnaill. It begins with an assertion of Clann Suibhne's descent from the O'Neills of Tír Eoghain, and their vassalage to the kings of Tír Chonaill,[24] suggesting that the kings of Tír Chonaill and Tír Eoghain are

---

23 Williams (ed.), *Poems of Giolla Brighde Mac Con Midhe*, poem no. 15. 24 *Verse 2:* 'Do cloinn Chonuill Néil[l] roimhe . crobhuing méin don chlainn eile . síol Neill is Niall da bfine …': Book of O'Conor Don, fo. 388a.

on relatively good terms at the time of writing. At the same time it refers to its subject as Toirdhealbhach from Islay, Mac Suibhne from the Bann, and mentions his expeditions overseas, 'Scots in your smooth ship, to plunder on the high sea'.[25] It repeatedly refers to Mac Suibhne as a king, and includes a lyrical passage on the good weather and fertility that attend his reign: 'Bright trout by the boat-filled Boyne ... – a man sleeps above an overflowing pool, while the twittering birds sweetly sing. Crimson apples on the surface of the Boyle, in the crimson wood ...'.[26] These details would suit a poem addressed to Toirdhealbhach, the first recorded Mac Suibhne lord of Fanad, confirming both his newly-acquired lordship and his relatively newly-acquired genealogical link with the Uí Néill. Toirdhealbhach reigned from 1358 to 1399, but if the rule of thumb holds, that patrons who are praised for their irresistible attractions to women are normally reasonably young, then the poem should belong to the first half of that period. It includes a statement that 'Mac Suibhne escapes from the wine to go courting on a hill ... A woman loosens her curling locks for him ... A feast is slowly poured out by blonde women for the hero of the Bann'.[27]

REFERENCES TO FIANNAIGHEACHT IN THE MACSWEENEY POEMS

Next in terms of date comes a two-part elegy for Ruaidhri Mac Suibhne, chief of Fanad, who died in 1518 at the age of 78, after having ruled in Fanad for 46 years.[28] The second part: '*Rachad i gceann scailti sgél*' ('I will set about publishing a tale'),[29] is simply a list of the veteran warrior's battles, which included the famous battle of Knockdoe in 1504, in which his master Aodh Ruadh Ó Domhnaill – not to be confused with the later Red Hugh – had turned out in support of the Great Earl of Kildare against MacWilliam de Burgh (a/de Búrca, Burke) of Clanricard, lord of Galway. Among his other exploits in a long career, he had on three occasions burnt Dungannon, the chief seat of Ó Néill, and had raided the cattle of the barons of Slane and Delvin in Meath, and burned their

---

25 *Verse 3:* 'Mac Suíbhne cenn a chine ...'; *Verse 4:* 'Toirrdealbach ó íath Íle ...'; *Verse 18:* 'Albanuigh ad luing leabhair . ar tuin̠n ardomhan d'fhoghail'; Verse 32: 'Mac Súibhne ón Bhan̠na bháin-si . erra gan doilghe ór nduais-ne . rí fa bhladh da mbé as-tír-si . gar don rígh-si é a n-uaisle.' **26** *Verse 23:* 'Bric gheala lámh ré longBhoinn ... codlaidh fer ós linn lom[h]náin . ré fedh comhráidh bhinn bhailbheóin'; *Verse 24:* 'Ubhla corcra ar bruinn Bhúille . a ccoill chorc̠ra ré chéile ...'. **27** *Verse 12:* 'Mac Suibhne ó fhíon ag ealódh . go síth ag suirge os gríanál ...; *Verse 26:* 'Re gribh mBregh na cc̠rann cc̠roibheg . do sgáoil ben a barr núalag ...'; *Verse 29:* 'Cuirn 'ga ndáil ar bharr Banna . go mall ag na mnáibh fionna'. **28** *AFM*, v, pp 1340–1; *LCS*, pp 66–7. **29** Appendix, no. 24.

houses. The first part of the elegy is simply a long and elaborate expression of grief, but it contains the significant first line '*Sealbh gan urraidh oighreacht Fhinn*' ('Fionn's inheritance is a property without an urradh'),[30] the latter word originally signifying a legal guarantor, a native-born free landowner qualified to act as guarantor, though later used in the more general sense of 'lord'.[31] It is just possible that the poet was thinking of the original legal sense in this context, since the Brehon law contains a maxim '*is urrad imorro in deorad crenus selb*' ('the *deorad* / exile' – a term often applied to a foreign mercenary – 'who buys a holding of land is classed as an *aurrad* [a native landowner]'.[32] Such an allusion would be very appropriate to the naturalization of the MacSweeney family which was far advanced by the early sixteenth century. The next question is, how are we to interpret the phrase 'Finn's inheritance', alluding to the legendary Fionn mac Cumhaill, whose warrior-bands, the Fianna, were said to have served Cormac mac Airt, highking of Tara, in the second century AD? Does it refer to the territory of Fanad, not because it is a place particularly prominent in Fiannaigheacht folklore, but because it is inhabited by galloglass, who identify themselves as the latter-day Fianna?

In a paper delivered to the Ninth International Celtic Congress (Paris 1991) the late Dr Máirtín Ó Briain pointed out, in reference to the poems of Cináed ua hArtacáin, that as early as the tenth century a parallel was being drawn between mercenary soldiers employed by Irish kings in the high Middle Ages and the legendary Fianna. For example in the fourth *Dindshenchus* poem on Tara, Cináed describes Cormac's palace as 'the great house with thousands of [mercenary] soldiers' (*In tech mór mílib amus*).[33] Kuno Meyer has remarked on the changing image of Fionn mac Cumhaill over time from the roaming hunter-warrior of the earliest literature to his position in the twelfth century and later as Cormac mac Airt's captain of the household, of the mercenaries and of the huntsmen (*táisech teglaig 7 amus 7 gilla con*).[34]

Since Fionn was head of the mercenaries of the highking of Tara, the 'inheritance of Fionn' could also be understood as referring not to the land of Fanad, but to the office of constable of Ó Domhnaill's galloglass, a position Ruaidhri Mac Suibhne had filled. Mac Suibhne of Fanad's

---

30 Appendix, no. 27.   31 Fergus Kelly, *A guide to early Irish law* (DIAS, Dublin, 1988), pp 5, 223.   32 D.A. Binchy (ed.), *Corpus iuris Hibernici* (DIAS, 6 vols, Dublin, 1978), vol. 5, p. 1631.1. 33 Edward Gwynn (ed.), *The Metrical Dindshenchus*, i (Dublin, 1903, rpr. 1991), p. 30; and see Cináed Ó hArtacáin's poem on 'Achall', dedicated to the Norse leader Amlaíb Cuarán, in ibid., pp 46–53.   34 S.H. O'Grady (ed.), *Silva Gadelica*, 2 vols (London and Edinburgh, 1892), 1, p. 90; Kuno Meyer, *Fianaigecht* (Todd Lecture Series, no. 16, Dublin, 1910), pp xv–xvi, xxvi–xxvii. See Katharine Simms, 'Gaelic warfare in the Middle Ages', in *A military history of Ireland*, ed. Thomas Bartlett and Keith Jeffery (Cambridge, 1996), p. 102.

military contract with O Domhnaill, which gave him billeting rights for his soldiers throughout Tír Chonaill and wages during the actual campaigns,[35] brought him greater wealth and power than an ordinary chieftain of a *tuath* could expect. This is why his role as servitor is given such a high profile in the poems, while being romanticized by the comparison with Fionn MacCumhaill. The theme is taken up in another poem in the Book of the MacSweeneys addressed to Toirdhealbhach Mac Suibhne, probably the son and successor of the aforementioned Ruaidhri, since the first line of his poem echoes the first line of his father's elegy, '*Geall re hinbhe oighreacht Fhinn*':

Fionn's inheritance is a pledge for wealth, the wealth that is earned from exploit – when engaged in battle he has by his great strength surpassed [all] in the inheritance of Fionn throughout Ireland. Few have heard of him being forced to retreat. More than any [other] mercenaries it is second nature to Toirdhealbhach that the ford of battle is breached by him, when he sets out on expedition … He seizes a battle-axe and waits not to bind his wounds – A warrior's wife at his command, a request he will not obtain without battle, according to the saying of the gold-ringleted queen, an avenging husband is not likely to follow her … Ravens and scald-crows gather when he takes weapon in hand, grateful for what they get from the slaughter … A man with an incurable wound looks again at the gash, far through the wound it went so the shaft pinned him to the ground … A man when drunk promises your death, who never travels to confront you. Tongues run after drinking, promising to repel you in the battlefield … The verdict of the well-rewarded bardic schools is that it is not right to compete against him, he has excelled Muirne's son [Fionn], the Clann Suibhne have taken every pledge.[36]

In the same spirit, the castle of Domhnall son of Toirdhealbhach Mac Suibhne at Rathmullan is compared to its advantage with Fionn's palace of Allen in '*Leithéid Almhan i nUlltaibh*' ('The counterpart of Allen is in Ulster'), one of the poems of Tadhg Dall Ó hUiginn, translated by Eleanor Knott.[37]

---

35 *LCS*, pp 42–4. 36 *Verse 1:* 'Geall re hinbe oighrecht Fhinn . an ínbhe ó oirbhert do thuill. fedh glíadh o choimhnert do chinn . a n-oighreacht Fínd ar fiadh Floinn'. *Verse 4:* 'Terc do chúala á chlódh ar gcúl . tar búann[aibh?] as dó budh dúal Toirrdhealbach an tráth fa dtriall . áth gliadh budh oirbhernach úadh'. *Verse 5:* 'Ga breith sa tochar as-tegh . ag neimh a ghona ni ghabh rug ar thúaigh tar lámhaibh ledh . fegh a álaigh dh'úaim nír an'. *Verse 6:* 'Ben féinnedh da furail féin . fulair nach gébha gan ghlíaidh do rádh ríoghna na n-edh n-óir . nar doigh fer díoghla na díaigh'. *Verse 7:* Brainéoin ag tocht ar gach táobh . ar nochtagh da ghabhail glíad buidhech badhbh da fhúair a n-ágh . arm da lámh an úair do íarr'. *Verse 9:* Fer ón guin ni leighis líaigh . don cneidh sin do chuir a thsuil fada anónn tre crecht do-chúaidh . gur fhúaidh do cronn echt re huir'. *Verse 16:* 'Fer dherbus t'oigid[h] fá fhíon . id ghoire a tennta ní tríall rioth tengadh ag tochd o ól . gealladh dod chlógh a ngort glíad'. *Verse 25:* 'Derbaid[h] sgol na toirbert trom . na budh oirces cor 'na chenn o mac Múirne do-beir bárr . clann tSuibhne do-gheibh gac geall': (RIA MS 475 (24/P/25), fo. 73r). 37 Eleanor Knott (ed.), *The bardic poems of Tadhg Dall Ó hUiginn* (2 vols, London 1922, 1926), 1 (text), pp 195–201, 2 (transl.), pp 130–4.

The parallel between the legendary Fionn and the galloglass of the sixteenth century is also underlined in an address by the celebrated master-poet Eochaidh Ó hEoghusa to Eoghan Óg Mac Suibhne na dTuath, constable of Tír Chonaill, and foster-father of Aodh Ruadh (Red Hugh), '*Roinn leithe air anbhuain Éireann*':

Ireland's troubles are divided in half ... Two groups for some time have ruled this plain of Feidhlimidh ... To keep control of sunny Ireland, without fierceness or feuds, without battle or warfare is part of her ruler's obligations. Nevertheless the heaviest burden in regard to the warm-streamed territory is on the professional soldiers, confronting violence and trouble. Often they spill their blood in battles for Conn's land. The sharp-bladed group ever had short lives. Cumhall fought much under Conn of the Hundred Battles, every warlike encounter fought by Cormac mac Airt, and by his father Art was also fought by Fionn's Fianna, at the Battle of Ventry and another day at Magh Léna, those first professional soldiers of Ireland, laughing and gaming in the face of danger. It is no reproach to these heroes of yore that the Race of Suibhne do twice as much in defence of Ireland. Eoghan Óg Mac Suibhne is entrusted with a heavy responsibility by the O'Donnells, to take the van and rearguard of the army. Eoghan neither can nor would sleep without a battle, often exchanging wounds in defence of the O'Donnells, taking the gap of danger when all others refuse, as Cú Chulainn did at the battle of Ros na Ríogh.[38]

38 *Verse 1:* 'Roinn leithe air anbhúain Éireann ...' *Verse 2:* 'Da droing a-tá re tréimsi . ós cionn an chláir Fheidhlim-si ...' *Verse 6:* 'Beith d'Éirinn na n-íath solus. fáoi gan fhíoch gan fholtanas. gan cliathaigh gan chor ccatha . bladh d'fhiachaibh a hardfhlatha.' *Verse 8:* 'Gidh edh is íad a buanna . re hucht éigne is anbhúana . críoch bhúadhach na mbuinne tte . as truime úalach impe.' *Verse 9:* 'Minic dhoirtid crú a ccathaibh . fan ccrich[-s]e Cuinn Céadchathaigh . drong reannfhaobhrach nár ríadh treas . gearrsháoghlach ríamh a réimeas.' *Verse 13:* 'Re linn Cuinn os cionn Banbha . fa mór ccath da comhardha . ro rad sháorChumhal slios seang . fa lios ráoncumhann Ráoidhleann.' *Verse 14:* 'Ni bfhúar Chormac mór mac Airt . ní fhúair Art na n-éucht ordairc . gleó nach bfhúaradar fían Fhinn . fa fhíadh bfhúarabaidh bFheidhlim'. *Verse 15:* 'Fa Fhionntráigh na n-inbear tte . ar Magh Léana lá eile . ga líon éantachair do bfearr . ag díon réaltachaidh Ráoileann'. *Verse 17:* 'Cluithe ₇ gáire a ngábhadh . a n-anbhúain a n-imbádhadh . san ccrích cuirr shédbhúadhaigh sin . do céadbuannuibh fhuinn Eimhir'. *Verse 18:* 'Re hainbhúain re hucht gcogadh . ni guth dóibh nach dearnadar . leath a ndéaninn Síol Suibhne.ag díon Éirionn iathghuirme'. *Verse 22:* 'Ar Eogan Óg mac Suibhne . curthar le cath Modairne. earr is díghend gach deacra . dream na sítheang súaitheanta'. *Verse 23:* 'Ris theag[h]mus tús a ngábaidh . air chuirid crú riDáluigh . cuire lonn o bhreacshrath Breag . trom a ndeacrach fa dheairedh'. *Verse 26:* 'Úain codail ni chaith Eogan . da gcaitheadh ní choideoladh . gan ró díbfeirge a ndhál cath . do cládh fhírfheirge Ulltach'. *Verse 27:* 'Minic fúair iomláoid álaidh . ag cosnamh chrú rioghDhálaigh . fa dhórus bfhrithir bfedhma . crithir sholas sheinEamhno'. *Verse 28:* 'Minic iomcras feidhm catha . ar impidhe a ardflatho . diúltaid fían Eamhna uile . a ngrían bearna báoghlaighe'. *Verse 29:* 'Cú Chulainn an crotha ghloin . fa cend meic Fachtna Fhathaig[h] . do-roighne mur do-ní [a]-niogh . ní fa coimhdhe don chuigeadh ...': (RIA MS 2 (23/F/16), p. 47).

SERVITORS TO THE O'DONNELLS

Such explicit references to the O'Donnells as employers come again and again in the poems. Domhnall Mac Suibhne, lord of Fanad (1570–1619) was addressed by a flattering poet as king of Rathmullan, mercenary of the O'Donnell kings (*buanna ríogh fhréimhe Dálaigh*), irreproachable Mac Suibhne, full moon of a high mercenary (*ré imlán ardbhuanna*), lover of the O'Donnells' poets (*a leannán clíar crú Dálaigh*). The author playfully adds that he lay as a lover with Mac Suibhne without his lady wife's permission, but she should not be jealous of him [as opposed to possible female rivals?].[39]

HOSPITALITY TO POETS

What was entailed in being a poet's lover is described by the famous Fearghal Óg Mac an Bhaird apparently at a time when he was absent in Munster (where he went to study in the bardic schools), but still anxious to deny a rumour that he would abandon Domhnall Mac Suibhné's service on his return. He protests he would not desert Mac Suibhne, chief of Fanad:

It is not without reason I loved him above the nobles of Ireland – he gave me his confidence and his royal shoulder [at the feast] – he consulted me above all, he shared his bed with me, he kept me at his elbow in the midst of all, gave me his gold-embroidered suit and noble steed. However many times I visited his house I never returned empty.[40]

The theme of extravagant hospitality to poets recurs throughout the poems to the MacSweeneys. It is, of course, a standard motif of the bards, who hoped that praise for a patron's generosity would prove a self-fulfilling prophecy, but it is particularly marked in the MacSweeney poems, especially those to Domhnall Mac Suibhne of Fanad and his wife Gráinne. Domhnall had come to the chieftainship at an unusually young age, after the untimely death of two of his elder brothers,[41] and the poems

---

39 *Verse 6:* 'Leis mur leannán do luidh me . gan chead d'inghin Maoil Mhuire . na biodh sé uirthe 'na éd . ni mé bud chuirthe a coiméd'. From 'Toghaim leannán do Leith Chuinn': RIA MS 475 (24/P/25), fo. 8or. 40 *Verse 7:* 'Gan adhbhur ni tucas toil . do tar uaisliph foid fiondtuin . ni chuir se [...] . liom a run 's a rioghguala'. *Verse 8:* 'Cnu mullaigh maicne Suibhne . liom tar cach a comairle . troig tseang n ... 's as liom colbha a chaoimhleabtha'. *Verse 9:* 'Liom a leathuille a lar chaich . liom fos. a erradh orsnaith . nech nac [...]. 's a each aigentach uasal'. *Verse 10:* 'Da meince teiginn da thigh . mo [...] gaidh tsoilbir . ri is omhan [...] aill treasa . folamh uaidh nior filleasa'. From 'Ní tréicfe mé Mac Suibhne': RIA MS no. 475 (24/P/25), fo. 79v. 41 *AFM*, v, pp 1636–7, and see Appendix, no. 9.

indicate that his leadership was at first disputed by other kinsmen. This is the usual context in which patrons are particularly lavish in paying poets, in order to publicize the legitimacy of their succession. In the poem '*Cia chosnas Clann Dálaigh?*' ('Who protects the O'Donnell dynasty?') we are told it is

A man who does not turn his back on battle, who leads his warriors to the van of the conflict, who does not boast of his exploits. Often he has been awarded the palm of generosity for the amount of his rewards [to poets] ... Oileach is supreme for the gifts dispensed. Though a man arrive early he is slow [to leave?].[42]

Another poem to the same Domhnall says

What he dispenses to every stranger means they do not seek to go away from him – a reason for guests to stay – it is customary to frequent the northern parts. He disarms angry guests in relation to their every whim with miracles of hospitality. A difficult party who went to exhaust his generosity has an eye on his axe! ... He pays no heed to whatever of his property is not yet given away. If he had the cloak of perpetual success in wooing, Mac Suibhne would not keep it long. ... [43]

THE GALLOGLASS AXE

The reference to Mac Suibhne's galloglass axe as his greatest treasure has symbolic value. The axe distinguished the professional soldier from the Irish nobles fighting on horseback with spears. The Annals of Connacht record an occasion when an Ó Conchobhair prince, presumably because he had lost his spear in the heat of conflict, 'was harassing [the enemies'] rear on horseback and performing deeds of prowess upon them with an axe belonging to one of his own footsoldiers'.[44] It is possible that in practice

---

42 *Verse 2:* 'Fer n [...] lo [...] tromm comhluinn . re cathaibh ni chuirid druim ...'. *Verse 3:* 'Teid ré n-ógaibh ar fhed troda . a tos aigh g[er?] b'annamh [...] ...'. *Verse 4:* 'Fer nac m[a?]oidend méd a thoirb[...] . tuc aoinneac is coir na [chlo?] . ger thend oll – as a fhoghlaim . do bferr bronn [...]'. *Verse 5:* 'Minic do ghebhid geall oinigh . dh'iomad na nduas dhailis se. róighne caigh do char na caraid . [...]'. *Verse 6:* 'Nir cuireadh riam ag ríar chléire . an clu a c[...]th nac cosain soin ...'. *Verse 7:* 'Méd an duas ag dol a clecht – . crodh o Cuinn ni crodh gan tóir . sgol 'ga fegain fein a foghlaim . uir mhéd[aigh] rer Domn[aill] doibh'. *Verse 20:* 'Gell gac criche do crich Oiligh. d'iomad na ndúas dháiles sud . ge luath le fer an tann tána[i]c . mall [...]': RIA MS 475 (24/P/25), fo. 79r–v. 43 *Verse 7:* 'As fiú a ndáilend da gac deóraidh . dul ar ccúl nac iarrann uadh . cred an fáth fa n-anann áoidhe . gnath tagall in táoibi túad'. *Verse 8:* 'Le fertaibh féile do fóiredh . ferg na n-áoidhedh da gach tail . súil aran túaigh ag dáimh dhoiligh . do chuaid[h] do tráigh oinigh air'. *Verse 30:* 'Ni ara laimh da mbeth gan bronnadh . na bidh sé 'ga airemh air . ge tarrla ar an mbrat búaigh suirgi . ni búan ag Mac Suibhni sin'. From 'An cumhall cédna ag cloinn Eóghain': RIA MS 475 (24/P/25), fo. 8ov. 44 See *AC*, pp 504–5. See also a couplet from a poem to Henry son of Eoghan Ó Néill (chief 1455–83), which may allude

the MacSweeney constables went into battle on horseback. A Catalan pilgrim to St Patrick's purgatory in 1397 recalled meeting the Great O'Neill's constable of the galloglass, Eoin Mac Domhnaill, at the head of a troop of a hundred horsemen.[45] However in the poems to Domhnall Mac Suibhne he is almost always shown fighting with the traditional axe, and there are some hints that his one was specially decorated: 'During the battle the man at Domhnall's side has little to apprehend, an ogham inscription is on his axe whose bounty is victory';[46] 'You win command of every fight with your poison-charmed brown-based weapon. Ireland is united by the slender axe';[47] 'A man heard the noise from your axe during the battle though he was far away ...'.[48] This poem also remarks that Domhnall picked his warriors only from those men of Fanad who were strongest – no man sat at his elbow in the banquet but he who had earned it in battle.[49] Another poem tells of the gold-embroidered birds on his battle-standard, and refers to the prudent practice of bringing a medical attendant to the battlefield, though this cowardly precaution is attributed to the enemy:

A crowd of fair women who grew envious (?) surround her till noon. Beautiful trees seen in the sewing, Gráinne embroiders them with golden birds ... Hard to chronicle after you every tale in your satin banners, flightless birds in the sewing, designed by you (?) with golden wings ... O grandson of Ruaidhri, ... it is no help to one you wound in the conflict to have a doctor in a house nearby.[50]

SPARTAN WARRIORS

The long spears which were also used by the footsoldiers are frequently mentioned in the context of their shafts being used as tent-poles when the army bivouacked for the night: 'No surprise when Domhnall takes his rest

to a similar incident: 'gabhais a n-uair firéigin . tuaid n-amais an t-Éinrísin . An tuadhsin i tréinEogain. re mbuannuib co mbéilsníthir'. From 'Gach síl co síl rígEogain', TCD MS 1363 (H.4.22), p. 132.   45 D.M. Carpenter, 'The pilgrim from Catalonia/Aragon: Ramon de Perellós, 1397', in *The medieval pilgrimage to S. Patrick's Purgatory* ed. Michael Haren and Yves de Pontfarcy (Enniskillen, 1988), p. 109.   46 *Verse 4:* 'Le Domnall ar fhedh an áigh . beg dograind an té re tháoibh . craebh oghaim tarla 'na thuaigh . búaidh faghla is crobaing don cráoibh'. From 'Fada Fánaid re rath ríogh', RIA MS 475 (24/P/25), fo. 72v.   47 *Verse 36:* 'Dot arm bundonn go mbriocht neimhe . neart gach troda tárraidh tú ; táth na Banbha ar an tuaigh thana . tarla fa bhuaidh cara clú'. From 'Ní ar aois roinntear rath buanna', poem no. 3 in Ó Foghlú, 'Four bardic poems from *Leabhar Chlainne Suibhne*' (TCD Thesis no. 2732).   48 *Verse 18:* 'do clos a fuaim ar fedh troda . fer od túaigh ger fhoda hé'. From '[F]uair Domnall oighreacht an enigh', RIA MS 475 (24/P/25), fo. 76v.   49 Ibid., Verse 29: 'D'feraib Fanad na lann líomtha . laoich 'ga togha ar tresi a lámh . nir geab fa fion ara uille . acht fer bud díol uirre a n-ágh'.   50 *Verse 4:* 'Bró fhionnban da tánaic tnuidh . 'na timchal go tanaic nóin . croinn áille ar fheghain san uaim . Gráinne ga n-uaim dh'énaib óir'. *Verse 23:* 'Decair a dhenaim ad diaigh . gac énsdair at engaibh after plunder sitting on the mountainside. Every man withdraws his spear from what constituted the sleeping-quarters last night';[51] 'For Mac Suibhne in the morning no presage of sleep, the birds of a mansion are his orchestra after he has burnt it to the ground'.[52] References like these occur in what I have come to know as the 'Spartan life of warriors motif', characterized by boasts about how tough the chief and his soldiers are, lying all night in their armour, drinking water from the brook instead of banquets of wine and so on.[53] Only one of the poems to Domhnall lord of Fanad looks forward to a period of peace, apparently in celebration of the end of the succession struggle that won the young man his chieftainship:

War has ended now that Fanad has found a worthy prince. Domhnall wielded an experienced axe before taking the kingdom, he does not avoid conflict since acquiring the title ... Even though he need not fight now that he is inaugurated, he still seeks his former reputation ... He will have to abandon his trade of arming at moonrise. A feature of his title is that he may not plunder ... Farmers who have ploughed little will soon be weary of it. Wine and music abound under his rule.[54]

Once again the poet's theme is the dual role of the MacSweeney lords, both as territorial princes in their own right, and military commanders under the warlike O'Donnell kings, and interestingly he hints that the roles are incompatible. I hope I have said enough to convince you that these unpublished poems urgently need editing.

APPENDIX

THIRTY-TWO BARDIC POEMS ADDRESSED TO THE MACSWEENEYS
(published editions marked with an asterisk)

1. 'An Cumhall céadna ag cloinn Eoghain?', by Pádraig Ó Gnímh.
Addressed to Domhnall Mac Suibhne (*fl.* 1570–d.1619).
Source: RIA 475 (24/P/25).

sróil . ealta gan etil san úaim . benta uaib go n-etibh óir'. *Verse 24:* 'A úa ruaidri ... ní fhóir nech ó'd ghoin a ngliaidh . da mbeath liaigh sa toigh re thaoib'. From '[D]á néll oinig san aird tuaidh', RIA MS 475 (24/P/25), fo. 76v. **51** *Verse 9:* 'Sgís ar domhnall a ndíaigh fhoghla . narb iongnadh dó suidhi ar sléibh . beired gac fer uaidh a fhogha an tegh súain a rabha arér'. From 'An cumhall cédna ag cloinn eóghain': RIA MS 475 (24/P/25), fo. 8ov. **52** *Verse 10:* 'Siad aige na crannaib ciuil . ar madain nir mana súain . do Mac Suibne is crannghal cheoil . eoin bruidhne ar n-a hadhnadh úaidh'. From 'Fada Fánaid re rath ríogh': RIA 475 (24/P/25), 72v. **53** Katharine Simms, 'Images of warfare in bardic poetry' in *Celtica*, 21 (1990), pp 612–13. **54** 'Do sguir cogadh criche Fanad', poem no. 4 in Ó Foghlú, 'Four bardic poems from *Leabhar Chlainne Suibhne*' (TCD Thesis no. 2732).

2. 'Cia a-deir gur imthigh Éamonn?', by Fearghal Óg Mac an Bhaird.
   Elegy on Éamonn (mac Maolmhuire mhic Dhonnchaidh) Mac Suibhne (na
   dTuath branch, but resident in Munster) (d. 1580).
   Source: RIA 2 (23/F/16) &c.

3. 'Cia chosnas buanacht Banba?', by Flann Mac an Bhaird.
   Addressed to Domhnall Mac Suibhne (*fl.* 1570–d.1619).
   Source: RIA 475 (24/P/25).

4. 'Cia chosnas clann Dálaigh?', by Domhnall Ó Dálaigh.
   Addressed to Domhnall Mac Suibhne (*fl.* 1570–d.1619).
   Source: RIA 475 (24/P/25).

5. 'Cia léar múineadh Maol Mhuire?', by Gofraidh Óg Mac an Bhaird.
   Addressed to Maolmhuire (mac Toirdhealbhaigh) Mac Suibhne, *fl.* mid-
   17th cent.
   Source: Stoneyhurst School Library MS A/II/20ii, TCD1411 (H.6.7) &c.

6. 'Críoch an ghaisgidh goin Donnchaidh', by Flann Mac an Bhaird.
   Elegy on Donnchadh (mac Toirdhealbhaigh) Mac Suibhne (Fanad branch–
   'consabal').
   Source: RIA 475 (24/P/25).

7. 'Cuid ronna a n-anbuain Éireann', by Pádraig Óg Mac an Bhaird.
   Addressed to Maolmhuire (mac Donnchaidh mhic Mhaolmhuire mhic
   Mhurchaidh) Mac Suibhne (*fl.* mid- or late 17th cent.).
   Source: Stoneyhurst School Library MS A/II/20ii, TCD 1411 (H.6.7) &c.

8. 'Dá néall oinig san aird tuaidh', by Aonghus Dorcha Ó Maoilghirigh.
   Addressed to Domhnall Mac Suibhne (*fl.* 1570–d.1619).
   Source: RIA 475 (24/P/25).

9. 'Dá uaithni fulaing fa Fhánaid', by Eoghan (mac Gofradha) Mac an Bhaird.
   Addressed to Aodh Buidhe and Toirdhealbhach (Clann Thoirdhealbhaigh)
   Mac Suibhne (*fl.* late 16th cent.).
   Source: RIA 475 (24/P/25)

*10. 'Dál chabhlaigh ar Chaistéal Suibhne', by Artúr Dall MacGurcaigh (?).
   Addressed to Eoghan Mac Suibhne (*fl.* early 14th or late 15th cent.).
   Published with transl. in W.J. Watson, *Scottish verse in the Book of the Dean
   of Lismore* (Scottish Gaelic Texts Society, Edinburgh 1937), pp. 6–13; D.
   Meek, 'Norsemen and noble stewards' in *CMCS*, 34 (1997), 1–49.

*11. 'Dlighidh coire cnáimh', by anon.
   Addressed to Walter (mac Lochlainn mhic Bhaitir) Mac Suibhne (*fl.* early
   17th cent.).
   Published with transl. in A. O'Sullivan and M. Herbert, 'The provenance of
   Laud Misc. 615' in *Celtica*, 10 (1973), 174–92, at 183–88.

12. 'Dóibh fein creidid Clann tSuibhne', by Flann Og Mac Craith.
    Addressed to Domhnall Mac Suibhne (*fl.* 1570–1619).
    Source: RIA 475 (24/P/25).

13. 'Do sguir cogadh críche Fánad' by anon.
    Addressed to Domhnall Mac Suibhne (*fl.* 1570–d.1619).
    Source: RIA 475. Unpubl. transl. in Seán Ó Foghlú, 'Four bardic poems
    from *Leabhar Chlainne Suibhne*' (M.Litt. thesis, TCD, [1992] 1993). Thesis
    Catalogue no. 2732, p. 141.

14. 'Fada Fánaid re rath ríogh', by Uilliam Ó'n Cháinte.
    Addressed to Domhnall Mac Suibhne (*fl.* 1570–d.1619).
    Source: RIA 475 (24/P/25).

15. 'Fuair Domhnall oighreacht an einigh', by Donnchadh Ó Cléirigh.
    Addressed to Domhnall Mac Suibhne (*fl.* 1570–d.1619).
    Source: RIA 475 (24/P/25) and Stoneyhurst School Library MS A/II/20 ii.

16. 'Geall re hinbhe oighreacht Fhinn' by Domhnall (mac Fearghail) Mac an
    Bhaird.
    Addressed to Toirdhealbhach Mac Suibhne (*fl.* late 16th cent.).
    Source: RIA 475 (24/P/25).

*17. 'Iad fein chinneas ar Chlainn Néill' by Tadhg Dall Ó hUiginn.
    Addressed to Eoghan Óg MacSuibhne na dTuath (chief 1570–d.1596).
    Published with transl. in Eleanor Knott (ed.), *The bardic poems of Tadhg Dall
    Ó hUiginn*, 2 vols, Irish Texts Society (London, 1922), poem no. 26 (text in
    vol. 1, transl. in vol. 2).

*18. 'Leannáin fileadh Síol Suibhne', by Eoghan Mac an Bhaird.
    Addressed to Ruaidhri Óg (mac Ruaidhri mhic Mhaolmhuire) Mac Suibhne
    (*fl.* mid–17th cent.)
    Published with transl. in Lambert McKenna, 'Some Irish bardic poems' in
    The Irish Monthly, 56, p. 35; published without transl. in L. Mac Cionaith
    (ed.), *Dioghluim Dána* (Dublin 1938), no. 102.

*19. 'Leithéid Almhan i nUltaibh', by Tadhg Dall Ó hUiginn.
    Addressed to Domhnall Mac Suibhne (*fl.* 1570–d.1619).
    Published with transl. in E. Knott (ed.), *The bardic poems of Tadhg Dall Ó
    hUiginn*, no. 27.

20. 'Mór re chuma caithréim deisi', by Cú Uladh (mac Conchobhair Ruaidh)
    Mac an Bhaird.
    Elegy for Maolmhuire (and his father Toirdhealbhach d. 1544) Mac Suibhne.
    Source: RIA 475. Unpubl. transl. in Seán Ó Foghlú, 'Four bardic poems
    from *Leabhar Chlainne Suibhne*' (M.Litt. thesis, TCD, [1992] 1993). Thesis
    Catalogue no. 2732.

21. 'Ní ar aois roinntear rath buanna', by Brian Mac an Bhaird.
    Addressed to Domhnall Mac Suibhne (*fl.* 1570–d.1619).
    Source: RIA 475. Unpubl. transl. in Seán Ó Foghlú, 'Four bardic poems
    from *Leabhar Chlainne Suibhne*' (M.Litt. thesis, TCD, [1992] 1993). Thesis
    Catalogue no. 2732.

22. 'Ní ben [...] (aceph.) [al. Ní céim nach cumhain linne]', by anon.
    Elegy on the sons of Toirdhealbhach Mac Suibhne (Fanad) (late 16th cent.).
    Source: RIA 475 (24/P/25).

23. 'Ní thréigfe mé Mac Suibhne', by Fearghal Óg (mac Fearghail mhic
    Dhomhnaill Ruaidh) Mac an Bhaird.
    Addressed to Domhnall Mac Suibhne (?d.1619).
    Source: RIA 475 (24/P/25).

24. 'Rachad i gceann sgaoilte sgéal' by anon.
    Elegy on Ruaidhri Mac Suibhne (d. 1518).
    Source: RIA 475 (24/P/25).

25. 'Roinn leithe air anbhuain Éireann', by Eochaidh Ó hEoghusa.
    Addressed to Eoghan Óg Mac Suibhne na dTuath (chief 1570–d.1596).
    Source: RIA 2 (23/F/16) &c.

26. 'Rugadh da chluiche ar Chloinn Suibhne', by Cú Uladh (mac Conchobhair
    Ruaidh) Mac an Bhaird.
    Elegy for Maolmhuire (and his father Toirdhealbhach d. 1544) Mac Suibhne.
    Source: RIA 475. Unpubl. transl. in Seán Ó Foghlú, 'Four bardic poems
    from *Leabhar Chlainne Suibhne*' (M.Litt. thesis, TCD, [1992] 1993). Thesis
    Catalogue no. 2732.

27. 'Sealbh gan urraidh oighreacht Fhinn' by anon.
    Elegy on Ruaidhri Mac Suibhne (d. 1518).
    Source: RIA 475 (24/P/25).

*28. 'Tánag adhaigh go hEas Caoile', by Tadhg Dall Ó hUiginn.
    Elegy on Maolmhórdha (mac Maolmhuire) Mac Suibhne [Connacht
    branch?] d. 1581.
    Published with transl. in E. Knott (ed.), *The bardic poems of Tadhg Dall Ó
    hUiginn*, no. 25.

29. 'Toghaim leannán do Leith Cuinn' by anon.
    Addressed to Domhnall Mac Suibhne (*fl.* 1570–d.1619).
    Source: RIA 475 (24/P/25).

30. 'Triar do thoghas ós iath Mogha', by Baothghalach Dubh MacAodhagáin.
    Addressed to Murchadh (mac Éamoinn) Mac Suibhne and two younger
    brothers (na dTuath branch in Munster? late 16th cent.?).
    Source: Maynooth B 6.

*31. 'Tugaim aghaidh ar Mhaolmhórdha', by Tadhg 'Ruadh' or Tadhg 'Dall' Ó hUiginn and Tadhg (mac Dáire) Mac Bruaideadha–a *crosántacht*. Addressed to Maolmhórdha Mac Suibhne (?d. 1581). Published in *The Irish Book Lover*, vol. xxvii.

32. 'Uaisle cinidh Clann tShuibhne' by anon. Addressed to Toirdhealbhach (mac Maolmhuire) Mac Suibhne (?d. 1399). *Source:* The Book of O'Conor Don (transcription by Eugene O'Curry in RIA 626 (3/C/13).

James V, king of Scotland – and Ireland?

ALISON CATHCART

When only 12 years old, in 1524, King James V of Scotland wrote to Henry VIII of England referring to him as his 'derrest and richt Uncle'.[1] By the time James began his personal rule, following his displacement of the Angus administration in 1528, such customary formalities had disappeared and his affection for his uncle was much more ambiguous.[2] During his minority James, arguably, was under the influence of his mother, Margaret Tudor, elder sister of Henry VIII. In attempting to gain influence within Scotland Henry had sought to create alliances with various Scottish nobles and Margaret, for a brief period during 1522–3, had become something of a pawn in Henry's meddling. At the same time, the English king did not hold back from interfering in Scottish affairs, political and ecclesiastical and throughout the years of his minority King James had watched as Henry tried to manipulate politics in Scotland by conspiring with factions within and without the realm.[3] While King Henry's motives can be viewed as dynastic and acquisitive, seeking to assert English claims to overlordship of Scotland, it has been argued that his real aim was simply to secure Anglo-Scottish stability which would then leave him free to concentrate on his main interest: recreation of the continental empire enjoyed by Henry V.[4] Such amity was welcomed by James who wanted to secure his own kingship and in December 1528 a truce was signed at Berwick which stated that a final treaty would be negotiated within five years.[5] A return to peace, therefore, was mutually beneficial. Henry VIII had become increasingly preoccupied with his divorce from Catherine of Aragon, while King James, unsure of European allies in the eventuality of breaking with England, was reluctant to face an English army with the memory of Flodden still so vivid. Henry and James continued to watch each other warily, but relations in the following decade were shaped by the overriding concern of both for their standing in

---

1 *LP Henry VIII*, iii, nos 3521, 3523; *SP Henry VIII*, iv, pp 95–6. 2 Gordon Donaldson, *Scotland: James V–James VII* (Edinburgh, 1965), p. 38. 3 Ibid., pp 31–42; *Letters of James V*, pp 86–7, 145. 4 D.M. Head, 'Henry VIII's Scottish policy: a reassessment', *SHR*, 71, no. 171 (1982), 1–24, esp. 1–2, 8–9; S.G. Ellis, *Tudor Ireland. Crown, community and the conflict of cultures, 1470–1603* (London and New York, 1985), p. 15. 5 *SP Henry VIII*, iv, pp 501–6; Donaldson, *Scotland*, pp 40–1.

international terms. Unfortunately for King Henry, his dispute and eventual break with Rome left him isolated and vulnerable for a period during the 1530s, a situation which James V was able to exploit effectively.

Henry's break with Rome placed King James in a powerful bargaining position *vis-à-vis* the papacy, resulting in increased royal control over appointments as well as financial dividends from church revenues.[6] Henry VIII tried, unsuccessfully, to persuade James to break with Rome, as this would give England an ally in Europe, but James had little incentive in the light of the advantageous position Henry's policy afforded him. Relations between England and Scotland need to be viewed in this international context but the internal situation also impacted greatly and, with the situation on the borders far from stable, relations between the two countries soon deteriorated.[7] By 1532–3 cross-border raiding had gained in intensity, underlining the fact that, while neither side wanted to abide by the conditions of the truce, neither actually wanted war. In fact, in the light of Henry's position in Europe, war was to be avoided at all costs, while James, despite the level and extent of border warfare, stated that he 'abhors the thought of war with his uncle'.[8] Despite making similar noises regarding Anglo-Scottish peace, it was due to the insistence of Francis I of France that a treaty was contracted in 1534. But this treaty did little to ensure lasting stability as Anglo-Scottish relations remained inextricably linked to fluctuations in European diplomacy.[9] Scotland's renewal of the Auld Alliance with France and King Henry's alliance with the emperor, Charles V, in the latter years of the 1530s, combined with King James's assertions of his status as an 'imperial' monarch, saw the two countries inch closer to renewed hostilities.[10] Nonetheless, a superficial cordiality was maintained in communications between the two kings. James emphasized the 'close kinship' between them and asserted he would 'persevier in perfyt kyndneis' towards Henry, who was confident of Anglo-Scottish stability.[11] Henry wanted to prevent James V making a European marriage-alliance which would further isolate England and, even as late as 1536 when James was fully involved in marital negotiations, English ambassadors

6 See *Letters of James V*, pp 206, 242–4, 285. For a more general discussion of King James V's relations with the papacy, see Donaldson, *Scotland*, pp 43–62; Jenny Wormald, *Court, kirk and community, Scotland, 1470–1625* (Edinburgh, 1981), pp 3–26, 75–108.   7 Head, 'Henry VIII's Scottish policy'.   8 Jamie Cameron, *James V. The personal rule, 1528–42* (East Linton, 1999), pp 219–20.   9 Ibid., p. 286; Head, 'Henry VIII's Scottish policy', 12; *Letters of James V*, pp 242–3, 260, 272.   10 R.A. Mason, 'This realm of Scotland is an empire? Imperial ideas and iconography in early renaissance Scotland', in Barbara Crawford (ed.), *Church, chronicle and Learning in medieval and early renaissance Scotland* (Edinburgh, 1999), pp 73–91; idem, *Kingship and the commonweal: political thought in renaissance and reformation Scotland* (East Linton, 1998), pp 78–103.   11 *Letters of James V*, pp 219, 272, 300; *LP Henry VIII*, vii, no. 1141.

in Scotland preferred to think that King James would not make such an alliance.[12] Henry persistently asked for a personal meeting with his nephew but James continued to stall: James responded to Henry's proposal for a meeting at York in 1536 by stating that 'his lords would not consent to his going further than Newcastle'.[13] When King James sailed to France in September 1536, subsequently marrying Madeleine, daughter of Francis I, in January 1537, it was clear that the 'Auld Alliance' was being maintained.

Most examinations of Anglo-Scottish relations in the reign of James V have concentrated on the wider European context of King James's search for a foreign bride and Henry VIII's break with Rome.[14] This context is vital for understanding the development of Anglo-Scottish relations during this decade, but attention also needs to be directed elsewhere. One largely overlooked dimension of Anglo-Scottish relations is the role that events in Ireland played. Henry was actively involved in Ireland but James's position requires deeper analysis. Diplomatic correspondence and intelligence reports regarding the Scottish king's interest in Ireland offer further insights into James's policy towards his uncle during the crucial decade of the 1530s. James V did not view the treaty with England as a cornerstone of Scottish policy, but until he secured a European ally his hands were tied. He was reluctant to break with England until assured of support from an ally, but in the meantime was happy to aggravate King Henry, diverting his attention from King James's diplomatic endeavours in Europe. The extent of James's direct, personal involvement in Irish resistance to Henry during the 1530s remains questionable but Scottish activity in Ireland was of growing concern to the English throughout the decade. The offer of the kingship of Ireland to James in 1540, made by eight 'gentylemen of Ierlande' on behalf of 'all the greate men in Irelande' has been largely overlooked.[15] They asserted they 'wolde houlde of Hym, and take Hym for thayre Kynge and Lorde, and that thay wolde come in to Scotlane to make hym omayge'.[16] This suggests that James's involvement in Ireland was greater than hitherto has been

---

12 Head, 'Henry VIII's Scottish policy', 13; Donaldson, *Scotland*, pp 48–99; *SP Henry VIII*, v, pp 47–9.   13 *LP Henry VIII*, xx no. 928.   14 Compare, e.g., Head, 'Henry VIII's Scottish policy' with the views of C.P. Hotle, 'Tradition, reform and diplomacy: Anglo-Scottish relations, 1528–42', (PhD thesis, University of Cambridge, 1992) which puts greater emphasis on Scottish affairs.   15 Apart from Michael Lynch, *Scotland: a new history* (London, 1991), p. 161; idem, 'National identity in Ireland and Scotland, 1500–1640', in C. Bjørn, A. Grant and K.J. Stringer (eds), *Nations, nationalism and patriotism in the European past* (Copenhagen, 1994), p. 128; Hiram Morgan, 'British policies before the British state', in Brendan Bradshaw and John Morrill (eds), *The British problem, c.1534–1707. State formation in the Atlantic Archipelago* (London, 1996), p. 73; C. Kellar, *Scotland, England and the reformation, 1534–1561* (Oxford, 2003), p. 64.   16 *SP Henry VIII*, v, p. 178; *LP Henry VIII*, xv, no. 710.

recognized and begs the question: what was he trying to achieve? Irish-Scottish military co-operation had existed on an unofficial basis for centuries but the extent to which it received Scottish crown sanction has not been fully explored. What follows probes some of these unanswered questions by examining King James's involvement in Ireland during the 1530s within the context of Anglo–Scottish relations.

The early 1530s saw James V embark on a policy of personal communication with some of his West Highland chiefs. Such a policy was not new for the Scottish crown as James IV had adopted similar measures to deal with the fallout from the forfeiture of the Lordship of the Isles in 1493. James IV, however, communicated with the Highland and Island chiefs through Giolla Easpaig Caimbeul (Archibald Campbell), second earl of Argyll. In contrast, James V wanted to assert his position above that of the house of Argyll and ensure that the Highland chiefs dealt directly with him. Consequently in 1531 King James removed Giolla Easpaig (Archibald), fourth earl of Argyll, from his powerbase in the West Highlands and promoted Alasdair Mac Domhnaill (Alexander MacDonald) of Dunivaig and the Glens as chamberlain of Kintyre in the earl's place. Keeping Argyll out of the west for a number of years allowed James to increase communication with both Mac Domhnaill and Eachann Mac Gill'Eathain (Hector MacLean) of Duart.[17] During this time James made gifts to Alasdair Mac Domhnaill of 'ane dosane of bowis and vi dosane of arrowis' as a sign of royal patronage and to ensure the continued cooperation of the Highland chiefs with the crown.[18] In 1533 Mac Domhnaill and Mac Gill'Eathain attacked Man and captured the English ship, the 'Mary Willoughby' (despite English intelligence of the planned attack),[19] but activity in the Irish Sea was not limited to minor sporadic raids. James V's connections with Mac Domhnaill and Mac Gill'Eathain extended into Ireland where Alasdair Mac Domhnaill had land, an established kin network and local alliances with the native Irish.

The MacDonalds of Dunivaig first acquired land in Ireland in 1399 when Eoin (John) Mac Domhnaill of Islay, younger brother of Domhnall (Donald of Harlaw), second Lord of the Isles, married Marjory Bisset, heiress of the Glens of Antrim. The establishment of a branch of Clann Domhnaill (the Clan Donald) in Ireland ensured continued migration

17 *TA*, vi, pp 43, 57, 124. Although it is unclear exactly how long Argyll was absent from the west, no charters were issued by him September 1531xJanuary 1533 (see Glasgow University Library, Argyll Transcripts, made by Niall Campbell, 10th duke of Argyll, i, pp 24–5) and he did not receive a remission for his misdemeanours until March 1533 (*RSS*, ii, p. 1525). 18 *TA*, vi, pp 92, 95. 19 *TA*, vi, pp 134, 136; *LP Henry VIII*, vi, p. 610. The 'Mary Willoughby' later became part of the fleet which sailed to the Isles in 1540–1.

between Ireland and the west of Scotland, and also provided a refuge for discontented Scots. In the 1420s, James the Fat, the last remaining member of the Albany-Stewart faction sought protection from the MacDonalds in Antrim following James I's attack on his family. The refuge offered to James the Fat and the possible alliance with the English was a very real threat to the king and the existence of a branch of the island kindred across the sea remained problematic for successive monarchs.[20] By opening lines of direct communication with Alasdair Mac Domhnaill, King James not only gained a stronger foothold in the Isles, but he could also use this to lever himself into Irish politics and gain some degree of control over military cooperation across the Irish Sea. James may well have viewed Alasdair Mac Domhnaill's ability to operate in two political worlds, Ireland and Scotland, as a threat to his authority within Scotland. By bringing the Highland chief into a closer alliance with him, James was attempting to neutralize Mac Domhnaill while also securing stability in the Western Highlands and Isles. It is, however, James's wider agenda in Ireland that deserves closer analysis.

King James maintained communication with Mac Domhnaill while the latter was in Ireland during the early years of the 1530s. Mac Domhnaill was involved in the feuding amongst the native Irish in the north, upheaval which the English viewed with suspicion, no doubt because the north was also a region of intense hostility to Tudor encroachment. From an English point of view the problematic situation in the north was heightened by Scottish intervention, and affairs in the region were closely monitored. But despite relatively precise knowledge of the extent of Scottish intervention, in the 1530s Henry appeared unconcerned. In 1532 Henry VIII was informed by Henry Percy, fourth earl of Northumberland, of the arrival of 4,000 Scots in the north of Ireland and although comforted by the 'ferre distances of Machonell [i.e., Mac D(h)omhnaill] from Edinburgh', the English were aware that Mac Domhnaill had been in communication with James. It proved difficult for Northumberland to unearth much information concerning Scottish interest in the north of Ireland although he was able to inform King Henry that the purpose of Mac Domhnaill's mission to Ireland was contained 'in secret articles devised by the archbishop of Glasgow, the bishop of Aberdeen, Henry Kemp, and Davy Wood, no more being privy thereto, which articles were delivered to John Canois at his departure' from King James. It was also noted that in response to communication received from Mac Domhnaill, the king sent '500 archers from the Out

20 Cf. Michael Brown, *James I* (Edinburgh, 1994), pp 62–7, 100–5.

Isles in great haste'.[21] The following year Henry was told that the Scots were 'busily inhabiting a great part of Ulster' and advised that they 'must be driven away'.[22] This level of involvement on the part of the Scots in the north of Ireland was not welcomed by the English regime.[23] The employment of Scottish mercenaries by native Irish kings in their wars against each other would only serve to continue unrest, making the task of extending Tudor authority in the region increasingly problematic.

In the previous decade English policy towards Ireland had taken a new turn. Henry VIII believed that Gaelic Ireland could be more easily brought under Tudor authority by reaching something of a political compromise with the native Irish instead of relying on a military solution.[24] But imposing direct rule through an English lieutenant sent over from London proved a costly affair, so Henry relied increasingly on the deputyship of the Anglo-Irish FitzGerald earls of Kildare as an intermediary between London and Dublin.[25] While he disliked the semi-autonomous influence of the FitzGeralds in Ireland, a position they achieved through manipulation of the deputyship, under current circumstances he was unable to govern Ireland effectively through any other means.[26] His real preoccupation was Europe and relations with Rome and Ireland did not merit King Henry's attention, or resources. Since 1532 Thomas Cromwell had been directing Tudor policy in Ireland and, as far as he was concerned, in order to push through with political and religious reform the influence of the earl of Kildare needed to be curtailed.[27] Henry did not need much persuasion. By late 1533 the decision had been taken to remove Kildare from the post of lord deputy and, as the next step, recommendations were sent over for reform under an English-born governor, Sir William Skeffington.[28]

Kildare, however, was not oblivious to the situation. He had watched the advancement of many of his critics within the Irish administration and realized that this represented a challenge to his authority. In response, during August 1533 he began to move ordnance from Dublin Castle to his

---

21 *LP Henry VIII*, v, no. 1246. Subsequent communication suggests that the 'Machonell' in question is Alasdair Mac Domhnaill of Dunivaig and the Glens, also referred to as 'Alexander John Canois', or 'Cannochson', i.e., Alasdair son of Eoin Cathánach, having been fostered with the O'Cahans in north Antrim.   22 *LP Henry VIII*, vi, no. 1587.   23 *AU*, iii, pp 585 [AD 1532], 615 [AD 1536]; *AFM*, v, p. 1413 [AD 1532].   24 Ellis, *Tudor Ireland*, pp 108–22.   25 For further explanation of the role of the lord deputy in Ireland, see idem, *Reform and revival. English government in Ireland, 1470–1534* (London, 1986), pp 12–31.   26 Idem, *Tudor Ireland*, p. 121.   27 Idem, 'The Kildare rebellion and the early Henrician reformation', *Historical Journal*, 19:4 (1976), 809; idem, *Tudor Ireland*, p. 113; Mícheál Ó Siochrú, 'Foreign involvement in the revolt of Silken Thomas, 1534–5', *RIA Proc.*, 96 C, 2 (1996), 51.   28 Ellis, *Tudor Ireland*, pp 122–3.

own strongholds. A few months later, however, the earl was recalled to London.[29] He vacillated for some time, arguing that ill-health was responsible for his non-appearance, but after securing the right to appoint his son, Thomas, Lord Offaly, to act as deputy in his absence he left for London in February 1534. Once there, however, the earl was refused permission to leave. Learning of plans for government in Ireland Kildare sent a message to his son informing him of the imminent arrival of Sir William Skeffington as lord deputy. In protest Offaly, in a symbolic gesture, resigned from his post as vice-deputy on 11 June. His renunciation of the post came at a time when Henry was acting against both the pope and the emperor while Cromwell was busy pushing a huge legislative programme for Ireland through parliament. Although not an indication of direct opposition to Tudor authority, that was exactly how Henry viewed Offaly's actions and the English king reacted in a predictable manner. Kildare, in London, was deprived of his office and imprisoned in the Tower (where he died in September 1534), a move which pushed Offaly, in Ireland, into full-scale rebellion.[30]

Offaly's main aim in instigating revolt was preservation of the position of the FitzGerald family in Ireland. Although previous earls of Kildare had rebelled against being deprived of the deputyship, opinion varies as to whether on this occasion King Henry was caught off-guard.[31] If Henry VIII was 'completely unprepared' for such a reaction then it could explain his initial inactivity and degree of uncertainty as to how to respond.[32] However that may be, Henry clearly viewed the matter as simply another minor outburst which would eventually be put down, just like previous rebellions. Henry was too concerned with European manoeuvrings to pay attention to the situation in Ireland, ensuring that it would not be resolved quickly or cleanly. It was only as the revolt dragged on that King Henry began to realize the seriousness of the threat, especially as reports suggested that an army of 10,000 Spaniards was on its way to provide reinforcements for the rebels. Although he had no way of knowing how reliable these reports were (and the army Charles V was amassing was in

---

29 Ó Siochrú, 'Foreign involvement', 50.   30 Ellis, *Tudor Ireland*, pp 124–5.   31 Laurence McCorristine, *The revolt of Silken Thomas, a challenge to Henry VIII* (Dublin, 1987), pp 61–71, puts forward the propensity of the Geraldines to rebel upon the loss of office, only to be subsequently reinstated. Ó Siochrú, 'Foreign involvement', 51, states that the English were 'certainly aware of the possibility of a revolt in Ireland, with foreign complications, long before it actually occurred'. In contrast, Ellis, *Tudor Ireland*, p. 126, argues that Henry VIII was 'completely unprepared' for it.   32 McCorristine, *Silken Thomas*, p. 62, argues that the traditional policy of the English government had given the Geraldine earls a clear message: 'resistance and retaliation was the road to restoration'. Ó Siochrú, 'Foreign involvement', 56, argues that even in October 1534 Offaly still had hopes of regaining the office of lord deputy.

fact to be sent against the Turks and left in May 1535), Henry could not afford to ignore them.[33]

Meanwhile English intelligence kept Henry VIII regularly informed of the extent of Scottish involvement which, although not directly related to the rebellion, continued to aggravate the north. In early 1534 a letter from 'Canossius Magugyr, Lord of Fermanachac [Cú Chonnacht Mag Uidhir of Fir Manach]' to Henry expressed grievance on the part of those who supported him. Mag Uidhir complained that the rebels, including Conn Bacach Ó Néill, Aodh Dubh Ó Domhnaill and Kildare had 'done much damage to O'Ragylly [Fearghal Ó Raighilligh of east Bréifne], ... MacMannam, ... O'Neyll and others who have served the king'.[34] It is unclear how far the O'Neills and the O'Donnells were involved in the rebellion at this early stage but the knowledge of Offaly's participation in fomenting unrest alongside his northern Gaelic allies who opposed English authority would not help his cause in London. Regional unrest in the north of Ireland, combined with the threat of Spanish aid for the revolt, meant that King Henry was forced, finally, to act decisively. Following the earl of Kildare's death in September, his replacement, Skeffington, arrived in Ireland in October 1534 with a force of over 2,000 men.

As Henry's earlier ambivalence gave way to a new determination to crush the revolt external support was vital for Offaly. Thus, he played the religious card, portraying his revolt as a Catholic crusade against heresy in an attempt to capitalize on Henry's break from Rome in the previous year and it won him some notable sympathizers. The appeals from Ireland to Charles V were made in good faith as the Spanish had sent a mission to Ireland as early as 1529 to determine the extent of the opposition to English royal policy and to offer Spanish support, although direct contact between Charles V and the FitzGerald faction was not established until 1534.[35] Charles V, for his part, viewed revolt in Ireland as a welcome distraction to be encouraged, though he stopped short of direct intervention. For example, late in October 1534 Charles V debated whether he should

do anything now ... to stir up the rebellion in Ireland, considering the offers made by divers princes there ... This would greatly hinder the king of England from helping France. Touching Scotland ... it would be well to ... help on a marriage between the Scotch king and the princess of England ...This will entertain the Scotch king, and prevent him from binding himself to France or making a closer treaty with England.[36]

33 Ellis, *Tudor Ireland*, p. 125.   34 *LP Henry VIII*, vii, no. 211. Thomas, Lord Offaly, is referred to as Kildare, although as yet he had not succeeded his father to the title of earl. 35 Ellis, *Tudor Ireland*, p. 125; Ó Siochrú, 'Foreign involvement', 52–5, 57.   36 Cf. *LP Henry VIII*, viii, no. 1336.

As foreign support did not translate into more practical assistance by February 1535 the situation was desperate and Charles V was informed that there was 'no longer any hope for Kildare's cause'.[37] Indeed, the following month Maynooth Castle, the stronghold of the Kildare earls, fell to the English. Yet the Irish had far from given up hope and were taking active steps to galvanize further support from Catholic powers. Offaly, now earl of Kildare, sent Charles Reynalds on a mission to Rome via Scotland and Spain, looking for aid from those who would help plead their case at the papal court, and who would welcome trouble for Henry VIII. His first port of call was Scotland early in 1535. Arriving in Rome in May 1535, he had an audience with Paul III, arguing that Kildare was a defender of the Catholic faith and that Gerald (Gearóid Óg), the ninth earl, had actually been imprisoned in the Tower because he supported Catherine of Aragon.[38]

James V was aware of events in Ireland but until 1535 his involvement had been limited to the north of the country where he had direct links, not only with Alasdair Mac Domhnaill, but also with Maghnus (Manus), son of Aodh Dubh Ó Domhnaill, lord of Tír Chonaill. In 1534 the king had received a communication from Maghnus, and in his reply King James V expressed his pleasure that Ó Domhnaill wanted to continue the relationship between the two families and 'their custom of meeting personally', and he encouraged Ó Domhnaill's plan to come to Scotland himself 'to achieve what his predecessors began and have left unfinished'. The O'Donnell rulers of Tír Chonaill had maintained continued communication with the Scottish court throughout the personal reign of James IV and the long minority of James V.[39] In 1534 the O'Donnells once again sought to renew this alliance with the Stewart monarchy, while also hoping to gain Scottish support for their wars with other native Irish kindreds in the north of Ireland. James's declaration to Maghnus Ó Domhnaill that he would 'refuse no just request' appears to reiterate many of the platitudes his father expressed which offered encouragement but did not commit to further involvement. James V signed off his letter urging Ó Domhnaill 'to come as soon as he possibly can … and he will learn more when they meet'.[40] Such a visit did not materialize, no doubt due to the turn of events in Ireland, but Ó Domhnaill had received a warm response from the Scottish king. Although Maghnus Ó Domhnaill was an ally of the Geraldines, opinion is divided as to when he actively became involved in

37 *LP Henry VIII*, viii, no. 189.   38 Ó Siochrú, 'Foreign involvement', 58.   39 *TA*, i, pp cxxi, 242; iii, p. lxxvii; iv, pp xxxvi, 415–16, 434; v, p. 255; *RMS*, ii, p. 3856; *The Letters of James the Fourth 1503–1513*, ed. R.K. Hannay and R.L. Mackie (Edinburgh, 1953), p. 89; *ER*, xiii, pp lxxx–lxxxi, lxxxiv, 527.   40 *Letters of James V*, p. 275.

the revolt. Maghnus's father, Aodh Dubh, the reigning O Domhnaill, was loyal to Henry VIII, and Maghnus was seeking Scottish aid for his own wars in the north as opposed to any other agenda.

It was an opportune time for Maghnus to seek aid from the Scots as King James's cooperation with the West Highland chiefs gave him a greater degree of leverage within native Irish politics in the north. At this point, James V's policy was unlikely to have had any ulterior motive but was driven solely by his desire to ensure that he, and not the Campbells of Argyll, was controlling the situation in the west while at the same time gaining some influence over Scottish involvement in Ireland. With Argyll safely detained in Edinburgh, the king had removed the main obstacle to his attempts to intervene both in Highland affairs and in Irish-Scottish mercenary activity.[41] Certainly his very positive response to Maghnus Ó Domhnaill suggests James was more than willing to capitalize on this offer. Aided by the posturing of Alasdair Mac Domhnaill of Dunivaig and the Glens in both the West Highlands and the north of Ireland, and combined with a tradition of Ó Domhnaill relations with the Scottish crown, James was well positioned to involve himself in native Irish politics – should he so wish. However, an opportunity, albeit unexpected, to influence politics at a wider level was afforded him in 1535 by the arrival at court of Offaly's servant.

Charles Reynalds received a positive welcome at the Scottish court in 1535. King James did not offer any tangible support in the form of men or munitions but before Reynalds's departure for Rome the king did provide him with 'commendatory letters' on account of his 'friendship with the earl'.[42] The idea of framing the rebellion within a religious context still prevailed and before heading to Rome, Thomas's servant was seeking commendation and support from other Catholic monarchs in their fight against English authority and the Reformation. James's actions at this time are open to interpretation for he was actually in the process of establishing a tentative peace with King Henry.[43] It may have been foolish for James V to give Reynalds, and Kildare, such recommendation. Were Reynalds to be intercepted by the English on his trip to Rome, Henry would have had

---

41 Cameron, *James V*, p. 238, clearly shows Argyll was not 'out of favour' with James during this period as Donaldson had earlier argued (Donaldson, *Scotland*, p. 51) as he regularly witnessed royal charters, was justiciar, hereditary master of the royal household, served on the Borders in 1533 and ratified the Anglo-Scots peace in 1534 at Holyrood.   42 *Letters of James V*, p. 284.
43 Ó Siochrú, 'Foreign involvement', 58–60; Head, 'Henry VIII's Scottish policy', p. 12. As part of a treaty between Henry VIII and Francis I, the French king insisted on an Anglo-Scottish peace which resulted in both kings making 'insincere concessions' to each other. Ó Siochrú interprets James as establishing direct contact with the Geraldine rebels through Reynalds.

firm evidence of James's support for the Irish revolt.[44] But King James, no doubt, was aware that he had the upper hand at this point. Henry's position was severely weakened by European diplomacy; his alliance with Francis I, forged in the previous year, had disintegrated and he could not afford the outbreak of hostilities with his nephew. Indeed, he actively sought to reinforce the tentative Anglo-Scottish peace. But when English ambassadors arrived in Edinburgh to negotiate with James, he gave few concessions. They asked that James forbid Scots to travel to Ireland, a request which he flatly refused, arguing that 'the prohibition would rather provoke them to go thither than otherwise'.[45] Although the English made it clear that a Scottish mercenary presence in Ireland was unwelcome, James V was not prepared to give way to his uncle although, like his uncle, did not want a return to open hostilities. Having refused English pleas to limit Scottish activity in Ireland, King James also refused his uncle's request for a meeting in England in early 1535. Although safe passage and expenses were offered, James stated that 'it was impossible for him to absent himself from his country a single day'.[46]

James was able to deal aggressively with his uncle, safe in the knowledge that in 1535 Henry was not in a strong position. There was growing discontent in the north of England,[47] the Kildare rebellion was a source of major embarrassment, and James's refusal to meet with his uncle increased English suspicions regarding the extent of Scottish involvement in Ireland. Such misgivings were soon to be corroborated by reports from Ireland. In June 1535 Skeffington informed King Henry that 'O'Neill and Manus O'Donnell have done their best to draw the Scots out of the Isles hither, and are trying to make a truce until they come', while Eustace Chapuys, the Spanish ambassador, reported that King James intended 'to send thither 3,000 or 4,000 men'.[48] But these reinforcements would arrive too late for Kildare who submitted to royal authority in August 1535 having been severely weakened by the fall of Maynooth Castle earlier in March. Nonetheless, the native Irish in the north of Ireland would welcome support against Tudor authority as English forces were pressing northwards to subdue the region. By October the lord deputy, the chief justice and others had met with most of the main Irish leaders in the north although it was observed that 'the north will not be quiet except certain

44 I would like to thank Mícheál Ó Siochrú for discussing this point with me.   45 *LP Henry VIII*, viii, no. 429.   46 Ibid.   47 Ó Siochrú, 'Foreign involvement', 58; J.J. Scarisbrick, *Henry VIII* (2nd ed. New Haven and London, 1997), p. 139 stated that 'in 1534 and 1535 Chapuys reported the makings of a rebellion under the leadership of Lord Sandys and Darcy and others, which was ready to enlist the emperor's and Scottish support'.   48 *LP Henry VIII*, viii, nos 429, 885; ix, nos 173, 515. It is unclear whether these forces actually arrived in Ireland.

Scots, who must be expelled'.[49] Thus by the end of 1535 the situation had altered dramatically. Henry VIII had regained control and set about restoring order throughout the country in the wake of a revolt that had challenged his authority for over a year. The failure of the Kildare rebellion, however, did not mean an end to resistance to Tudor government. Support for Kildare continued with the formation of the so-called Geraldine League and the native Irish in the north were to become pivotal players in this movement, albeit after the death of Thomas, the tenth earl.

When Earl Thomas submitted to Lord Leonard Gray, signalling the end of the revolt, he was promised his life would be spared. On arrival in London he was able to spend some weeks hunting or at other pastimes.[50] Once Henry had decided on the course of action to take, Thomas, along with his five uncles who also had been taken to London, was sent to the Tower. And while Henry may have appeared to be prevaricating once again, he deliberately allowed time to pass before taking action against the rebels so as to ensure the pacification of Ireland. However, as the situation dragged on with the FitzGeralds remaining in the Tower the uneasy atmosphere in Ireland intensified. The execution of Kildare and his five uncles in early 1537 was a clear message to both Irish and continental observers that King Henry would not tolerate such resistance to his authority. Harsh action ensured the message was received loud and clear, but it did not eliminate opposition, and in some quarters, heightened it. The movement against Tudor authority in Ireland now centred on Gerald FitzGerald, the only remaining male member of the immediate family of the Kildare Geraldines. Gerald was a half-brother of Thomas, the tenth earl, and in the care of his aunt, Eleanor MacCarthy. The Geraldine League which consisted of former allies of the late earl galvanized themselves in support of Gerald who was adopted as a figurehead. While the native kindreds in the north had been something of a side-issue during the rebellion, Henry now had to pay them much greater attention.

The native Irish had not been dormant during the period of Kildare's imprisonment. Maghnus Ó Domhnaill's communications with King James had continued following the end of the revolt and in August 1536 James V sent further aid to Ireland in the light of 'some new disturbance', although English intelligence felt it was 'not a thing to which much importance need be attached'.[51] But James was supporting Maghnus Ó Domhnaill's position within the local context as well as in wider Irish political affairs

49 *LP Henry VIII*, ix, nos 116, 515. **50** McCorristine, *Silken Thomas*, pp 122–3; Ó Siochrú, 'Foreign involvement', 66. Gray was uncle-in-law of Thomas, earl of Kildare. **51** *LP Henry VIII*, xi, no. 286.

and in July 1536 wrote two letters to the papacy which convey this.[52] The first concerned a disputed appointment to the see of Raphoe. Formerly the office had been held by Cornelius Ó Catháin but he had been deprived in 1534 following his acceptance of the English Reformation. The other possible candidate was Edmund Ó Gallchobhair. James requested that the dean of Derry, Art Ó Gallchobhair, should be appointed to the see and consecrated by the bishop of Derry, Ruaidhri Ó Domhnaill. Edmund and Art Ó Gallchobhair were from different branches of the kindred and as the O'Gallaghers were hereditary inaugurators of the Ó Domhnaill kings, it may be for this reason that Art Ó Gallchobhair was the preferred candidate.[53] Raphoe was a Columban foundation originally under the jurisdiction of Iona and in 1532 Maghnus had written his famous *Life* of Colum Cille, the Ó Domhnaill kings seeing themselves, of course, as descendants of the saint whose cult had spanned the Irish Sea: in effect, Maghnus was attempting to gain Scottish support for the appointment of a preferred candidate, playing perhaps on the symbolism of Colum Cille as representative of such Irish-Scottish unity, and portraying James as defender and protector of the Catholic church in both Scotland and Ireland. Religious connections between Scotland and Ireland had certainly been strong in recent years: payments were made during the reign of James IV to Irish priests and friars on several occasions,[54] while Maghnus was a strong supporter of the Franciscan community in Ireland.[55]

Of more obvious political significance was King James's other letter to Clement III concerning a dispensation required for Maghnus's proposed second marriage. His first wife, a daughter of Conn Ó Néill, had died in 1535.[56] This marriage had seen Maghnus isolated from much of his kindred, including his father and brothers, because of the long history of

52 *Letters of James V*, pp 321–2.   53 M. Carney (ed.), 'Agreement between Ó Domhnaill and Tadhg Ó Conchobhair concerning Sligo Castle (23 June 1539)', *Irish Historical Studies*, 3 (1942/3), 292–4, 293, n. 3. Art Ó Gallchobhair was from the 'Sliocht Aodha' while Edmund was from the 'Sliocht an Easbuig' and there was rivalry between these two branches of the kindred. It is suggested that Edmund Ó Gallchobhair was acting as bishop of Raphoe, despite opposition, until his death in 1543 after which Art was appointed to the see. Until that time Art Ó Gallchobhair, first cousin of Edmund, was dean of Raphoe, and dean of Derry. According to the *AFM*, v, p. 1439 note g, the bishop of Derry and Ó Firghil (Friel), the erenagh of Kilmacrenan were necessary for the inauguration of the Ó Domhnaill king, although the erenagh of Kilmacrenan was 'the ecclesiastic whose presence was indispensable' (see also, Katharine Simms, *From kings to warlords. The changing political structure of Gaelic Ireland in the later middle ages* [Woodbridge, 1987], pp 28, 30).   54 *TA*, ii, pp 159, 268, 367; iii, pp 64, 69, 71–3, 285, 289, 291; iv, p. 187.   55 Brendan Bradshaw, 'Manus "the magnificent": O'Donnell as renaissance prince' in Art Cosgrove and Donal McCartney (eds), *Studies in Irish history presented to R. Dudley Edwards* (Naas, 1979), pp 27–8.   56 Bradshaw, 'Manus "the magnificent"', pp 27–8; Carney, 'Ó Domhnaill and Ó Conchobhair', p. 283.

conflict between the O'Neills and O'Donnells. Nonetheless it proved a wise political move, ensuring good relations between Maghnus and the O'Neills, which paid dividends in terms of their support. But while this first marriage had been advantageous in the locality, his subsequent marriage would catapult Maghnus into prominence in Irish affairs more generally.[57] His choice of marriage partner was Eleanor MacCarthy, aunt of Gerald FitzGerald. Following the execution of his half-brother Thomas, earl of Kildare, and his uncles, Gerald subsequently succeeded to the earldom of Kildare as the eleventh earl. In the context of Maghnus's support for the Geraldine League this was a highly significant alliance but he needed a dispensation to gain legal recognition of the validity of the union. Through successive generations the FitzGerald family had maintained quite close connections with Irish kindreds from the north of the country. Sisters of both Gearóid Mór (Gerald), the eighth earl, and of Gearóid Óg, the ninth earl of Kildare, had married into the main Dungannon branch of the O'Neills, while a brother of Gearóid Óg had been fostered by the O'Donnells. Combined with Maghnus's first marriage to a daughter of Conn Ó Néill, the ties of consanguinity and affinity were too close to be permissible.

James's letter to the papacy on behalf of Maghnus was a clever mix of religious and diplomatic persuasion. He appealed on behalf of Maghnus as 'a distinguished Irish chieftain' whose 'attitude to the apostolic see is excellent', and argued that the marriage would 'bring the almost continuous fighting in the island to an end' and 'render a service to Irish peace'. James combined this with emphasis on the religious issue and mentioned specifically that 'Irish rulers well affected to the Roman Church may unite to preserve the country from the new doctrine'. It was a plea that reflected the attempts of the Irish to portray their revolt against Tudor authority as a religious crusade against the imposition of heretical beliefs by Henry VIII. James's support for Maghnus at the papal court is not evidence that he was actively encouraging continued resistance to English influence, but there can be little doubt that King James was aware of the political significance of Maghnus Ó Domhnaill's second marriage in the current Irish climate and was willing to assist in ways he felt acceptable.

If the Irish had sought external aid during the revolt, they needed it even more in its aftermath, and considering the Scottish king's support of Maghnus during 1536, Ó Domhnaill may well have attempted to capitalize on this. It has been argued that the 'diplomatic activity of the period of

57 Bradshaw, 'Manus "the magnificent"', pp 28–31.

the Geraldine League from 1537 onwards was to reveal how well established was the link between Donegal and the Scottish court'.[58] That may
be the case but evidence suggests that by 1536 King James had become
distracted by other concerns, mainly his marriage. On 1 September of that
year he travelled to France, remaining there for most of the next nine
months. He married Madeleine, daughter of Francis I, on 1 January 1537
and brought his frail bride back to Scotland in May. The fact that he was
absent from Scotland for so long indicates his confidence in the stability of
both Scotland's internal politics and Anglo–Scottish relations, despite his
contemptuous treatment of ambassadors Henry VIII had sent to Scotland
in March 1536: Henry had sent the ambassadors to ask King James to
break with Rome, but the latter's response was to subject them to a
'sermon on obedience to the church'.[59] The marriage of King James and
Madeleine reinforced the Auld Alliance, secured a European ally and
reduced the likelihood of any hostile action by the English against the
Scots in the king's absence. Within this context, James had little to gain
from encouraging further Irish unrest while the execution of Kildare and
his five uncles in 1537 brought home to James the seriousness of the
situation. James used the rest of his sojourn in France to distance himself
from the political situation in Ireland.

Due to his prolonged stay in France in 1536–7 and with continuing
marriage negotiations in 1537–8 following the premature death of
Madeleine (which resulted in James finding a second French bride, Mary
of Guise, whom he married in 1538), James V's interest in Ireland slowly
began to diminish. At no point, however, did he sever connections with
Maghnus Ó Domhnaill who, in July 1537, was inaugurated as ruler of Tír
Chonaill and the two men remained in communication.[60] Ó Domhnaill
wrote to the Scottish king in 1537 and spoke of his 'great goodwill towards
James and his realm'.[61] But James's reply in November of the same year
conveys a distinct change in attitude. The Scottish king encouraged Ó
Domhnaill and conveyed his hope that the Irish chief would 'keep the
other Irish lords so disposed', a clear reference to the fact that stability and
peace in Ireland was now on King James's agenda. But Ó Domhnaill could
no longer rely on the Scots king for intervention in local affairs as James
reverted to the policy of his father of offering a sympathetic ear, but little
of practical value. In response to Ó Domhnaill's 'request for engines and
guns and skilled men for the recovery of certain castles' (including
Carrickfergus, the most strategic fortress on the northeast coast of

---

58 Ibid., p. 22.   59 Cf. Cameron, *James V*, p. 287.   60 *AFM*, v, p. 1439.   61 *Letters of James V*,
p. 339.

Ireland), James V replied that it was 'rather late in the year; even if they were available, wintry weather would be an obstacle'. As something of a sweetener, James informed Ó Domhnaill that he was in the process of having more guns made and when they were ready the king would 'not fail to consider his advantage and honour'.

External support, therefore, was lacking at a crucial juncture and Maghnus's attempts to build up a strong connection with the Scottish court were not bearing fruit, or so it appeared. His custody of Gerald FitzGerald placed the Tír Chonaill ruler in a crucial bargaining position with the English administration, but without some foreign assistance there was little the Geraldine League could do to advance resistance to the Henrician reformation which was being pushed through in Ireland. In 1537–8 King James's attention was focused on another French marriage and despite worsening Anglo-Scottish relations the Scottish king did not want a major diplomatic incident with his uncle. But even if James's interest in Irish affairs was waning he continued to encourage from a safe distance. In 1538 he wrote a letter to Clement VII's successor, Paul III, again regarding the appointment to the see of Raphoe.[62] He reiterated his choice of Art Ó Gallchobhair, dean of Derry, as bishop and informed Paul III that Clement VII had submitted to the bishop of Derry the claims of the rivals Edmund Ó Gallchobhair and Cornelius Ó Catháin, and that the bishop had found neither claim valid. While James repeated the view that settlement of this issue would help the position of the church in Ireland, he made little of the imposition of King Henry's Reformation.

James V's support of Ó Gallchobhair's claims to the see of Raphoe no doubt reinforced Maghnus's regional status, but the wider situation was of concern to quite a few individuals. The Geraldine League stepped up their campaign to enlist the support of external parties. The marriage of Maghnus and Eleanor in 1538 also brought Tadhg, son of Cathal Óg Ó Conchobhair (of Sligo), amongst others, into the fold thus forming an alliance of principal lords of the north of Ireland.[63] In 1538 Ruaidhri Ó Domhnaill, bishop of Derry, arrived in Rome with letters from Gerald FitzGerald expressing Irish opposition to Henry VIII's rule. Again the religious crusade was emphasized asserting the 'dread that the Antichrist of England will come … to put such order in the churches of Ireland as he has done in England'. The Irish asked for 'certain ships with galleys and pinnaces of Biscay, with some men of Biscay, artillery and powder, and 30,000 men of war' in return for '100,000 ducats of gold out of the land'

---

62 Ibid., p. 348. 63 Carney, 'Ó Domhnaill and Ó Conchobhair', 284–5.

and numerous 'Moors of England'. The response was favourable. The
pope said he would ask 'all Christian princes' to aid the 'good Christian
people of Ireland' and would specifically appeal to both the French king
and the Scottish king, 'as their kingdoms are near Ireland', to assist the
Irish 'against the tyrant of England'.[64] But King James's support had
already been requested as the bishop had travelled to Rome via Scotland.
His efforts were later reinforced by messengers sent from Ó Domhnaill, Ó
Néill and FitzGerald 'to have aide from them in this matter'.[65] One of
these messengers, Art Ó Gallchobhair, dean of Derry, was captured by the
English on his way to Scotland and he confessed that Ó Domhnaill already
had men in Scotland soliciting aid from the Scots. Upon his release,
Ó Domhnaill sent Ó Gallchobhair to 'procure the Scottes of the Iles to
come … against the said rebellion'.

It would appear that these renewed requests from Ireland and the
papacy had the desired response in terms of support from Scotland,
although the extent to which this was crown-sanctioned is questionable. In
May 1539 Cromwell was informed that Ó Domhnaill and Ó Néill relied
heavily on 'the Scots of the Out Isles, and those of Ireland, of whom Alex
Karragh, alias Macdonnell, is chief'.[66] It was asserted that there were
about 2,000 Scots in the north under the leadership of 'Alexander
Carragh, captayne of the Scottes of this lande' and that Mac Domhnaill's
'knowledge and power' in Ireland worked towards James's 'purpoos'.[67]
The activity of Scots in the north is not doubted, but it is unclear what
James's purpose was. It has been argued that King James continued to
send military assistance to the Geraldine League and was prepared to
come to Ireland until the League was defeated at Bellahoe in 1539.[68]
Thomas Lynche, a merchant of Galway who had been in Tír Chonaill

---

64 *LP Henry VIII*, xiii, pt i, nos 77; 272.   65 *SP Henry VIII*, iii, pp 136–42, 243, 253; Carney,
'Ó Domhnaill and Ó Conchobhair', 285.   66 *LP Henry VIII*, xiv, part i, nos 1027, 1245.
Kenneth Nicholls, 'Notes on the genealogy of Clann Eoin Mhóir', *WHN & Q*, series 2, 2/8
(1991), 18 states: 'Alexander Carrach, son of Sir John of Dunniveg … succeeded his nephew
and namesake by "tanistry" on the latter's death in 1536 … "Alexander Karrogh, otherwise
called MacDonell" – a style which seems to indicate that he was recognized as overall head of
Clan Donald – figures prominently in the records of the Dublin administration during 1538 and
1539, being referred to as the "great captain" or "head captain" of the Scots in Ireland'. *AU* (iii,
p. 590) refers to Alasdair Carrach, son of Mac Domnaill, although this is unlikely to refer to any
formal status (I would like to thank Kenneth Nicholls for drawing my attention to this
reference). As Wilson McLeod, '*Rí Innsi Gall, Rí Fionnghall, Ceannas nan Gàidheal*: sovereignty
and rhetoric in the late medieval Hebrides', *CMCS*, 43 (2002), 25–48, has argued, the use of
titles and labels in Irish written sources follows no hard-and-fast rules. Although *Mac Domhnaill*
is used in a Gaelic source to indicate the head of *Clann Domhnaill*, it should not be taken as such
on all occasions.   67 *SP Henry VIII*, iii, pp 136, 270.   68 Morgan, 'British policies', p. 73.

with 'a ship of wine', informed the English that 'Odownell and Ownele wold have three thousande Skottes, and have sent for to seke to motche; but ... the King of Skottes wilnat that any of his men goo out of the countrey, in feare of the guerr of Ingland'.[69] Despite this suggestion that James V was unwilling to offer aid at this time, the prevailing view of the English was that in May 1540 King James was preparing to go to Ireland.

English intelligence reports were correct in asserting that preparations were underway for an expedition in 1540.[70] But despite speculation concerning James's intended destination, assumed to be either Ireland or France, in fact, preparations were being made for an expedition to the Isles following the outbreak of rebellion under Domhnall Gorm Mac Domhnaill the previous year. English sources, however, convey the belief that James intended travelling to Ireland, a view grounded in the knowledge of the offer made to James V of the kingship of Ireland in 1540.[71] The confession of 'Connor More Ochonnour, servaunt and messenger to yong Geralde, son of the late Erle of Kildare', taken in April 1539, asserted that 'the Bishop Odonell and the Abbot Osheill been goon into Scotlande abowte Mydlent last past, in message from Oneile and Odonell, to have aide from thens in this matter'. Later reports stated that the eight Irish gentlemen who visited James 'at the Courte in Lente last' brought the offer of the kingship of Ireland from 'all the greate men in Ierlande'. But such an offer was a last desperate attempt by the Geraldine League to gain King James's support and intervention in Ireland. The League had the view that Henry had 'no tight or title' to Ireland but by 'usurpacion' but needed external support to help overthrow him.[72] They turned to James who, earlier in the 1530s, had shown considerable interest in affairs in Ireland and although a much larger carrot was offered to secure his involvement, in 1540 it was too late.

James's main alliance with the Irish was through Maghnus Ó Domhnaill who in 1538 married Eleanor MacCarthy, aunt of Gerald FitzGerald. Maghnus's guardianship of the young FitzGerald heir had enhanced his position in the north temporarily, but regardless of the political advantage Ó Domhnaill gained via his marriage into the FitzGerald family, the Irish lord could read the writing on the wall. There was a high level of resentment on the part of the native Irish towards the programme of Anglicization and religious reform instigated by Cromwell

---

69 *SP Henry VIII*, iii, p. 141, note 1.   70 *LP Henry VIII*, xv, no. 697; *SP Henry VIII*, v, p. 372.
71 *SP Henry VIII*, v, pp 178–81, *LP Henry VIII*, xv, no. 697; Carney, 'Ó Domhnaill and Ó Conchobhair', 285.   72 *SP Henry VIII*, iii, pp 175–8.

which, combined with Henry VIII's reaction to the Kildare rebellion, meant that Ireland was being treated with renewed drive. Maghnus had begun to comprehend the reality of the situation. In 1537 Aodh Dubh Ó Domhnaill, lord of Tír Chonaill, died and despite Maghnus's prominence, it would appear that a brief succession dispute broke out between him and his brother Aodh Buidhe, before Maghnus's eventual inauguration as Ó Domhnaill in July or August 1537.[73] On a national level resistance to Tudor authority had not produced any lasting results and, aware that the Geraldine League could not succeed without external assistance, Maghnus acted decisively. In May 1540 Maghnus sent Gerald to the continent for his own safety, conveniently ridding himself of the focus of opposition to the Tudor regime.[74] The next month Maghnus submitted to Henry promising that henceforth he would 'lyve in due and faythfull obedyens as his true and most humblye subjecte'.[75] Although he secured the welfare of the young Gerald his surrender to Henry effectively meant – highlighting his political awareness and knack for self-preservation – his abandonment of the League (as a consequence of which his wife, Eleanor MacCarthy, left him). The Irish themselves were unable to resist Henry and with the change in the international situation no foreign aid would be forthcoming. Ó Domhnaill was able to forecast the way the political winds were blowing and recognized that his political future would be secured through an outward, superficial submission to the Tudor state rather than holding on to the tenuous hope of James's intervention.

Unlike Maghnus, many of the other key figures in the Geraldine League continued to hold out hope that they could throw off King Henry's oppressive regime. Following Maghnus's renunciation of the League, Conn Ó Néill took over communications with King James. His response to Ó Néill in June 1540, if it refers to the offer of kingship, suggests that James V was open to the idea. James wrote of Ó Néill's 'remarkable goodwill, now clearer than ever', continuing that he would 'reciprocate it in a practical manner when a justifiable occasion arises'. But if James was intrigued and interested by such a move, the reality of the European situation ensured that he was reluctant at this time to take any decisive action. He wrote that 'the points raised regarding Henry VIII are difficult and weighty' and that he had 'not made up his mind upon them, as he and Henry have been for some years under a treaty which still

73 *AFM*, v, p. 1437.   74 *SP Henry VIII*, iii, pp 211–13; Bradshaw, 'Manus "the magnificent"', pp 28, 32–3.   75 *SP Henry VIII*, iii, pp 217, 302–3, 311–17 reveal that Kildare was on his way to St Malo; *LP Henry VIII*, xi, nos 704–799.

stands'. But he assured O Néill that when the opportunity presented itself, the Irish would 'not be disappointed'.[76] No such opportunity arose.

Ó Domhnaill's submission to English royal authority had quite possibly come about because of the waning interest of King James in Irish affairs. For a brief period in 1534–6 Scottish crown support for the Irish had appeared promising, but James's marriages had been a major distraction while the execution of the leading Kildare FitzGeralds had caused the king to distance himself from the situation. Although the prospect of gaining the kingship of Ireland would have been attractive for a monarch aggressively asserting his imperial status, by the turn of the 1540s neither the domestic nor the European situation encouraged this move. James V was concentrating on quelling unrest in the Western Isles following the rebellion of 1539 while trying to deflect English requests for a meeting. King Henry was still attempting to persuade James to follow his lead and instigate religious reform, thus shifting the balance in Europe. The European situation was changing as France and Spain moved closer towards war, thereby destroying the alliance against England that had earlier existed. Henry VIII's alliance with Spain ensured that Anglo-Scottish relations would have wider ramifications. Therefore, up until 1536 King James was able to use Ireland as a means by which he could aggravate his uncle at a time when Henry was facing increased pressure from the European powers following his break with Rome. Three years later in 1539 the situation had changed considerably and James had to balance internal unrest with a fluctuating European situation and the awareness that political affairs in Ireland were rapidly developing. He still maintained a confident and aggressive policy towards England and his uncle, failing to meet King Henry at York in 1541.[77] But James V's window of opportunity for intervention in Ireland, if he wanted to exploit it, was not open for long. By 1541, when the Irish parliament passed an act to make Henry king of Ireland, it was firmly closed.[78]

76 *Letters of James V*, p. 400.　77 Head, 'Henry VIII's Scottish policy', p. 16 note 4.　78 The author would like to acknowledge Steve Boardman, Charles McKean, Roger Mason and Alex Woolf for discussions regarding different aspects of this paper, and the Strathmartine Trust.

Having the right kit: West Highlanders fighting in Ireland

DAVID H. CALDWELL

My intention in this essay is to comment on some of the equipment used by the West Highlanders who went to fight in Ireland from the twelfth to the seventeenth century, and assess its effectiveness. The main focus of my attention is the evidence from Scottish sources. I have used the term West Highland to include all the Hebrides and mainland Argyll. Much of this area formed the lordship of the Isles, and coincides with the distribution of a vigorous tradition of medieval sculpture – 'West Highland sculpture' – a crucial source of images for many of the items of equipment discussed.

SHIPS

The most important items were the ships, often called galleys and birlings (Gaelic *birlinn*), which provided transport. They have recently been the subject of other much fuller studies, especially by Clark, MacAulay and Rixson.[1] These show that there is a paucity of quality information on them. No significant fragments survive and contemporary documentation is of limited value in describing their characteristics or manufacture. The main sources for them are representations on seals and West Highland crosses and grave-slabs.

These indicate that they were clinker-built, open-hulled craft, with high prows and sterns. They were propelled by the muscle-power of rowers or else by the wind catching a rectangular sail hung from a central mast. An early representation of such a ship can be seen on the seal of Aonghus Mór Mac Domhnaill of Islay (fig. 1) which probably dates to the late thirteenth century.[2] It may be the earliest representation of such a ship with a stern rudder. Images of similar ships appear on West Highland sculpture of the fourteenth to the sixteenth century, prompting the

---

1 Wallace Clark, *The Lord of the Isles voyage* (Naas, 1993); John MacAulay, *Birlinn longships of the Hebrides* (Cambridge, 1996); and Denis Rixson, *The West Highland galley* (Edinburgh, 1998).
2 J.H. Stevenson and Margaret Wood, *Scottish heraldic seals* (Glasgow, 1940), iii, p. 483.

1 Seal of Aonghus Mór of Islay, late 13th century (British Library).

assumption that the basic form of the vessels changed little over a long period of time.

It seems clear that they are the direct descendants of Viking longships and that there was a continuous tradition of construction and use from the settlement of Scandinavians in Britain and Ireland in the ninth century. A report to the Scottish Privy Council, dated 1615,[3] indicates that by then these vessels were being identified as a West Highland phenomenon, but this had not always been the case. Apart, of course, from their use by the Irish, there is reason to think that craft of this type had been in service in the Firth of Clyde as well, at least at an earlier date. One appears before the gate of the castle on the fifteenth-century seal of the burgh of Rothesay (fig. 2). One of the finest representations of one (fig. 3) occurs on the fifteenth-century seal of the burgh of Renfrew.[4] It should be noted, however, that while this image is detailed enough to show oar-ports, none are present. Perhaps it was not intended to be rowed.

3 *Register of the privy council of Scotland preserved in the Scottish Record Office* [1545–1691], edited by J.H. Burton and others, 16 vols (Edinburgh, 1877–1970), 3rd ser., vol. x., *1613–16*, pp 347–8. 4 Stevenson and Wood, *Seals*, i, pp 78–9.

2 Cast of seal of the burgh of Rothesay, 15th century
(National Museums of Scotland).

Rixson has suggested that there might have been a change in the design
of West Highland galleys in the later sixteenth century to ships more in a
Mediterranean tradition of galley design, but in my opinion his evidence
is slight and not convincing. It depends on a handful of heraldic
representations of ships on stone carvings, seals and a map of Ulster of
the late sixteenth or beginning of the seventeenth century, probably by a
cartographer with little real local knowledge.[5] This apart, it appears that
these ships remained in use with relatively little modification of their basic
design for a period of several hundred years. It is therefore not unreasonable to assume that they were good at their job. It is possible to suggest at
least some of their key qualities.

They could be made from local resources, especially of wood. Although
our knowledge of the tree cover in Argyll and the Western Isles in our
period is not as complete as we would like, there is good reason to think
that there were suitable forest resources in Argyll and some of the islands.[6]
It might reasonably be guessed that the keels and frames were of oak, and

5 Rixson, *Galley*, pp 100–2.   6 Ibid., pp 104–9.

3 Cast of seal of the burgh of Renfrew, 15th century
(National Museums of Scotland).

the masts of pine, but the planking might either have been of oak or pine. While making them was a skilled job, there was no need for elaborate equipment – certainly not launch-slips and dry-docks.

The fact that they could be rowed as well as sailed gave them considerable versatility, and it is probable that an experienced crew could often row themselves away from any threat posed by larger, more cumbersome craft. This appears to have been the view, based on experience, of the English naval commander, Captain George Thornton, charged with countering the threat to English interests in Ireland posed by West Highland galleys in the late sixteenth century.[7]

With their shallow draft they were ideal for beaching, being manoeuvred in amongst rocks, and being taken up rivers. Their size and lightness relative to crew numbers meant that they could easily be lifted out of the water, and, indeed, transported overland from one stretch of water to another. In 1263 it was the Hebridean contingent of King Hákon's invasion fleet which carried their ships, perhaps because theirs were

7 *CSPI, 1592–6*, p. 412.

smaller than the Norwegians', across the 1½-mile *Tairbeart* from Loch Long to Loch Lomond. In 1611 an order was given out for all the boats and birlings on Loch Lomond to be transported to Loch Katrine, as part of a campaign to capture an island stronghold of the MacGregors.[8] This would probably have involved two portages, going via Loch Arklet.

Surely the key characteristic of these vessels is that they could carry relatively large numbers of men, and also booty on the return voyages. The 1615 report to the Scottish Privy Council, previously mentioned, lists the number of galleys and birlings in the Western Isles, explaining that galleys have between 18 and 24 oars and birlings between 12 and 18, and that three men should be reckoned to each oar. Several other 'boats' of eight oars are also mentioned.[9] These figures suggest crews ranging from 72 to 24 men.

Few early accounts of expeditions provide both the number of ships and men. Firstly there is the raid by Domhnall Ballach Mac Domhnaill of Dunyvaig in the mid-fifteenth century (1452?) on the islands in the Firth of Clyde and the coast of Renfrewshire, allegedly with a force of 5,000 or 6,000 men in 100 galleys. This would compute at 50 or more men per ship. Then there is the expedition of Domhnall Dubh, the heir of the lordship of the Isles, to Ireland in 1545 with 4,000 men in 180 galleys, giving an average of about 22 men to each boat. In 1569 a Bristol merchant spotted 32 galleys and other boats marshalled in the Sound of Islay with 4,000 men for an invasion of Ireland by Somhairle Buidhe Mac Domhnaill, suggesting an average of 125 per boat. Finally, there are the reports of a landing in 1589 at Erris on the west coast of Ireland of a force of up to 600 men (Macneils of Barra?) in seven galleys. This would work out at 85 or 86 per boat.[10]

It would be foolish to place too much reliance on the accuracy of these figures, but with the exception of Domhnall Dubh's fleet, they at the least convey the impression that these ships were effective troop carriers. In any case, Domhnall Dubh may have been looking to recruit extra men in Ireland.

There is also the matter of how much cargo they could carry, specifically the booty which was one of the main attractions for those who went to fight in Ireland. Booty very often came in the form of cattle on the hoof, and a relatively early insight into this comes from a mid-thirteenth-century praise poem to Aonghus Mór Mac Domhnaill of Islay which

8 Anderson, *Early sources*, ii, p. 625; *Reg. privy council Scot., 1610–13*, p. 126.   9 *Reg. privy council Scot., 1613–16*, pp 347–8.   10 W.A. Craigie (ed.), *The Asloan manuscript* (Scot. Text Soc., Edinburgh, 1923), i, pp 221–2; *SP Henry VIII*, iii, p. 529; *CSPI, 1569–73*, p. 416; ibid., *1588–92*, pp 232, 242, 251.

recounts how the graceful long ships (*longbhárca*) of Islay raided Ireland and lifted many cattle.[11] Are we to take from this and other accounts of cattle-lifting that the beasts were transported back to Scotland alive? That there was a business in medieval times in shipping live beasts from some of the Western Isles to the Scottish mainland cannot be doubted, like the ninety-six Islay cows and their calves at Ross in Knapdale in 1506, representing some of the rents extracted by the crown.[12] These, of course, were not necessarily transported in the galleys and birlings under consideration.

On the other hand, it was reported that a Scottish force took only the hides and tallow of over 1,000 cattle gathered as booty when they sailed off from Erris in Mayo in 1589.[13] Perhaps this was the norm, rather than the shipping of live booty. Whatever the case, mercenaries from the West Highlands did not expect to return home empty-handed and their appetite was presumably for as much as they could get.

The reconstruction of a birling, the *Aileach*, in 1991 gives an opportunity for an assessment to be made of our knowledge of such craft and an evaluation of documentary accounts of their exploits. She was built by an Irish boat-builder in Moville, Co. Donegal, using traditional skills and ideas and a plan based on representations of birlings in West Highland sculpture. She thus has a high, near vertical, stem and stern-post. She has a length of 40 feet (12.19m) and 16 oars (that is, eight a side). On the basis of the Privy Council report of 1615 she should have had a crew of at least 48, three pulling on each oar.[14]

I do not feel competent to remark on Clark's generally favourable comments on the *Aileach*'s qualities as a boat well-suited for the seas she sailed. What is clear, however, is that she could hardly have ventured to sea with 48 men, never mind equipment and booty on top of that. Her complement was only about 10 or 11, and she normally had only one person pulling on each oar, sometimes two, and even so it was found to be easier to row with fewer than eight oars a side, the thwarts (benches for the rowers) being too close together for comfort.

Are we to conclude from this that documentary sources exaggerate the capacity of such vessels, and therefore, the size and effectiveness of raiding parties in Ireland, or are we to dismiss the *Aileach* experiment as misleading? I am more inclined to believe the latter. The builders of the

11 Osborn Bergin, 'An address to Aonghus of Islay', in *Scottish Gaelic Studies*, 4 (1934–5), 57–69, at p. 65; reprinted in idem, *Irish bardic poetry*, ed. David Greene and Fergus Kelly (Dublin, 1970), pp 169–74, trs. at pp 291–4.   12 *Rotuli scaccarii regum Scotorum. The exchequer rolls of Scotland* [1264–1600], ed. John Stuart and George Burnett et al., 22 vols (Edinburgh, 1878–1908), xii, p. 709.   13 *CSPI, 1588–92*, pp 232, 242.   14 Clark, *Lord of the Isles voyage*, passim.

4 Detail of a galley on the cross-shaft of Raghnall of Islay,
late 14th century (National Museums of Scotland).

Aileach took the representations of ships on West Highland sculpture as
accurate representations of contemporary vessels but it is not improbable
that the carvers deliberately gave their ships more upright stems and
sterns than they had in reality, in order to give them more presence and
make them a good fit to the narrow upright panels available for their
representation on grave-slabs and cross-shafts (fig. 4, 7).

In a few cases, the ships on West Highland sculpture are not so
obviously constrained by the size and shape of the stone on which they are
carved and have a larger, longer look, more akin to their Viking ancestors.
Such is the representation of a ship on a fourteenth- or fifteenth-century

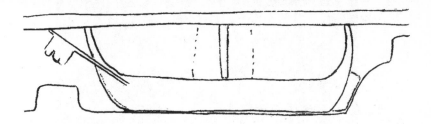

5 Detail of a ship on a 14th- or 15th-century grave-slab in Iona Abbey Museum.

slab in the Abbey Museum on Iona (fig. 5).[15] There is a graffito of a ship with a similarly proportioned hull in the entranceway to Dunluce Castle on the coast of Antrim, a stronghold of Clann Domhnaill of Islay.

It is also possible that there has been a basic misunderstanding of the size of birlings. The *Aileach* is not much more than half the length (12.9m against 23.33m) of the ninth-century Viking ship from Gokstad in Norway. The Gokstad ship has twice the number of oars as the *Aileach*, and early sources suggest that Viking ships of the size of the Gokstad ship would have had at least three men to each oar.[16] But it surely does not follow that a ship half the size of the Gokstad could have the same number of men per oar? Perhaps the *Aileach* should have been much bigger. Further research on galleys and birlings is clearly necessary.

PROTECTIVE CLOTHING

Another key item of equipment for West Highland mercenaries was a padded coat for protection in warfare (figs. 6, 7), and it is this we wish to concentrate on here rather than attempt a balanced overview of all their armour. There are many representations of these padded coats in West Highland sculpture.[17] They appear to be quilted vertically in long narrow rolls, extending to the knees, and drawn in at the waist. They have long sleeves, often shown with thin straps around the arm just above and below the elbow. These are interpreted as arm-bands designed to allow greater flexibility by reducing the drag on the arms. One effigy at Saddell abbey in Kintyre has decorated reinforcing elbow pieces (fig. 8), possibly of cuir-

15 RCAHMS, *Argyll. Volume 4. Iona* (Edinburgh, 1982), p. 221, no. 127.   16 A.W. Brøgger and Haakon Shetelig, *The Viking ships: their ancestry and evolution* (Oslo, 1953), pp 112, 227. 17 K.A. Steer and J.W.M. Bannerman, *Late medieval monumental sculpture in the West Highlands* (Edinburgh, 1977), pls 8A, 8C, 22A, 22B, 24C, 25C, 30A.

6

7

6 (*far left*) Effigy of Giolla
Bhrighde MacFhionghein (Gilbride
MacKinnon), Iona, probably dating
to the second quarter of the 14th
century (Crown copyright: Royal
Commission on the Ancient and
Historical Monuments of Scotland).

7 (*left*) Effigy of Domhnall Mac
Giolla Easpaig (Donald
MacGillespie), Finlaggan, Islay,
mid 16th century (National
Museums of Scotland).

8 Detail of warrior effigy at Saddell
Abbey, Kintyre, with reinforcing
elbow pieces, 14th or 15th century.

bouilli.[18] These garments were presumably fastened up the front, though
only on one effigy, at Oronsay priory, can little buttons be seen down the
front of the garment.[19] Some representations do seem to show an opening
or overlap at the thighs (fig. 9). On the other hand, a slit here in the lower
part of the garment might have been designed solely for allowing the
wearer to sit astride a horse. Some West Highland effigies of warriors
show straps for spurs around the ankles (fig. 7).

They were worn with a collar of mail (or perhaps a coif or mail-hood),
over the top, and also a type of metal helmet known as a bascinet. Gauntlets
are represented on some effigies but it is difficult to detect the presence of
any leg defences. Good examples of these outfits include the effigy of Giolla
Bhrighde MacFhiongheín (MacKinnon) in the Abbey Museum on Iona
which probably dates to the late fourteenth century (fig. 6), and the grave-
slab of Domhnall Mac Giolla Easpaig (Donald MacGillespie) at Finlaggan
on Islay dating to the mid-sixteenth century (fig. 7).[20]

In their survey of West Highland sculpture, Steer and Bannerman
identified these garments as aketons. The term aketon was used in medieval
sources to describe a quilted defensive coat, normally worn under armour.[21]

18 Ibid., no. 93. 19 Ibid., fig. 6. 20 Ibid., pls 8A, 30A. 21 Claude Blair, *European armour
circa 1066 to circa 1700* (London, 1958), p. 33.

Mentions of aketons so worn can be found in Scottish sources, like the aketon paid for in 1303 by the English administration as part of the armour of the earl of Ross. It is described as having been made out of a gambeson and the rest of the equipment bought for him includes another gambeson and a mail coat.[22] A gambeson was a quilted garment, and the implication of this account is that an old one was being altered to form an aketon for wear under the earl's mail coat, while a new one had to be acquired to act as a surcoat for wear over the mail. According to Wyntoun's chronicle of about 1400, William Spence was shot dead at the siege of Dunbar Castle in 1338 by an arrow that pierced his 'blazone' (shield), habergeon and actoun of three ply (of three layers of textile?), presumably in that order.[23]

It is clear, however, that the garments on the West Highland sculpture are not under-garments, and Scottish documentation indicates that aketons (Scots *actoun*) were often, if not normally, regarded as the main or only defensive covering for the body. This can be seen from an act of King Robert I

9 Effigy of a warrior at Kilmartin Parish Church, Argyll, 14th or 15th century (Crown copyright: Royal Commission on the Ancient and Historical Monuments of Scotland).

22 *CDS*, ii, no. 1416.   **23** F.J. Amours (ed.), *The Original Chronicle of Andrew of Wyntoun* (Scot. Text Soc., Edinburgh, 1908), vi, p. 83.

of 1318, ordering every man worth £10 in goods to have armour consisting of an actoun – or else an habergeon (a coat of mail) – and bascinet.[24] It might reasonably be supposed that this was the kit that had served the Scottish foot well in their wars against the English and in Ireland, and which was to be generally employed by them for some time afterwards. How long they remained the armour generally worn by the zemen (yeomen) as distinct from the nobles is obscured by lack of documentation and possible changes in the naming of these garments. It is probable that the doublets of fence that were required equipment for zemen according to an act of the Scots parliament of 1429/30 were essentially the same as actouns. So too the jacks with long sleeves ordered in 1456 and the jacks mentioned in an act of 1481, knee-length if worn without leg-harness, or else long enough to overlap the leg-harness.[25]

There are, however, much later examples of the use of the word actoun in a specifically Highland context. There is in an act of 1574 for the holding of wappenshaws (musters) which recognizes that the armour used by Highlanders is habergeons or actouns.[26] A report on the Hebrides, dating to the period 1577–1595, says that 6,000 fighting men could be raised there, 2,000 of whom should be clad with actouns and habergeons.[27] The implication of these texts is surely that, by the late sixteenth century, if not much earlier, actouns were different from the jacks and brigantines (defensive jackets reinforced with metal plates, in the latter, riveted together) regarded as normal wear for Lowland warriors. Jacks and brigantines had changed and developed with the times whereas the garments identified as actouns were essentially the same as those favoured by Robert Bruce and carved on West Highland effigies.

There is little to be gleaned from other Scottish documentary sources on the manufacture or appearance of these actouns. Hector Boece explained that the Scots (the context is actually the first settlers who came from Ireland) were clad in *loriciis, alii ferreis, alii pelliceis, vulgo nactones dicunt* – translated in the Mar Lodge MS from the 1530s as 'habergeons, sum of irne, sum of leddir, commonly callit nactouns'.[28] In his study of old Highland dress McClintock considered that it was probably actouns that John Major had in mind when he wrote in his history published in 1521 of the common people amongst the 'wild Scots' (Highlanders) going

24 *The acts of the parliaments of Scotland*, ed. Thomas Thomson and Cosmo Innes, 12 vols (Edinburgh, 1814–75), i, p. 113. 25 Ibid., ii, pp 18, 45, 132. 26 Ibid., iii, p. 91. 27 W.F. Skene, *Celtic Scotland: a history of ancient Alban*, 3 vols (Edinburgh, 1876–80), iii, p. 439. 28 Hector Boece, *Scotorum historiae a prima gentis origine* (Paris, 1527), fol. V, lines 48–9; George Watson (ed.), *The Mar Lodge translation of the History of Scotland by Hector Boece* (Scot. Text Soc., Edinburgh, 1946), i, p. 50.

into battle *in panno lineo multipliciter intersuto et coerato aut picato
cum cervina pellis coopertura.*[29] The
meaning of multipliciter intersuto
is not altogether clear, but it
might be translated as 'quilted',
and so 'in a quilted linen garment
well daubed with wax or with
pitch, with a covering of deerskin'. This surely should be
understood to mean that the
garment would appear to be of
quilted deerskin, the deerskin
being an alternative to the leather
of Boece's *History*.

So either actouns or habergeons were worn by Highlanders
as late as the sixteenth century,
and often, it has been supposed,
habergeons over the top of the
particular type of actouns under
discussion. There are, however,
no specific references to mail
habergeons being worn over
actouns in early documents about
Highlanders, and only a few
illustrations that may show this.
In Scotland itself there is the
effigy in the church at Rodel in
Harris (fig. 10), thought to be of
William Mac Leòid (MacLeod),
prepared in 1539.[30] Although
badly weathered, the outer, knee-
length garment with three-
quarter-length sleeves can be

10 Effigy of William Mac Leòid
(MacLeod), St Clement's Church, Rodel,
Harris, 1539 (Crown copyright: Royal
Commission on the Ancient and Historical
Monuments of Scotland).

29 H.F. McClintock, *Old Irish and Highland dress* (Dundalk, 1950), pp 3–4. 30 Steer and
Bannerman, *Sculpture*, pl. 34B.

11 Detail of a warrior with an axe from a hunting scene on the tomb of Alexander Mac Leòid (MacLeod), St Clement's Church, Rodel, Harris, 1528 (Crown copyright: Royal Commission on the Ancient and Historical Monuments of Scotland).

interpreted as a mail habergeon, but the undergarment provides little clue as to its nature.

On another MacLeod tomb at Rodel, that of Alexander Mac Leòid of Dunvegan prepared in 1528, one of the figures in a hunting scene carved in bas-relief (fig. 11) clearly wears a mail habergeon with two longer garments beneath, at least one with long sleeves (but why all this, a bascinet, mail collar, sword and axe – for hunting?).[31] One of these garments might be a typical West Highland actoun with narrow vertical quilting. The other, between it and the habergeon, may be a textile coat to

31 Ibid., pl. 32B.

12 Drawing of Irish soldiers and poor people, by Albrecht Dürer, 1521.
(Bildarchiv Preußischer Kulturbesitz, Berlin).

cushion the habergeon. A mail habergeon must always have been worn over a thick layer of clothing to prevent the mail links digging into the flesh. Is this Rodel carving indicating that a stiff quilted actoun covered in leather or deerskin was unsuitable as a support for mail?

The evidence for the armour worn in Ireland, much of it conveniently gathered together by Harbison, demonstrates that aketons (Irish *cotún*) were worn by native Irish warriors from the fourteenth century through to the sixteenth century.[32] Many of these were evidently garments worn under other armour, particularly habergeons (Irish *lúireach*), and might therefore be substantially different from the actouns worn by West Highlanders. One of the key pieces of evidence here is a drawing of Irish soldiers (possibly galloglass) and poor people dated 1521 by the German artist Albrecht Dürer (fig. 12). One of the warriors is clad in a long coat with vertical quilting, evidently an aketon of the type worn by West

32 Peter Harbison, 'Native Irish arms and armour in medieval Gaelic literature, 1170–1600', *Irish Sword*, 12 (1975), 173–99; xiii (1976), 270–84.

Highlanders. His companion, however, is wearing a mail habergeon over an unquilted coat, slit at the front.[33] The drawing is so meticulous and detailed that it seems not unreasonable to suggest that it is made of a single layer of thick hide or leather, like the 'buff coats' much worn by soldiers in the seventeenth century. It is possible that it is a coat of this type that is shown on the effigy of William Mac Leòid at Rodel, mentioned above. Two of the effigies at Iona also seem to be dressed in such unquilted garments.[34]

The predominance of actouns on West Highland sculpture of the fourteenth to the sixteenth century suggests that they were the normal garment for warriors in this part of the world throughout that period. They were garments specifically designed for wearing by themselves rather than as an undergarment. There are no representations of them in the medieval period elsewhere in the Highlands or Lowlands of Scotland and documentary sources allow the impression that they were not favoured outwith the West Highlands by the sixteenth century. They had presumably been superseded by other defensive garments such as jacks and doublets of fence. Whereas actouns, jacks and doublets might have been interchangeable terms in the fifteenth century for similar clothing, in the sixteenth century they were identified as different.

All this leads me to suggest that the actouns of the West Highlands may have been the medieval equivalent of the padded, all weather jackets – 'anoraks' – worn by many today, including those who sail for pleasure or sport. They were clearly developed as a light, relatively cheap, form of protection for warriors in battle, but their continued use by West Highlanders may relate more to other key properties like warmth and water-proofing that would have made them ideal for voyages by sea. Indeed, it might be of interest if further research could discover if such garments, coated with wax or pitch, could have offered any buoyancy to a man in the water.

WEAPONS

While no West Highland ships or actouns survive, several weapons do, particularly swords and axes. Most of these have an Irish provenance and are only identified as being possibly West Highland on the basis of their similarity to representations of them on West Highland sculpture. Some,

---

33 Steer and Bannerman, *Sculpture*, pl. 40D. **34** Ibid., pl. 8D; RCAHMS, *Argyll. Vol. 4. Iona*, pp 234–5.

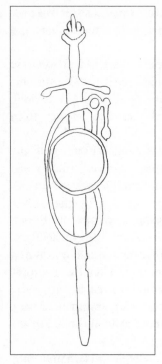

13 Detail of a buckler and
sword on a 15th-century
grave-slab at the old parish
church, Keills, Knapdale.

but by no means all, of those with an Irish provenance may have been lost by Scotsmen. We have to believe that many fashions in weapons were common to native Irish and West Highlanders. It is not my purpose, however, to explore their typology here. They have been listed and described elsewhere.[35] What I am interested in is the suitability of the weapons for the tactics adopted in warfare.

The shield on the effigy (fig. 6) of Giolla Bhrighde MacFhionghein (MacKinnon) is a convenient device for a heraldic design of a galley and animals which would probably have confirmed his identity and certainly indicated his status. As with the handful of other effigies with 'heater-shaped' shields (shaped like the base of an iron) there is probably no need to imagine that these are actual items of kit for fighting. There are two types of shields used by the Scots in battle, referred to in fifteenth- and sixteenth-century documents – bucklers and targes – the two often confused, or assumed to be the same, by modern writers. The former are small and circular and have a handle for the left hand. They were used along with swords, and were called for in legislation of 1425/6, 1429/30, 1456 and 1491 specifying appropriate military equipment for the Scots king's lieges.[36] Bucklers are represented on two grave-slabs (fig. 13), probably of the fifteenth century, at Keills chapel in Knapdale.[37]

35 J.G. Mann, 'A late medieval sword from Ireland', in *Antiquaries Jn.*, 24 (1944), 94–9; G.A. Hayes-McCoy, 'The gallóglach axe', in *Galway Arch. Soc. Jn.*, 17 (1937), 101–21; 'Sixteenth century swords found in Ireland', in *RSAI Jn.*, 78 (1948), 63–4; *Sixteenth century Irish swords in the National Museum of Ireland* (Dublin, 1959); Etienne Rynne, 'Military and civilian swords from the River Corrib', in *Galway Arch. Soc. Jn.*, 39 (1983–4), 5–26; Andrew Halpin, 'Irish medieval swords c.1170–1600', in *RIA Proc.*, 86C, no. 5 (1986), 183–230; J.G. Scott, 'Three medieval swords from Scotland', in D.H. Caldwell (ed.), *Scottish weapons and fortifications, 1100–1800* (Edinburgh, 1981), pp 10–20; D.H. Caldwell, 'Some notes on Scottish axes and long shafted weapons', in Caldwell, *Scottish weapons*, pp 253–314; Cormac Bourke, 'Antiquities from the River Blackwater III, iron axe-heads', in *UJA*, 60 (2001), 63–93. 36 *Acts parl. Scot.*, ii, pp 10, 18, 45, 226. 37 James Drummond, *Sculptured monuments in Iona and the West Highlands* (Edinburgh, 1881), pl. LX, no 1; *The Royal Commission on the Ancient and Historical Monuments of Scotland, Argyll. Volume 7. Mid Argyll and Cowal: medieval and later monuments* (Edinburgh, 1992), p. 90.

Targes are also circular but larger than bucklers, on the basis of surviving seventeenth-century Highland examples, about 500mm in diameter. They were designed so they could be held on the left arm. Although there are no representations of targes in West Highland art or specific mentions of them in medieval documents about West Highlanders it seems reasonable to assume that they were used by West Highlanders in the fifteenth century since it is clear that they were normally wielded along with axes, as required by acts of 1456 and 1481. The second of these specifically required every axeman without either a spear or bow to have a targe of wood or leather, modelled on an example to be sent to every sheriff.[38] It is known that they were also used in Ireland, being slung on the back when not actually in use.[39]

The skill and tenacity of the Scots under William Wallace and Robert Bruce, fighting on foot with spears, is well known, and the importance of spears in the early fourteenth century seems to be underlined by the fact that they, with swords, are the only weapons required for fighting men (defined as those with £10 worth of goods) in a Scottish act of parliament of 1318.[40] Some pieces of West Highland sculpture show warriors armed with a spear and a sword (fig. 9), and in some cases a small shield as well. These representations of spearmen may be early, fourteenth-century rather than later, though only the slab of Giolla Bhrighde MacFhionghein at (fig. 6) Iona can confidently be dated to the fourteenth century on the basis of its inscription, possibly the second quarter of that century, despite Steer and Bannerman's caution.[41] Giolla Bhrighde, who is said in later tradition to have fought at Bannockburn, is thus, with his actoun and bascinet, equipped according to the 1318 Act.

At Bannockburn the Scots gripped their spears firmly, although the sixteenth-century Scottish historian, John Major, describes how *spiculis* (darts – spears designed for throwing) were hurled before the two sides closed.[42] Major is unlikely to have been drawing on early sources for this information. Perhaps he was writing more to give an impression of an epic conflict rather than with absolute accuracy as a priority. Nevertheless, he may have been influenced by weapons and tactics still known, or remembered, in his day. Darts are mentioned in other sixteenth-century literary and historical sources, including Boece's *History*, for instance, in recounting the activities of King Custantín (Constantine I) in the ninth

---

38 *Acts parl. Scot.*, ii, 45, 132.   39 Harbison, 'Arms and armour', 197–8.   40 *Acts parl. Scot.*, i, p. 113.   41 Steer and Bannerman, *Sculpture*, p. 25, pl. 8A.   42 John Major, *Historia Majoris Britanniae tam Angliae quam Scotiae* (Edinburgh, 1740), p. 197; Archibald Constable and A.J.G. MacKay (eds), *A history of greater Britain, as well England as Scotland* (Scot. Hist. Soc., Edinburgh, 1892), p. 240.

14 Detail of a huntsman with a bow on a grave-slab at
St Maelrubha's Church, Arisaig, 15th century.

century. They are described as *missiles* in the original Latin, and *darts* in the translation by Bellenden.[43] A Scottish act of parliament of 1481 envisages that axemen should also be armed with a spear or a bow, and perhaps these spears should be interpreted as missiles.[44] None of this adds up to impressive evidence for the use of darts by any Scots in warfare in the medieval period. It is only considered here because of the more substantial documentation for darts by the Irish, including the galloglass, said in a report of 1543 to have three each, carried for them by their boys.[45] Might West Highland warriors have been similarly equipped?

The evidence for darts may be tenuous, but not so another missile weapon, bows and arrows. The Scots were encouraged to train as archers by acts of parliament of 1424 and 1456/7,[46] but there is little evidence that the bulk of the king's lieges adopted these weapons in military campaigns. In any case, by the 1470s the Scots foot had adopted pikes (very long spears) and they were to remain committed to them until the late seventeenth century.[47]

West Highlanders apparently did not adopt pikes but took to bows and arrows. Only two bows are depicted in West Highland sculpture. One, in the act of being fired by a huntsman (fig. 14), is on a slab of fifteenth- or sixteenth-century date at St Maelrubha's church, Arisaig, in Lochaber; the other is carried over the shoulder of a huntsman, with a quiver at his

43 Boece, *Scotorum Historiae*, fols CCXII recto, CCXIIII verso; John Bellenden, *The chronicle of Scotland compiled by Hector Boece translated into Scots* (Scot. Text Soc., Edinburgh, 1941), ii, pp 62, 67.   44 *Acts parl. Scot.*, ii, p. 132.   45 Harbison, 'Arms and armour', 273, 276; *SP Henry VIII*, iii, p. 444.   46 *Acts parl. Scot.*, ii, pp 6, 48.   47 Caldwell, 'Axes and long shafted weapons', pp 254–5.

15 Detail of a huntsman
with a bow on the tomb of
Alexander Mac Leòid
(MacLeod), St Clement's
Church, Rodel, Harris, 1528.

belt (fig. 15), on the 1528 tomb of Alexander Mac Leòid at Rodel.[48] An admittedly late source, one of the manuscripts of Pitscottie's *History* of *c.*1575 has Mac Gill'Eathain (MacLean) of Duart on Mull on the Flodden campaign in 1513 with a force of 600 men armed with bows and halflangs (swords with hilts long enough for two hands) and clad in habergeons.[49] The West Highland contingent which turned out for the battle of Pinkie in 1547 is described as 4,000 archers under the leadership of the earl of Argyll. At least some of these would have been Clann Domhnaill (Clan Donald South) and MacLeans, and it is not without significance that King James V made gifts of bows, including English and Flemish ones as well as Scottish examples, to Alexander Mac Domhnaill of Dunyvaig in 1532 and 1535, Alexander's son James in 1539, and Alan, brother of Mac Gill'Eathain of Duart in 1539.[50] Scottish bows were considerably cheaper

48 F.O. Blundell, 'Notes on the church and some sculptured monuments in the churchyard of St Maelrubha in Arisaig', *PSAS*, 45 (1910–11), 358, fig. 4, no. 2; Steer and Bannerman, *Sculpture*, pl. 32B. 49 Robert Lindesay of Pitscottie, *The historie and cronicles of Scotland* (Scot. Text Soc., Edinburgh, 1899), i, pp cliv, 274. 50 William Patten, 'The expedition into Scotland, 1547', in J.G. Dalyell (ed.), *Fragments of Scottish history* (Edinburgh, 1798), p. 60; *The accounts of the Lord High Treasurer of Scotland, 1473–1580*, 13 vols (Edinburgh, 1877–1978), vi, pp 95, 262; vii, 194, 256.

16 Detail of Raghnall (Ranald) of Islay from his cross-shaft,
late 14th century (National Museums of Scotland).

than English ones, reflecting not just local availability but that they were shorter. The traditional accounts of the Battle of Tràigh Ghruinneart on Islay in 1598 between the MacDonalds and MacLeans have Sir Lachlan Mac Gill'Eathain (MacLean) being struck down by an arrow.[51]

Apart from spears and pikes, it is known that the favourite weapon of the Scots was the axe. Barbour, in his account of the fight at Dalry between John of Lorne's men and Robert Bruce in 1306, describes how the men of Lorne fought effectively on foot with axes, even killing the horses of Bruce's party.[52] Barbour obviously knew that axes were the

51 Nicholas Maclean-Bristol, *Murder under trust: the crimes and death of Sir Lachlan Mor Maclean of Duart, 1558–1598* (East Linton, 1999), pp 238–45.   52 M.P. McDiarmid and J.A.C.

17 Detail of axemen from Derricke's *Image of Irelande* of 1581.

weapon used by West Highlanders, if not in 1306 then at least when he was writing in the 1370s. There are, however, few representations of battle-axes on West Highland sculpture. The most significant is an image, presumably of Raghnall (ON Rögnvaldr) of Islay (fig. 16), the eponym of Clann Raghnaill (Clanranald), on a cross set up to commemorate him in the late fourteenth century. It stood next to the chapel on the island of Texa but its shaft is now on display in the Museum of Scotland in Edinburgh. Apart from the axe Raghnall is equipped with a bascinet, actoun and sword.[53]

The shaft of Raghnall's axe is long enough to be gripped with both hands and an illustration of a battle between English and Irish from Derricke's *Image of Irelande* of 1581 clearly shows a force on the Irish side – perhaps galloglas rather than West Highlanders – armed with similar long-shafted axes, one of which is being wielded double-handed (fig. 17).[54] It is probable that many axemen had shorter staffs for one-handed use, thus facilitating the use of a targe.

Stevenson (eds), *Barbour's Bruce* (Scot. Text Soc., Edinburgh, 1980), ii, p. 46.   **53** Steer and Bannerman, *Sculpture*, pp 125–7, pl. 24C.   **54** John Derricke, *The image of Irelande with a discouerie of woodkerne* (rpr. Edinburgh, 1883), pl. 9.

18 A claymore, a two-handed Highland sword, early 16th century (National Museums of Scotland).

Swords are by far the commonest weapons depicted in West Highland sculpture, either as the sole weapon of a military effigy or as a main element of a scheme of decoration on a grave-slab. Many of these swords are for wielding in the right hand, with blades shaped for slashing and cutting as much as stabbing. Others appear to be halflangs, with hilts large enough for two hands. From the late fifteenth century larger 'twa-handit' swords or claymores (fig. 10, 18), with long hilts and blades, make an appearance in West Highland sculpture, the earliest securely dated one being on a slab of 1539 at Oronsay Priory.[55] We may reasonably doubt whether the prevalence of swords on the sculpture reflects an underlying reality in the equipment of those who fought. Swords were expensive, they required great skill in their manufacture, and many of their blades were imported. It is possible that relatively few warriors were armed with them prior to the sixteenth, or even the seventeenth century. Their frequency in sculpture could be attributed to the high status of those who commissioned the slabs and crosses and the symbolic value of a sword as an attribute of nobility. In any case, halflang and twa-handit swords would have been wielded in a similar way to axes, and may have been viewed as an up-market or more sophisticated alternative.

The effectiveness of West Highland warriors could not have depended on their use of axes and large swords alone. A force so armed would have been vulnerable to attack by cavalry and bowmen, and from the sixteenth century forces armed with firearms. Likely solutions to this problem were the use of bows to fend off such threats, and closing with the enemy as quickly as possible where axes and swords could have most effect. There is no compelling evidence that there were West Highland bowmen as a

55 Steer and Bannerman, *Sculpture*, pl. 26c.

distinct category separate from those warriors armed with axes and swords. Rather, it may be supposed that bows were increasingly carried by all, so that they might readily be identified as archers, as in an English eye-witness account of them at Pinkie in 1547.[56]

The Scottish army at Pinkie was drawn up with three battles (divisions) of pikemen in line abreast, flanked on one side by light horsemen, and on the other by Argyll's West Highland bowmen. The Scots were notably weak in mounted troops and there were clearly not enough to be positioned on both flanks, but were the bowmen considered the next best thing because of their mobility?

The mobility of Highland armies of the seventeenth and eighteenth centuries is well known, starting with the campaigns of Montrose in 1644–5, and continuing with the Jacobite forces of 1689, 1715 and 1745. Many of the men in these armies came from the West Highlands. The tactic that is particularly associated with them is the 'Highland Charge'. The Highlanders approached the enemy lines *en masse*, paused to fire their bows or guns only once before jettisoning them. They then rushed their enemy with targes and swords. Their opponents' pikes or bayonets were caught on the targes and deftly turned aside as sword blades wreaked havoc. The tactic was successful time after time against conventionally drilled and equipped armies. It has been suggested that it was invented by Alasdair Mac Colla, Montrose's right-hand man.[57] Mac Colla was a leading member of Clann Domhnaill with experience of the wars in Ireland.

Perhaps, however, the Highland charge was not such an innovation in the 1640s but had its roots in methods of fighting amongst West Highlanders in the medieval period. The key role of targes in the Highland charges executed as late as 1746 provides a link with medieval times. The combination of targe and sword is unusual, essentially a Scottish phenomenon, but makes sense if targes remained in use as axes were replaced by swords. The positioning of the West Highland con-tingent at Pinkie suggests that they could charge – after they had fired their bows? At Pinkie it never happened, but the expectation may have been there.

Did the success of West Highland warriors always depend on such mobility, whether armed with spears, axes or swords?

The continued use of galleys and birlings, of actouns, targes, bows and other weapons might be dismissed as the result of conservatism in a culture unprepared to adapt to modern ways. Conservatism there undoubtedly was, and an often deliberate and conscious desire to learn

56 Patten, 'Expedition into Scotland', p. 60.   57 David Stevenson, *Alasdair MacColla and the Highland problem in the seventeenth century* (Edinburgh, 1980), pp 81ff.

from the past and be different from other Scots. It would be wrong, however, to view West Highland society as static and totally lacking in innovation. The kit described in this paper gave the flexibility to move and fight fast, abilities prized by generations of warriors. Equipment may have been retained, adapted, and finally discarded, to allow such mobility. The desire to be quick and light in warfare is a thread to be traced through all the period, and offers a better explanation for events and tactics than conservatism alone.

Images of Scottish warriors in
later Irish bardic poetry

WILSON McLEOD

Warriors from the Scottish *Gàidhealtachd* played a crucial role in Irish affairs between the thirteenth and early seventeenth centuries, and this involvement is memorialized in a range of Irish bardic poems, often composed for the Hebridean chiefs themselves. Perhaps the earliest work in this vein is the anonymous 'Domhnall mac Raghnaill, rosg mall' ('Domhnall mac Raghnaill, of the stately gaze'), a fragmentary piece celebrating Domhnall mac Raghnaill (*fl.* 1212), grandson of Sumarliði (Somerled), and his host of *gallmhaoir* (Hebridean stewards).[1] The best-represented period, however, is the last stage of the bardic era, and of Irish Gaelic independence itself, from *c.*1575–*c.*1625; a range of poems, principally for members of Clann Eoin Mhóir (Clann Domhnaill 'South') but also for Caimbeul and Mac Leòid chiefs, illustrate their involvement in a range of campaigns and raids in Ulster and Connacht, some of them successful, some of them disastrous. Scottish Gaelic warriors are often depicted in conventional and stereotyped ways, conceptualized as exiled mercenaries returning to their motherland, an understanding that provides telling insights into the Irish Gaelic *mentalité* of the late medieval period.[2]

'CAITHRÉIMÍ AGUS MARBHNAÍ': DESCRIPTIONS OF CAMPAIGNS AND RAIDS

The most obvious kind of depiction of Scottish warriors in Irish poetry of the late bardic period is as warriors *per se*: vigorous leaders of raids and campaigns, feared opponents, loyal and sturdy allies. The vivid descriptions and forceful imagery presented in the poems bring a sense of freshness and immediacy not always conveyed by more conventional accounts.

---

1 NLS Adv. MS 72.2.2, f. 16; ed. and trans. by Wilson McLeod and Meg Bateman, in *Duanaire na sracaire / The song-book of the pillagers: anthology of Scotland's Gaelic verse to 1600* (Edinburgh, 2007), 74–81. See generally Katharine Simms, 'Images of warfare in bardic poetry', *Celtica*, xxi (1990), pp 608–19. 2 See Wilson McLeod, *Divided Gaels: Gaelic cultural identities in Scotland and Ireland c.1200–c.1650* (Oxford, 2004), pp 173–93.

Several late sixteenth-century poems composed for Ulster chiefs include Hebridean warriors in the lists of allies who will support them in attacking the English. For example, an anonymous poem to Toirdhealbhach Luineach Ó Néill (†1595), 'An sluagh sidhe so i nEamhuin?' ('Is this a fairy host in Eamhain Mhacha?'), gives an account of a hosting that Toirdhealbhach made at Armagh, encouraging him to fight the English and naming Clann Domhnaill among those gathered:

> Tig chuige do Chloinn nDomhnuill,
> cia an cath as fherr ionchomhluinn,
> cath loinnearlann ón tír thoir,
> mín doinndernonn ré ndornnchloibh.
>
> [Warriors] of Clann Domhnaill come to him,
> what battalion is more battle-worthy?
> A fierce-bladed battalion from the eastern land,
> their smooth strong hands around their sword-hilts.[3]

Tadhg Dall Ó hUiginn's address to Brian na Múrtha Ó Ruairc (†1591) beginning 'D'fhior chogaidh comhailtear síothcháin' ('To the warlike man peace is observed') is somewhat similar in tone, but the hosting and proposed march on Dublin and the Boyne are imagined, and the portrayal of the Clann Domhnaill warriors more figurative:

> Clann Domhnaill leis líon a dtionóil,
> mar tiad dairghe ós doireadhaibh,
> d'fhianaibh Fhódla, d'amhsain Íle
> gasraidh shídhe shoineamhail.
>
> Clann Domhnaill will be with him in their full strength,
> like oaks towering above the groves,
> an excellent and wondrous band of the soldiery of Fódla,
> the mercenaries of Islay.[4]

Several poems describe actual military campaigns to one degree or another: these presentations can be of particular interest to the historian, either to give information of a purely factual, narrative nature or to illustrate the contemporary impact or perception of specific events. A colourful example is the anonymous poem 'An síth do rogha, a rígh

---

3 Published in Tadhg Ó Donnchadha (ed.), *Leabhar Cloinne Aodha Buidhe* (Dublin, 1931), pp 94–7 (§ 12c–d) [translation WCM]; for a discussion of the poem, see Simms, 'Images of warfare in bardic poetry', p. 612.   4 Published in Eleanor Knott (ed.), *A bhfuil aguinn dár chum Tadhg Dall Ó hUiginn (1550–1591)/ The bardic poems of Tadhg Dall Ó hUiginn (1550–1591)*, Irish Texts Society, 22 and 23 (London, 1922, 1926), i, 108–19, ii, 72–9 (§ 55) (translation revised).

Fionnghall?' ('Is peace your choice, o king of the Hebrideans?'),[5] composed *c.*1590 for Aonghus Mac Domhnaill of Dunyveg (†1614), son of Seumas nan Ruaig (†1565), which uses the common literary device of the mock quarrel between poet and patron as a pretext for listing his chief's impressive military triumphs. The poet, apparently an Ulsterman, challenges Aonghus to make peace with him, announcing that despite Aonghus's fearsome reputation as a warrior he himself feels no trepidation:

Ó chuan Leódhuis go Loch Eireais
eagla romhad, a rosg gorm,
is t'eagla ar chách um Bhóinn mbraonghlais,
gan sgáth roimh, a Aonghuis, orm.

Do chreich tusa le tús th'oirbhirt
Inis Eóghuin, a fholt fionn:
ge atá duit fa chíos ód chéidchion,
mo throid síos ní léicthear liom.

Ge tá an chreach sin Cairrge Fearghuis
fá bhfríth guasacht lét ghruaidh mhín,
'na sgáth uaibh do ghnáth ar Ghalluibh
gan sgáth let ghruaidh mballaigh bím.

Do shaorais, 's ní saorfa oram,
gach aird dod thír, 's níor taom réidh,
ar sluagh Gall dearg-ghruadh dreachbhláith,
's ar mear-shluagh clann neamhthláith Néill.

Rugais an Rút le ruaig énlaoi
d'fhuil Uí Bhilin gerb fhuil ríogh,
's ní reacainn sin ret chéibh ccúlchais —
sibh do bhein mo dhúthchas díom.

From the Minch of Lewis to Loch Eireas[6]
you are feared, O blue eye,
and all fear you round the Boyne's grey water,
but I, Aonghas, am not afraid.

At the start of your career, you raised tribute
in Inishowen, O fair hair:
although it is your favourite dependency
I will not give up my suit.

5 For an analysis of the title *rí Fionnghall*, see Wilson McLeod, '*Rí Innsi Gall, Rí Fionnghall, Ceannas nan Gàidheal*: sovereignty and rhetoric in the late medieval Hebrides', *CMCS*, 43 (2002), pp 25–48 (at pp 36–8).   6 The location of 'Loch Eireas' is unidentified. It may refer to Erris in northwestern Co. Mayo, or possibly to Urris in Inishowen (both of these normally being

> Although your raid on Carrickfergus
> (which brought danger to your smooth cheek)
> keeps the Goill in constant terror,
> I am without fear of your freckled face.
>
> You have guarded – I will not deny it –
> every part of your land — no gentle fight –
> from the Lowland host, smooth-faced ruddy,
> and from the valiant merciless host of clan Néill.
>
> You won the Route with a single day's offensive
> from the Mac Uilíns, despite their royal blood;
> and I would not mention this to your curly ringlets:
> that you have deprived me of my native place.[7]

Significant in this poem is the mix of references to places where Aonghus apparently campaigned personally – Inishowen, Carrickfergus, the Route, Strangford Lough – with a 'mythological' reference to the Boyne, in other words to Tara, the centre of power and prestige, for Scottish as for Irish Gaels, in the panegyric code of bardic poetry.[8]

The most detailed of these catalogues of campaign and triumph is to be found in the Scottish poet Eoin Óg Ó Muirgheasáin's elegy for Sir Ruaidhri Mór Mac Leòid of Harris (†1626), 'Creach Gaoidheal i reilig Rois' ('A ruination for the Gaels in the churchyard of Ross'). The poet celebrates Ruaidhri Mór's wide-ranging raids all over Ulster and Connacht (many of these evidently in support of Aodh Ruadh Ó Domhnaill in 1595).[9] Although a *leitmotif* in bardic poetry, Eoin Óg's repeated emphasis on his patron's rewarding of poets with the spoils of battle seems somewhat excessive:

> Tús dá fhoghlaidh i n-iath Ír,
> nár ba foghlaidh Dia 'na dhiaidh –
> do bhiodh ós cách in gach céim;
> níor ghnáth béim dá ghníomh i ngliaidh.
>
> Sliocht Bhriain Bhallaigh níor dhíon dóibh
> a ngalaigh ar ghníomh a shluaigh;
> 's níor bh'fheirrde i dtealaigh dá dtóir;
> fóir Eilge um cheanaibh do chuaidh.

---

spelled Iorras in Irish). Either place would suit the sense here, but there appears to be no *loch* bearing the name.   7 McLeod & Bateman, *Duanaire na Sracaire*, 156–9 (ll. 36–56); W.J. Watson, 'An unpublished poem to Angus MacDonald of Dun Naomhaig', *An Gaidheal*, xix (1923), pp 36–8 (§§ 10–14).   8 See McLeod, *Divided Gaels*, pp 151–2.   9 For an account of Ó Domhnaill's campaign see *AFM*, s.a. 1595.

Aird Uladh d'argain dá fhéin
curadh do árdaigh a n-uaill;
easbhaidh daoine a theacht don tóir
ó neart slóigh an taoibhe thuaidh …

Tar Drobhaois tar Sligigh siar
gan shlighidh rochaoil 'na raon,
tug iarraidh ar ndíol na ndámh,
a lán diobh triallaidh re a thaobh.

Baile an Mhúta adhnaidh uaidh
gan adhbhaidh dúnta 'na dhiaidh;
comha is í dá déanamh dhóibh
fóir Sgí ní ghéabhadh gan gliaidh.

Dún Mheic Fheórais airgthear uaidh
go i daingne seólais tar sáil –
beag da bhfoghlaibh san tír thiar
is riar síl Olbhair an áigh.

Taibhgheóir a ndíola don dáimh
ó daighLeóid le díorma a shlóigh;
go bhfuair troimriar as gach taoibh
maoir uaidh fán gCoirrshliabh do chóidh.

Fir Chonnacht mar do an uaidh
a gcrodh ar sgolaibh do sgaoil
lorg a fhaghla tré Ath Luain
sgáth uaidh mar tharla ar gach taoibh.

Tugsad dá gcreachaibh ar gclódh
curaidh ba deacair do dhíol;
fáth daingin níor bh' fheirrde uadh
sluagh Eilge ó Ghaillimh dá ghníomh.

Sé an tan-soin dá dtaobhadh tóir
dá ghasraidh níor bhaoghal béim;
Goill fá Eas Dara 'na dhiaidh
treas do ghliaidh nách rabha réidh.

Groighe ó Chonnachtaibh ar gcúl
– Conallaigh do roinne a ríomh –
tug do dháimh daoineallach uadh
's buar Baoigheallach dháibh mar dhíol.

Crodh Bóghaineach d'éigsibh uaidh
di óroineach ní hé a-mháin,
ní thug ar ais uatha féin
réir 's na tuatha leis do láimh.

Crodh Fánad i ndíol na ndámh
síol nDálaigh do loc a luadh;
siris an deóraidh do dhíol
díon ag Inis Eóghain uadh.

A bhfuair riamh mun ráith-sin Ír
do riar buair nó d'fháinnibh óir
gan áireamh ar chrodh do chléir –
ag réir sgol do dháileadh dhóibh.

He began his career of reaving in Ireland
– may it not be that God's vengeance follows thereon –
he was leader in every foray;
never was fault found with his performance in the fight.

In face of his army's fighting the descendants of Brian Ballach
[i.e. the O'Neills of Clann Aodha Buidhe][10]
had no protection in their warriors;
their plight no better on the battle-hill when chased there;
the overthrow of the Irish troops was among his triumphs.

The pride of his troops was roused by the challenge
to plunder the Ards of Ulster;
because he led them on that raid many fell
through the might of that army from the north ...

On a wide ranging advance to the west
across the Drowes, over the river of Sligo,
he saw that the poets were rewarded –
a full company of them were with him.

He set Ballymote aflame;
in his track no house stands with closed doors;
there was an attempt at terms with them,
but the Skye troops would not accept; they would fight.

Dún Mheic Fheórais [Dunmore, Co. Galway?] was pillaged by him;
to that stronghold he directed his course across the sea.
Little of their reavings in the west country fell
as share to the fortunate descendant of Olbhar.

The descendant of noble Leod, bestower of satisfying rewards upon poets,
as he led his company of soldiers,
sent his stewards through Coirrshliabh [Co. Roscommon]
until he got full supply from every side.

10 I follow the view expressed by Kenneth Nicholls and Katharine Simms at the Edinburgh
conference that 'sliocht Bhriain Bhallaigh' is to be associated with the O'Neills of Clann Aodha
Buidhe and not with the O'Connors, as suggested by the poem's editor, John MacDonald.

Since the men of Connacht kept away from him
he distributed spoil taken from them upon the schools of poets;
through Athlone lay the path of his reaving;
on every hand whenever he chanced there was fear of him.

Soldiers that were hard to repel
began harassing them when they turned back –
it was the task of Irish troops from Galway –
that was no better way of security from him.

At that time should an army venture to attack,
his soldiers would earn no discredit;
the English from Eas Dara [Co. Sligo] were following him
– troops that were rough combatants in a fight.

Herds of horses taken from the people of Connacht
followed in the rear – Tír Chonaill men counted them –
these he gave away to his many poets,
and the cattle of Boylagh [Co. Donegal], too, as reward.

To give away the cattle wealth of Banagh [Co. Donegal]
to his poets was characteristic of his golden generosity,
and not that only, he did not take in return
from his clansmen that were with him the tribute due him.

Síol nDálaigh [the O'Donnells] prevented the cattle of Fanad
being driven away to be reward for the poets;
the foreign soldiers sought to exact payment,
but Inishowen provided protection from them.

All that he ever got in Ráth Ír [Ireland]
in booty of cattle or golden rings –
for the poets cattle unnumbered –
he divided out to schools (of poets) as recompense.[11]

Of course, not all Scottish Gaels who engaged in military activity in
Ireland during this period were successful, and a different aspect of the
enterprise is reflected in two laments composed by members of the Ó
Gnímh bardic family for members of Clann Eoin Mhóir. Brian Ó Gnímh's
'Mionn súl Éireann i n-Áth Cliath' ('The jewel of Ireland's eyes is in
Dublin') laments the death of Alasdair, son of Somhairle Buidhe Mac
Domhnaill of Antrim (†1590), at the hands of an English force led by
Captain Nicholas Merriman during a night-time skirmish in Inishowen in
May 1586. According to the Book of Clanranald, Alasdair was then

11 Published in John MacDonald, 'An elegy for Ruaidhri Mór', *Scottish Gaelic Studies*, viii
(1955–8), pp 27–52 (§§ 40–2, 44–54).

decapitated, with his head being sent to Dublin (hence the reference in the poem's opening line) and his body buried in the monastery at Burt.[12] The second poem, 'Do loiscceadh mé sa Mhuaidh' ('I have been burnt in the Moy'), bewails the death in September of that year of Domhnall Gorm Mac Domhnaill, another son of Seumas nan Ruaig of Dunyveg (†1565) and nephew of Somhairle Buidhe, at Ardnaree, along the river Moy across from Ballina, Co. Mayo. Domhnall Gorm was killed in the course of a notorious massacre of Scottish Gaels by English troops under the command of Sir Richard Bingham; some two thousand men, women and children, including Domhnall's younger brother Alasdair Carrach, are said to have died in the slaughter.[13] The poet – probably also Brian Ó Gnímh – expresses his devastation at his loss in unusually personal and passionate terms:

> Do loisceadh meisi sa Mhuaidh:
> a bhfad uaidh – anba an anbhuain –
>   lá m'uilcsi nírbh fhosgadh damh –
>   mo losgadh d'uisce is iongnadh.
>
> Ar ccur chaor ttuaithfeal tairrsi
> d'uisce fhuar don abhoinnsi,
>   mar budh uisge agus é ar goil
>   rom thuitsi agus mé ar marthoin. ...
>
> Do loisc lionn [mhór] an tuile
> sinn ar n-oighidh éanduine
>   ar bhfoscadh ar ghoimh na nGall,
>   ar losgadh, ar ndoigh Domhnall.
>
> Ar mbás síorruidhe is sinn beó,
> ar ndíothladh uile d'éincheó,
>   teacht fan Domhnall Ghormsa ar ghuin,
>   ar bhfonnsa comdhonn cumhduigh.
>
> Ar n-áitioghadh tíre ar ttreóir,
> ar sciath eadrána ar aindeóin,
>   ar ndíoboirtne a-nos a nimh,
>   ar líogfhoircli ar ndós díttin.

12 A summary account of Alasdair's death is given in *AFM*, s.a. 1586, and a more detailed narrative in the 'Black Book of Clanranald': see Seosamh Laoide, *Alasdair Mac Colla* (Dublin, 1914), p. 46, and Alexander MacBain and Revd John Kennedy (eds), *Reliquiae Celticae: texts, papers, and studies in Gaelic literature and philology left by the late Rev. Alexander Cameron, LL.D.*, 2 vols (Inverness, 1894), i, 301; see also *CSPI* 1586–8, pp 39–40, 43, and G.A. Hayes-McCoy, *Scots mercenary forces in Ireland (1565–1603)* (Dublin, 1937; rpr. 1996), pp 175–6. 13 The encounter is described in detail in *AFM* and *ALC*, s.a. 1586, and in *CSPI* 1586–88, pp 161–2, 164–6; see also Hayes-McCoy, *Scots mercenary forces in Ireland*, pp 174–5. English accounts of the massacre give a somewhat lower number of dead, closer to 1,400.

Scalded have I been in the Moy
though far away – cruel agony –
on that day of my suffering I had no escape –
though strange my burning by water.

After flooding with great billows
of chill water widdershins –
as if the water boiled –
the river has felled me, though still living ...

The great water of the flood
has burned us with one man's death –
our shelter from the sting of the Goill,
now Domhnall is our scald, our torture.

Our eternal death while alive,
the destruction of all by one death-mist,
coming with the slaying of Domhnall Gorm,
the noble ring-fence of our protection.

Our settler on the land, and our guide,
our shield between ourselves and discord,
our rock-bulwark, our protecting tree,
is now our banishment from Heaven.[14]

The surreal, almost phantasmagoric natural imagery of this elegy recalls the most famous 'war poem' of the period, Eochaidh Ó hEódhasa's fearful 'Fuar liom an adhaighsi dh'Aodh' ('Too cold I deem this night for Aodh'), composed for Aodh Mag Uidhir (†1600) as he fought a campaign in Munster from which he would not return.[15]

'ÓN ÁIRD THUAIDH THIG AN CHOBHAIR': SAVIOURS COMING OVER THE SEA

If these descriptions of raids and campaigns are usually grounded in the reality of actual military conflict, this line of bardic poetry is at its most stylized and stereotypical in depicting Scottish chiefs as potential saviours, urged to fulfil prophecy or destiny by defending or seizing Ireland, which is conventionally depicted as being in a weak or pitiful state. This kind of presentation, urging the seizure of the highkingship, is also extremely

14 Published in McLeod & Bateman, *Duanaire na Sracaire*, pp 210–17 (ll. 1–8, 25–36); Colm Ó Lochlainn, 'Ár ar Ard na Riadh', *Éigse*, v (1945–7), pp 149–55 (§§ 1–2, 7–9). 15 Published in Bergin, *Irish Bardic Poetry*, pp 124–7, 268–70; for a compelling analysis of Eochaidh's poem, see Louis de Paor, '"Do chor chúarta ar gcridhe"', in Pádraigín Riggs et al. (eds), *Saoi na hÉigse:*

common in poems to Irish chiefs, both in the later sixteenth century and earlier.[16] There are, however, differences of emphasis and nuance in the poems to Scottish chiefs: the idea of salvation coming from over the sea, and the defence or taking of the ancient motherland. This theme of return from exile is explored in more detail in the next section of this paper.

An illuminating example here is 'Dual ollamh do thriall le toisg' ('It is customary for an *ollamh* [high-poet] to travel on an embassy'), composed for Gill'Easbaig, earl of Argyll. The circumstances of the poem's composition are not entirely clear: by virtue of a dedicatory verse at the conclusion of the poem to Anne Douglas, first wife of the seventh earl (†1638), it would appear that the poem should be associated with that earl and not one of his predecessors and namesakes. It might possibly be connected to the efforts of Ó Néill and Ó Domhnaill to persuade Argyll to send soldiers to Ulster in early 1595, efforts which involved sending a messenger over to Scotland – a diplomatic task sometimes assigned to poets themselves.[17]

Ireland is adrift like an unsteered ship ('*Soitheach gan stiúir Banbha Breagh*'), the *ollamh* complains, urging Argyll to relieve her plight, thereby regaining his kindred's ancient sovereignty there:

> Do bhí a chíos ar Chruachaibh Aoi
> 's ar Bhóinn 's ar Gháille géasnaoi
> is ar lacht Bhuilleadh sing suthain:
> Cing Ardúir ór fhás[abhair] …

> A Mhic Cailín na gcolg nocht
> mar sin dlighear i d'fhurtacht;
> cíos ar Teamhraigh na tTrí bhFear
> do bhí ar sealbh far sinnsear.

> Cruacha Aoi [seat of power in Connacht], the Boyne,
> the swan-fresh Galey [Co. Sligo],
> the flow of the slender everlasting Boyle [Co. Roscommon]
> were under tribute to King Arthur, from whom you sprang …

> O Mac Cailein of the bare blades,
> thus she [Ireland] is due your assistance;
> your ancestors held possession of tribute
> over Tara of the Three Men.[18]

---

aistí in ómós do Sheán Ó Tuama (Dublin, 2000), pp 35–53. 16 See Brian Ó Cuív, 'Literary creation and Irish historical tradition', *Proceedings of the British Academy*, 49 (1963), pp 233–62. 17 See Hayes-McCoy, *Scots mercenary forces in Ireland*, pp 233–4; McLeod, *Divided Gaels*, p. 99. 18 NLS Adv. MS 72.2.2, ff 8v, 10, 11r (§§ 6a, 9, 11). On the Caimbeuls' Arthurian connection and 'British' pedigree, see William Gillies, 'The "British" genealogy of the Campbells', *Celtica*, 23 (1999), pp 82–95. *Mac Cailein (Mór)* is the traditional patronymic for the Caimbeul chief, tracing descent from Cailean Mór (†1296).

Similarly, in a poem to Somhairle Buidhe of Antrim, 'Fada cóir Fhódla ar Albain' ('Long has Ireland had a claim upon Scotland'), Tadhg Dall Ó hUiginn compares the chief to Caesar, returning from a distant campaign to defend the Roman homeland, and depicts a dream-like vision of Somhairle's anticipated return to Ireland amid a forest of majestic ships:

Do-bhéara Banbha, bean Chuinn,
do bhreith na Rómha romhuinn,
a fear féin ó Mhoigh Mhonaidh,
ag soin céill a gcualabhair.

Ar aghaidh mheic Mheic Domhnuill,
feadh éagcaoine a hanfhorluinn,
do chí an Bhanbha bhfairsing bhfinn
d'aisling suil tarla i dtoirchim.

Mac Alastoir d'fhurtacht cháigh
tiocfa, mar tháinig Séasáir,
don dulasa fa Bhóinn Bhreagh,
slóigh nách urusa d'áireamh.

Sluagh Shéasáir mar rug fan Róimh —
tre Ghoirt Luirc, líon a dtionóil,
tiocfa Séasair clann Cholla,
barr do dhéasaibh díoghlama.

Fásfaidh coill a ciomhsaibh trácht
do chrannaibh seólta síothbharc,
ó Mhuaidh shéadoirdheirc bhinn bhaoith
go Binn Éadoirmheic Éadghaoith.

Banbha, wife of Conn,
just as Rome did before,
that is the meaning of what you have heard,
will bring her own mate from the plain of Monadh [Scotland].

Before him, MacDhomhnaill's son sees,
intent on bewailing her sorrows,
the fair generous Banbha,
in a vision before he fell to slumbering.

Alasdair's son, to succour others,
will come, as did Caesar,
this time to Bregia's Boyne,
with hosts not easy to number.

As Caesar's army captured Rome
through Lorc's field, with full muster,
so will come the Caesar of the race of Coll,
the topmost wheat ear of the gleaning.

A wood will grow by the strands' edge
of masts of stately rigged vessels,
from the illustrious sweet lightsome Moy
to Binn Éadoir [Howth Head], son of Éadghaoth.[19]

Similar ideas are expressed in an anonymous poem to Sir Seumas mac
Aonghuis Mhic Domhnaill of Knockrinsay (†1626) – son of Aonghus mac
Seumais, the subject of 'An síth do rogha, a rígh Fionnghall?', discussed
above – beginning 'Bí ad mhosgaladh, a mheic Aonghais' ('Awake, o son of
Aonghus'), composed *c*.1600. Seumas's return to Ireland, the poet claims,
is destined by ancient prophecy delivered by Fionn mac Cumhaill himself:

Bí ad mhosgaladh, a mheic Aonghais,
ionnsuigh Fódla na bhfonn sídh:
dod dearc úaine ni tráth tathaimh,
a shnáth úaime Achaidh Ír.

Cian le hÉirinn an fheóir mhilis,
a mheic Aonghuis adhnas goil,
fad do chadail a gCeann Tíre
eang abaigh fán míne moir.

Gabh do bhrosdadh, ná bí ad chodladh,
cabhair Íle, a earla nocht,
tabhair thíarain do Thoigh Fhéilim
iarraidh soir ag Éirinn ort.

Ná déna thoir tathamh súaimhneach,
ar sén tturais tríall a le:
d'úaim na ríghi gabh do ghormlainn,
sgar re hÍle ttonnmhoill tte.

Mosgail th'aigneadh, eirg ad lúireach,
ná léig codladh, a chruth fial,
do ríoghraidh choirmthinn chláir Íle,
cáir oirchill na ríghi ríamh ...

---

19 Published in McLeod & Bateman, *Duanaire na Sracaire*, pp 126–39 (ll. 126–44); Knott (ed.),
Tadhg Dall Ó hUiginn, i, 173–9, ii, 115–19 (§§ 32–6). Tadhg Dall is probably also the author of a
second poem in this vein, composed for Somhairle Buidhe's wife, 'Mealladh iomlaoide ar Éirinn'
('The enticement of an exchange for Ireland'). See Pádraig Ó Macháin, 'Tadhg Dall Ó hUiginn:
foinse dá shaothar', in Pádraig Ó Fiannachta (ed.), *Léachtaí Cholm Cille XXIV (An Dán
Díreach)* (Maynooth, 1994), pp 77–113 (pp 103–11), and McLeod, *Divided Gaels*, pp 188–91.

Fionn mac Cumhaill nár char maoine,
a mheic Aonghuis fhuilngios frais,
do chlú níor úaisligh gan adhbhar;
tú an úairsin do labhradh leis.

Cuir a gcrích ar chan an fáidhsin,
fóir ar Bhanbha na mbrogh bfionn,
ná dearg a ghruaidh um Ghort Éibhir:
ort do lúaidh an féinnidh Fionn.

A Shémais, a shúil le flaithios,
fóir a hAlbain na n-eas mbinn
ar Bhóinn ttrédghlain na ttrágh sídhe;
ná brégnaigh glár fíre Finn.

Awake, o son of Aonghus;
draw near to Fódla of the magic lands.
for thy emerald eye 'tis no time of slumber,
thou binding cord of the Field of Ír [Ireland]

Too long seems to Ireland of the sweet grass,
o son of Aonghus, kindler of battle,
the length of thy sleep in Kintyre,
that vigorous land around which the sea is smoothest.

Rouse thee! sleep not.
In the west, thou bare-haired one,
bring to Feidhlimidh's House [Ireland] the help of Islay;
Ireland is looking for thee towards the east.

Slumber not gently in the east;
come hither under good auspices for a journey;
to unite the kingdom grasp thy blue blade;
part from warm Islay of the majestic waves.

Waken thy courage, don thy breastplate.
o noble figure, suffer not sleep to rest
upon the ale-stiffened princes of Islay's plain:
it were right to make provision for the former kingship ...

Fionn son of Cumhall who loved not riches,
O son of Aonghus, thou that withstandest the shower [of spears],
did not without reason exalt thy fame:
'tis of thee he spoke then.

Accomplish what that seer uttered;
help Banbha of the white castles;
cause not the cheek of Éibhear's Field [Ireland] to blush;
of thee the hero Fionn spoke.

O Seumas, thou hope of lordship, bring help
from Scotland of the melodious waterfalls
to the Boyne, bright with flocks of the elfin
strands; make not vain Fionn's true voice.[20]

'DEORAIDHEACHT': EXILE AND RETURN

One of the most striking features of Irish bardic poetry's depiction of
Gaelic Scotland is the apparent discomfort and uncertainty at the simple
fact of a Gaelic community existing outside Ireland. Again and again, in
poems from earlier centuries as well as in works from the period considered in this article, the Gaelic presence in Scotland is presented as an
unstable, impermanent phenomenon – something that should come to an
end with the return of the Scottish Gaels to Ireland, which is understood
as the only natural and normal place for Gaels to exist. The dominant
theme is exile, and Gaels in Scotland are often depicted as warriors on
a distant, but inherently temporary, foreign campaign, or as mere
mercenaries.[21]

Tadhg Dall Ó hUiginn's 'Fada cóir Fhódla ar Albain' makes the case in
terms of mythology, urging Somhairle Buidhe Mac Domhnaill to return
to the land of his forefather, Colla Uais. The poet retells the tale of the
three mythological Collas (Colla Uais, Colla Dhá Críoch and Colla
Meann), ancestors of the Oirghialla and of Clann Somhairle, who were
banished to Scotland by Muireadhach Tíreach before returning to Ireland
in triumph. The descendants of Colla Uais (in this case meaning Clann
Domhnaill) chose to return to Scotland, a matter of regret to the poet, but
this can now be put right:

> Na trí Colla, críoch a sgéal,
> clann Eochaidh díomsoigh Dhoimléan,
> déanamh dóibh ar fhiadh nAlban,
> triar ris nár chóir comhardadh.
>
> Dias don triúr do theacht i Ile
> go crích Bhreagh na mbeann sídhe;
> rogha an tsluaigh i Moigh Mhonaidh
> ó shoin uainn ar n-anamhain.

20 Published in Bergin, *Irish Bardic Poetry*, pp 161–6, 287–90 (§§ 1–5, 20–2).   **21** See McLeod,
Divided Gaels, pp 173–92.

Iongna do fhuilngeadar féin,
fir mhaordha na n-arm n-aighmhéil,
Colla 'sa shéinshliocht ó shoin,
a n-eighriocht orra d'easbhoidh.

Créad fa tiobhradh clann Cholla,
ar son ar fhás eatorra,
tar magh mbarrúrchas mBanbha
tal d'andúthchas allmhardha?

The three Collas, the end of their tale,
the children of proud Eochaidh Doimléan,
they made for the land of Alba,
three who would brook no rivalry.

Two of the three returned from there
to Bregia's land of the fairy mountains [Ireland];
the choice of the host remained
ever since in the Plain of Monadh [Scotland].

It is strange that they allowed themselves,
the stately men of the destructive weapons,
Colla and his ancient lineage ever since
to be deprived of their inheritance.

Why should Colla's sons,
owing to whatever rose between them,
give support to a strange foreign land
before the rippling cropped plains of Banbha?[22]

Fear Flatha Ó Gnímh's 'Éireannaigh féin Fionnlochlannaigh' ('These Hebrideans are Irishmen indeed'), composed *c*.1620 for Raghnall Mac Domhnaill, first earl of Antrim (†1636), has a rather more tactical objective, asserting that the Hebrideans – at least those descended from the Collas – are properly Irish, a useful argument for the earl as he jockeyed for position in Ireland under the new dispensation of the early seventeenth century.[23] The poem's rhetoric is particularly extreme, presenting these Scottish Gaels as alienated exiles for whom Scotland can never be home and return to Ireland is the only natural course of action:

22 McLeod & Bateman, *Duanaire na Sracaire*, pp 130–1 (ll. 29–44); Knott (ed.), *Tadhg Dall Ó hUiginn*, i, 173–9, ii, 115–19 (§§ 8–11); on the history of the Collas, see ibid., ii, 228–32. 23 On the significance of the term *Fionnlochlannaigh*, see McLeod, *Divided Gaels*, pp 128–30; on the maneuverings of the first earl of Antrim, see Jane H. Ohlmeyer, *Civil war and restoration in the three Stuart kingdoms: the career of Randal MacDonnell, marquis of Antrim, 1609–1683* (Cambridge, 1993), pp 19–27.

Eireannaigh féin Fionnlochlannaigh
dá bhfréimh ó na finnghealChoḷḷaibh,
an fheadhain shaor shuilbhearchonnail
nar thaobh Eamhain innbhearthonnaigh.

Aicme ad-roigh re robhuanaimsir
tar moir ngoilthe ngoibhéilinnsigh,
lucht sealbha na seinÉireann-soin
ó Ghurt Eamhna oiléininnsigh.

Triallaid tar cuan gcormbhogabaigh
sluagh dá bhfianaibh formaideagair
do ládh druim gér dhearmadobair
le clár Cuinn far chomhraigeadair.

Dronga go gcéill chomhairlemhir
do fhréimh Cholla chridhiorghalaigh
ó shoin um fhád n-oirearMhonaidh
a-tád thoir 'n-a dtighearnadhaibh.

Ré cian fa chuing fhéinnidheachta
ó fhiadh Fhloinn don leomhainealta;
deigh-sheal raith an ríoghoireachta;
maith deireadh na deoraidheachta.

Tír dúthaigh chláir chríchfhionnMhonaidh
dháibh níor dhúthaigh mhátharbhunaidh;
fan tír fhoirbhthe fhéithinnbhearaigh
díbh níor ghoirthe achd gnáthallmhuraigh.

These Hebrideans are Irishmen indeed
owing to their springing from the fair-bright Collas,
the noble, well-spoken worthy band
that stayed not in Eamhain of the wave-girt estuaries.

The race that long long ago sped
across the boiling sea of isles and bays,
the folk that had possessed Ireland of yore
leaving the field of island-Eamhain.

They pass out over a sea [reminiscent] of mild matured ale,
that host with their bands of enviable array;
backs were turned – though it was mistaken work –
to Conn's Plain for which they had fought.

Hosts of quick decisive spirit
of the race of Colla the joyous-fighting
abide ever since in the coast-land of Monadh
in the east as rulers.

For long, under yoke of military service,
that lion-band stayed far from Flann's land [Ireland];
an upturn in fortune (?) for the royal assembly;
and happy, too, the end of their exile.

The land of the plain of fair-bordered Monadh
was for them no original-motherland;
in that perfect land of calm estuaries
they could not be called anything but mere foreigners.[24]

Returning to Ireland, the Clann Domhnaill *Fionnlochlannaigh* are destined
to be triumphant and victorious:

Gasraidh do dhruim dúthrachttogha
tar tuinn anfaidh áithneartmhara,
Fád Dá Thí ar tí a luathrochtana
's a-tád ar tí a tháithreachtana.

Banbha Chuinn badh críochcoganta
do dhruim fhaghla 's éachtaigeanta
sirthe ón bannbhras bárccuideachta
adhnas crithre a gcéadchaigealta ...

Ceann brughadh is breitheamhmaicne,
ceann na gcuradh gcaithinnilte,
ceann riaghla agus rochomairce,
fearr ón Iarla an aithimirce.

A band of set choice coming over
the stormy surface of the keen strong sea,
the land of Dá Thí [Ireland] awaits their speedy arrival,
and they are set on reaching it.

Border-harried shall be Conn's Banbha
by reivings and valiant prowess;
the forays, which make the sailors eager-paced,
awake again the flames of their former smouldering ...

Prince of yeoman and brehons,
prince of battle-harnessed warriors,
prince of law and good guardianship,
the Earl has made that return the grander.[25]

24 Published in Lambert McKenna, 'Poem to the first earl of Antrim', *Irish Monthly*, 48 (1920), pp 314–18; Láimhbheartach Mac Cionnaith (ed.), *Dioghluim Dána* (Dublin, 1938), pp 290–3; and (in part) Mícheál B. Ó Mainnín, '"The same in origin and blood": bardic windows on the relationship between Irish and Scottish Gaels, *c*.1200–1650', *CMCS*, 38 (1999), pp 1–52 (pp 23–5) (§§ 1–6). I have made some minor adjustments to the translation. 25 'Éireannaigh féin Fionnlochlannaigh', §§ 8–9, 13.

CONCLUSION

With the final conquest of Ireland at the beginning of the seventeenth century, Scottish Gaelic involvement in military activity in Ireland diminished very rapidly. The era of 'pan-Gaelic' warfare may be said to have reached its decisive end in the War of the Three Kingdoms with the career of Alasdair mac Cholla Chiotaigh of Colonsay, who campaigned across the breadth of Scotland and Ireland only to fall in the end at the battle of Knocknanuss in Co. Cork in 1647. Alasdair's death, memorialized in Ireland in the famous harp tune 'Máirseáil Alasdruim', was lamented grievously by the great vernacular poet, Iain Lom of Keppoch:

Fhir nan gearrghruaige duibhe,
Tha mi deurach 'gad chumha
O'n là reub thu cuan sruthach nan ròd ...

Cha bu tais 's cha bu tlàth thu
Marcachd suas roimh 'n bhragàda
Air each aigeannach àrd nan ceithir bròg.

Cha bu chladhaire truid thu
Dol an aghaidh an trupa;
Ceum air th'adhart 'nan uchd b'e do nòs ...

Fhuair mi sgeul o Dhùn Chanain
A bhrist leus air mo shealladh,
Mo chreach léir nach robh Alasdair beò;

Agus firinn o'n chlàrsair
Tighinn air tìr am Port Phàdraig,
Cha d'rinn m'inntinn fhéin fàilte r'a cheòl.

You with the short black hair, tearfully do I lament you,
ever since the day you cleft the foaming sea
with its open roadsteads ...

You were not faint-hearted or feeble
as you rode up at the head of the brigade,
on a high mettlesome steed well shod.

You were not a coward in battle
as you advanced to meet a squadron,
to march to face them breast to breast was your wont ...

I got news from Dungannon
that has dimmed my eyesight,
my utter woe that Alasdair was dead.

And the truth from the harper
when he landed at Port Patrick [Galloway];
my mind made no glad response to his music.[26]

---

26 'Cumha Alasdair mhic Cholla' ('Lament for Alasdair mac Cholla'), published in Annie M. MacKenzie (ed.), *Òrain Iain Luim: The songs of John MacDonald, Bard of Keppoch*, Scottish Gaelic Texts, 8 (Edinburgh, 1965), pp 34–9 (§§ 2, 8–9, 15–16).

Securing the Jacobean succession: the secret career of James Fullerton of Trinity College, Dublin

DAVID EDWARDS

This crown [of England and Ireland] is not like to fall to the ground for want of heads that claim to wear it, but upon whose head it will fall is by many doubted

(Thomas Wilson, *The State of England*, 1600)[1]

Retrospect is a dubious gift for the historian. Incautiously handled, it has the capacity to telescope events into a straight line, allowing what subsequently happened to seem inevitable, pushing everything else to the margins and out of view. We recently witnessed the 400th anniversary of the Anglo-Scottish regnal union of 1603, when the Stewart king of Scotland, James VI, inherited the thrones of England and Ireland after the English royal family of more than a century, the Tudors, died out. Despite the various commemorative events, and the accompanying platforms for research output, a number of myths based entirely on retrospect continue to prevail. Two of these require urgent correction – the myth of King James's 'unopposed' succession (in fact, he had many opponents, and was greatly worried by them); and the myth that Ireland posed no threat to him (potentially it did, but not in the way that historians have traditionally viewed it).

Much remains to be discovered about the decade or more of complex and highly secretive intrigue that had prepared the ground for the Jacobean succession. A particularly glaring lacuna is the absence of any systematic examination of the role played by special agents and 'intelligencers' in negotiating by stealth the progress of King James's claim to the English and Irish thrones with the key figures of both kingdoms. The following paper investigates the activities of one such agent, a Scottish academic from Ayrshire, James Fullerton.

---

1 Thomas Wilson, 'The state of England, Anno Dom. 1600', ed. F.J. Fisher, in *The Camden Miscellany XVI*, Camden Society, 3rd ser., 52 (London, 1936), p. 5.

Retrospect has done Fullerton few favours. Because he ended his career as a so-called 'mere favourite' of Charles I and failed to secure one of the great offices at the royal court before his death,[2] English constitutional historians have dismissed him as of little significance in the political history of the Stewart monarchy. He was, we are told, 'an ordinary courtier of the second rank', his proximity to King Charles has been called 'surprising',[3] and his usefulness has been called into question as 'not so obvious'.[4] One biographer of Charles I even misnames him.[5] Had scholars examined his early life, however, his later high standing as a trusted royal servant would be entirely understandable – not at all 'surprising'. Before 1603, from his post at the just recently-founded Trinity College, Dublin, Fullerton was involved in all kinds of secret diplomacy with the English and Irish on behalf of the Scottish king, the barest outlines of which have survived. Notably, he helped to neutralize the threat that various military forces in Ireland posed to the Stewart cause, initially in the North Channel, at the outbreak of the Nine Years War, and later at the time of King James's accession. He also played a crucial role in developing secret links with Sir Robert Cecil, the great English minister, without which the Scottish king's chances of succeeding would have been seriously weakened.

It is no bad thing if what follows raises more questions than it can provide answers to, in regard to the tensions and uncertainties surrounding the establishment of the Stewart multiple monarchy, or triple crown. For too long historians have ignored the fact that King James's bid for the kingdoms of England and Ireland was a calculated gamble. That the gamble paid off is a tribute not just to the political skills of the king and those of the English ruling elite that favoured him – an indisputable fact, as far as it goes – but also to other players in the drama, such as Fullerton and his kind. But before discussing Fullerton's role in the succession, it will first be necessary to revisit in some detail the other definitive event of 1603, the end of the house of Tudor, in order to place the agent's actions in their proper context.

---

2 The phrase is Gerald Aylmer's: G.E. Aylmer, *The king's servants: the civil service of Charles I* (London, 1961), p. 92. See also Kevin Sharpe, 'The image of virtue: the court and household of Charles I, 1625–1642', in David Starkey et al., *The English court: from the Wars of the Roses to the civil war* (London, 1987), p. 232.   3 Aylmer, *The king's servants*, p. 317.   4 John Bruce (ed.), *Correspondence of King James VI of Scotland with Sir Robert Cecil and others*, Camden Soc., 1st ser., 78 (London, 1861), p. xliv.   5 Charles Carlton, *Charles I: the personal monarch* (London, 1983), pp 15–16, renders him as 'Sir Jasper Fullerton'.

I

Early on the morning of Thursday 24 March 1603, at Richmond Palace in Surrey, the last Tudor monarch of England, Queen Elizabeth I, passed away in her sleep. Her death was no great shock. For one thing, she was old, in her seventieth year; for another, suffering from rheumatism, chronic insomnia and 'melancholy' (as contemporaries called depression), and emaciated from refusing to eat, her health had been fading for weeks.

According to reports, across England and Wales her passing was marked more by feelings of relief than sadness. Since the glory days of the defeat of the Spanish Armada her star had waned, with the last 15 years of her rule marked by the rising demands of seemingly endless war, political and religious tension, mounting official repression, and an economic decline bordering on recession.[6] As the future Bishop Godfrey Goodman put it, 'the people' longed for change, 'being very generally weary of an old woman's government'.[7]

Some felt the relief of her death more acutely than others. In Edinburgh, her expected successor, King James VI of Scotland, was exultant. On 19 March he had been confidently informed by an overly-eager English suitor that Elizabeth would definitely die within two or three days, only for her to cling to life a little longer, provoking fears that she might recover and reign on. In England senior statesmen shared the Scottish king's concerns. For years the members of Elizabeth's privy council had been preparing for the day when they might have to act on their own initiative to preserve what they defined as the best interests of the English Protestant state.[8] Having determined that James should succeed her, and expecting to reap great rewards for engineering his succession, Sir Robert Cecil and the rest of the councillors were nevertheless worried that a plot might materialize to foist a rival candidate on the throne. Accordingly they had met – without consulting the queen – to decide on the best course of action. That the details of their discussions are not known is hardly surprising. It was treasonous, clearly in breach of a statute of 1581 that had prohibited on pain of execution any who 'not only wished her Majesty's death, but also by divers means practised and sought to know how long her Highness should live, and who would reign after her decease'.[9] Not that Cecil and

---

6 R.B. Outhwaite, 'Dearth, the English crown, and the "Crisis of the 1590s"', in Peter Clark (ed.), *The European crisis of the 1590s* (London, 1985); John Guy (ed.), *The reign of Elizabeth I: politics and culture in the last decade* (Cambridge, 1995).   7 Godfrey Goodman, *The court of King James the First* (2 vols, London, 1839), i, pp 96–7.   8 John Guy, 'Tudor monarchy and its critiques', in idem (ed.), *The Tudor monarchy* (London, 1997), pp 97–8.   9 23 Eliz. I, Cap. II (1581), part V, printed in G.W. Prothero (ed.), *Select statutes and other constitutional documents of*

his colleagues had had much choice in meeting unofficially or behaving independently. For forty-four years Elizabeth had refused to name a successor, and despite repeated promptings by Cecil and others in the last weeks of her life, she had continued to evade the subject.[10] Consequently, when at last she took to her deathbed, her councillors failed to ensure she was provided with proper medical care. As an eyewitness later recalled, at Richmond the ailing queen was left alone, 'very much neglected'.[11] To avert a succession crisis or civil war, even a foreign invasion, it had become politically desirable that Elizabeth die and James VI of Scotland be made James I of England as quickly as possible.[12]

The subsequent story of the Jacobean succession – messengers riding frenziedly between London and Edinburgh, the king's departure from Edinburgh on 5 April, his entry into England, at Berwick, the following day, and his triumphant procession southwards, reaching the Tower of London on 7 May – is much better known than the grim little waiting game that had preceded it.[13] This is only to be expected. The English and Scottish governments expended much effort in creating an official record of 1603 in which the advent of James in England, and the resultant 'Happie Unione' of England and Scotland, was shown as being celebrated by everyone. Chronicles, pamphlets, even poems were produced, all emphasizing James's exclusive legitimacy to rule and insisting on the universal joy that greeted his accession.[14] Suffice it to say, these officially sponsored records do not tell the whole story.

Although in the event no serious opposition to James materialized in England, at the time nobody in authority could be certain that a rival claimant would not emerge.[15] Despite all the propaganda to the contrary, James was debarred from inheriting the English and Irish thrones by one

the reigns of Elizabeth and James I (Oxford, 1913), p. 78.   10 Months after her death a note was written of two meetings, supposedly on 22 and 23 March, between the queen, Cecil and other councillors. It claims that on both occasions Elizabeth indicated James was her chosen successor. Although some historians continue to believe the note is accurate, I think others are correct to dismiss it as a convenient fabrication written by Cecil's secretary to provide retrospective justification for Cecil's actions on James's behalf (Penry Williams, *The later Tudors: England 1547–1603* [Oxford, 1995], pp 386–7; Paul Johnson, *Elizabeth I: a study in power and intellect* [paperback ed., London, 1988], p. 436).   11 Goodman, *Court of James*, i, pp 16–17.   12 For the circumstances of Elizabeth's final days see, e.g., Mandell Creighton, *Queen Elizabeth* (2nd ed., London, 1899), pp 297–303; J.E. Neale, *Queen Elizabeth I* (Pelican ed., London, 1971), pp 393–7; Johnson, *Elizabeth I*, pp 433–7. In addition, Mark Nicholls, *Investigating the gunpowder plot* (Manchester, 1991), chs 7–8, contains much valuable new information.   13 G.P.V. Akrigg, *Jacobean pageant: the court of James I* (London, 1962), ch. 2, gives the best account of the procession south.   14 Ibid.   15 Williams, *The later Tudors*, pp 383–7; Joel Hurstfield, 'The succession struggle in late Elizabethan England', in idem, *Freedom, corruption and government in Elizabethan England* (London, 1973), pp 104–34.

rather important document – the will of Henry VIII, which in 1547 had identified the English Greys, not the Scottish Stewarts, as the rightful royal heirs in the event of the Tudors dying out. James's concern that this 56-year-old item might be dusted off for use against him was not helped by his awareness that, for many English people, the fact that he was a Scot counted hugely against him. For more than three hundred years Anglo-Scottish relations had been characterized by mutual loathing.[16] True, relations had thawed somewhat since the 1560s because of the spread of Protestantism in both kingdoms,[17] but as some of King James's English allies were at pains to point out in secret correspondence, by 1600 this thawing was not yet sufficiently advanced to overcome such ancient antipathy.[18]

Religion was not nearly so unifying or integrative a factor as James, Cecil and the rest would have wished. In 1603 approximately a third of the English population was Catholic. They could not be ignored, as England's Catholic enemies in Europe would merrily exploit any opposition on their part. But neither could they be accommodated. Any attempt by James to reassure the English Catholics of his good intentions would necessarily mean antagonizing the majority of English Protestants. Already, in the early 1590s, James had angered many in England by his half-hearted punishment of pro-Spanish Catholic conspirators in Scotland.[19] The fact that his wife, Anna of Denmark, was known to have converted to Catholicism in 1593 served only to heighten Catholic expectations and Protestant suspicions of him.[20] Lastly, being the son of Mary, Queen of Scots, the greatest Catholic martyr of the sixteenth century, compounded all these difficulties where it mattered most – among sections of the English political elite. As Michael Questier has put it, fearing revenge, those in England who had led the campaign to have Mary executed – nobles, courtiers, senior officials, MPs – 'did not want to see him [James] crowned in London ever'.[21]

Hence the propaganda of the English and Scottish governments. Far from being the only possible successor to Elizabeth, bound to succeed, all

16 William Ferguson, *Scotland's relations with England: a survey to 1707* (Saltire Soc., Edinburgh, 1994), chs 3–4; R. Campbell Paterson, *My wound is deep: a history of the later Anglo-Scots Wars, 1380–1560* (Edinburgh, 1997).   17 Jane Dawson, 'Anglo-Scottish protestant culture and integration in sixteenth-century Britain', in S.G. Ellis and Sarah Barber (eds), *Conquest and union: fashioning a British state, 1485–1725* (London, 1995), pp 87–114; Gordon Donaldson, *Scottish church history* (Edinburgh, 1985), pp 137–63.   18 E.g., the advice of the earl of Northumberland: Bruce (ed.), *Correspondence of James VI*, pp 53–61.   19 Michael C. Questier, 'The politics of religious conformity and the accession of James I', *BIHR*, 71/174 (Feb. 1998), 20.   20 M.M. Meikle, 'A meddlesome princess: Anna of Denmark and Scottish court politics, 1589–1603', Julian Goodare and Michael Lynch (eds), *The reign of James VI* (East Linton, 2000), p. 138.   21 Questier, 'The politics of religious conformity', 20.

that was needed to prevent James's succession was the appearance of a plausible rival candidate to the throne. While everyone waited for Elizabeth to die, other candidates besides James were touted to succeed her. Indeed, as many as a dozen potential rivals existed,[22] four of whom have since been acknowledged by historians as genuine contenders.[23] James's cousin, Lady Arabella Stewart, was fancied by some, including at least two prominent courtiers, Henry, Lord Cobham, and Sir Walter Raleigh.[24] Arabella boasted the same English descent as James, from a daughter of Henry VII, but though her gender counted against her, she enjoyed the advantage of having been born and raised in England.[25] Late in 1599 reports that she might marry the Archduke Matthias, a continental prince with the power to enforce her claim, had greatly alarmed James, and immediately he had set about trying to hinder the marriage.[26] An alternative candidate was the Spanish Infanta, Isabella de Austria, co-ruler of the Spanish Netherlands, who was distantly descended from the Lancastrian prince, John of Gaunt. The preferred choice of hard-line Catholics, the Spanish king, her brother Philip III, failed to push her claim effectively, so that she was never more than an outside bet. She was, moreover, personally disinterested in pursuing her claim.[27]

More serious than is often assumed were the potential claimants that existed among the English male nobility.[28] The Tudor monarchs had managed, without too much savagery, to curb the ambitions of nobles of 'the blood royal' during the sixteenth century.[29] However, now that the Tudors faced extinction, interest grew in the exalted lineages of certain noblemen and made them natural targets for plotters hostile to a Scottish, Spanish, or female succession. The principal English candidate in 1603 was Edward Seymour, Lord Beauchamp, eldest son and heir of the earl of Hertford and his wife Katharine Grey, sister of the 'Nine Days Queen' of 1553, Lady Jane Grey. By the terms of Henry VIII's will, Beauchamp, not

---

22 Wilson, 'The state of England', 2–5.   23 E.g., Williams, *The later Tudors*, p. 384; Hurstfield, 'The succession struggle', p. 108.   24 Mark Nicholls, 'Two Winchester trials: the prosecution of Henry, Lord Cobham, and Thomas, Lord Grey of Wilton', *BIHR*, 68/165 (Feb. 1995), 26–48. 25 Akrigg, *Jacobean pageant*, pp 113–15.   26 Maurice Lee, *The 'inevitable' union and other essays on early modern Scotland* (East Linton, 2003), p. 103.   27 A.J. Loomie, 'Philip III and the Stuart succession in England', *Revue Belge de Philologie et d'Histoire*, 43 (1965), 492–514; Lee, *The 'inevitable' union*, p. 103; Jenny Wormald, 'Gunpowder, treason and Scots', *Journal of British Studies*, 24 (1985), 155. It has been argued that, prior to the Essex rebellion of 1601, Sir Robert Cecil himself gave serious consideration to backing Isabella, but the evidence is slight: L. Hicks, 'Sir Robert Cecil, Father Persons and the succession', in *Archivum Historicum Societatis Iesu*, 24 (1955), 95–139.   28 Joel Hurstfield almost totally ignored the domestic claimants in his treatment of the question, concentrating instead on the Infanta and her alleged supporter, Cecil: Hurstfield, 'The succession struggle', passim.   29 M.L. Bush, 'The Tudors and the royal race', *History*, 55/183 (Feb. 1970), 37–48.

King James, should have succeeded Elizabeth I, being the most senior representative of the Greys.[30] Fortunately for James, however, in 1561, on learning of Beauchamp's birth, and in order to protect Queen Elizabeth's right to rule, the English government had declared the infant lord illegitimate.[31] So Beauchamp remained thereafter, but as the queen herself could testify, being declared a bastard was not necessarily a lasting barrier to royal succession. Indeed, by deciding to remain unmarried, ruling as a virgin queen, Elizabeth ensured that those of her subjects opposed to foreign claimants would one day naturally look to Beauchamp to succeed her.[32] In 1596, as the end of her reign came into sight, Beauchamp's father, Hertford, had risked imprisonment in the Tower and possible execution for attempting to have his son's birth legitimized before the court of Arches.[33] Six years later, in November 1602, Arabella Stewart had caused alarm in London and Edinburgh when it was learned she had looked for a secret marriage alliance with Beauchamp in order to unite their separate royal claims.[34] In the event Beauchamp and his father ignored Arabella's overtures, but before Queen Elizabeth died a rumour spread that the two men were deliberately absent from London, plotting again. They continued to be closely watched.[35]

Another possible contender, at least in legal terms, was William Stanley, sixth earl of Derby, whose great-grandmother on his mother's side was Mary Tudor, younger daughter of Henry VII. Yet, probably because his claim was inferior to those of both Beauchamp and Arabella Stewart, Derby made no obvious attempt to throw his hat in the ring either before or after Queen Elizabeth's death. It should be noted that the fate of his elder brother Ferdinando, the fifth earl, might have dissuaded Earl William from pursuing his royal rights. In 1594 Ferdinando had denounced those who were then plotting to advance the Derby claim to the crown, only to be poisoned by the plotters.[36] It was probably because of his perceived

30 Mortimer Levine, *The early Elizabethan succession question* (Stanford, CA, 1966), pp 17–29. 31 Norman Jones, *The birth of the Elizabethan Age: England in the 1560s* (Oxford, 1993), pp 102–6.   32 E.g., the MP John Hales, who in 1564 wrote a pamphlet naming Beauchamp as the true heir to the throne, and spent the rest of his life under restraint: Robert Tittler, *Nicholas Bacon: the making of a Tudor statesman* (London, 1976), pp 117–22.   33 G.E.C., *Complete peerage*, sub 'Hertford, earls of'.   34 D.N. Durant, *Bess of Hardwick: portrait of an Elizabethan dynast* (London, 1977), pp 201–13, gives a sensible account of Arabella's plight, based mainly on HMC, *Calendar of the manuscripts of the marquis of Salisbury*, 24 vols (London, 1883–1976), xii, pp 681–96.   35 Nicholls, *Gunpowder plot*, p. 118. An indication of the extent of their scheming is perhaps suggested by the fact that not a single document bearing on their claim has survived among their family papers at Longleat: see Marjorie Blatcher's 'Introduction' in HMC, *Manuscripts of the marquess of Bath at Longleat, Volume iv: Seymour Papers, 1532–1686* (London, 1968), p. xvi.   36 G.E.C., *Complete peerage*, sub 'Derby, earls of'; C. Nicholl, *The reckoning: the murder of Christopher Marlowe* (London, 1994), pp 247–8, 258–9. For background to the Derby

timidity that English Catholic and French Protestant onlookers focussed their energies on finding a suitable continental groom for Earl William's eldest daughter, a son-in-law who would be strong enough to lead the earl into declaring the Stanley claim (The French King, Henri IV, was among those considered by Protestant plotters).[37]

Lastly, there was the de la Pole claim, an entitlement dating back to the mid-fifteenth century through descent from George, duke of Clarence, brother of Edward IV. In 1603 the main candidate capable of activating this was George Hastings, fourth earl of Huntingdon, a rich and powerful magnate. The fact that in 1601 he arranged the marriage of his teenage grandson and heir, Henry, Lord Hastings, to a daughter of Ferdinando, late earl of Derby, does not sit easily with the suggestion made by some historians that the Hastings family avoided getting involved in the succession question.[38]

Opposition to King James of Scotland during 1603, and the English government's fear of it, was further advanced than is often thought. In the week-and-a-half before Elizabeth's death, in order to head off any Catholic threat, the privy council ordered the detention of prominent recusants, and all seminary priests were banished from England and Wales on pain of death. But the government was only moderately concerned by Catholics. Recognizing the much greater risk posed by nationalistic Englishmen opposed to a foreign succession, public meetings and assemblies were outlawed, and in London extra guards were posted at the most important buildings in the city.[39]

The prospect of dissent was palpable, reaching even into the ranks of the English ruling class. Immediately after Elizabeth died there is evidence that some at least of the country's nobles were prepared to propose an alternative to James. At a meeting of the 'great council' held on the morning of the queen's death (24 March) it is recorded that 'some speech of divers competitors' was had. It is not stated which of James's competitors were discussed – the source is an 'official', pro-Jacobean one, written afterwards to legitimize the Scottish king's succession[40] – but it is

plot see A.H. Dodd, 'North Wales and the Essex revolt of 1601', *EHR*, 59 (1944), 357–9. 37 Loomie, 'Philip III', pp 500, 509n; *CSPV*, ix, p. 367.   38 This suggestion is explicitly advanced in Bush, 'The Tudors', p. 48, and implicitly in other accounts, by virtue of the Huntingdon claim being completely overlooked. The basis for not taking it seriously derives from what is known of the behaviour of the third earl, Henry, who was anxious to disassociate himself from the succession issue. Earl Henry died in 1595, when the succession struggle was only beginning. His brother and heir, Earl George, has never been studied. For the 1602 marriage see G.E.C., *Complete peerage*, sub 'Huntingdon, earls of'.   39 Nicholls, *Gunpowder plot*, pp 113, 120 nn; *APC, 1601–04*, pp 491–2.   40 BL, Sloane Ms 1786, fol. 5v. For a brief commentary on this source, and other versions of it, see Nicholls, *Gunpowder plot*, pp 124 and

surely significant that other names were touted at such a critical moment. Equally revealing is surviving information about how the great council was persuaded to endorse James's candidature. According to the 'official' version of the meeting, those present agreed to have James proclaimed king only when Cecil, Lord Chancellor Egerton, and the earl of Nottingham had stated that Elizabeth's last act was to signify that the king of Scotland should succeed – a claim that was very probably a lie.[41] An impression of how heated the meeting got is suggested by another source, Bishop Goodman's memoir, which though written many years later is generally accepted by scholars as reliable. Goodman spoke to 'credible persons' who had been at the great council on 24 March. He was told that James's greatest supporter among the English nobility, the earl of Northumberland, had warned that 'if any man' made trouble for the king, 'he [Northumberland] would instantly raise an army against him'.[42] It is also known that Northumberland had at least fifty armed retainers close by.[43] Ultimately, then, it seems that in March 1603 the king of Scots secured the English and Irish thrones not simply by universal approval, as his supporters had it. Deceit and the threat of force were also factors, a small but powerful clique of English ministers and nobles having decided that he, rather than some other claimant, should be crowned.

II

Modern dictators were by no means the first to recognize that, at base, all power is derived from the barrel of a gun. Having ruled Scotland for nearly twenty years James VI was well acquainted with the usefulness of force. From the late 1590s, as the death of Elizabeth I began to loom near, he had been at pains to ensure that everyone understood his willingness, if necessary, to invade England to impose his claim at gunpoint. Though his legal right to succeed was far from clear-cut, following the failure of Henri IV of France to enter the race,[44] as a ruling monarch James was the only one out of all of Elizabeth's possible successors capable of putting a large army in the field. Theoretically, the Infanta, Isabella, could have called upon the forces of the Spanish Netherlands to support her, but in reality neither she nor her husband, the archduke of Austria, controlled

---

136 n. 7, where it features as part of a somewhat different interpretation.   **41** See n. 10 above. Elizabeth, we know, was virtually comatose for the last three days of her life, when Cecil, Egerton and Nottingham allegedly 'visited' her; moreover, Bishop Goodman states that during her last days, only clergy entered her chamber.   **42** Goodman, *The court*, pp 24–7.   **43** Nicholls, *Gunpowder plot*, p. 118.   **44** Loomie, 'Philip III', 509–13.

the army there, enjoying only nominal authority.[45] The best the strongest English claimant, Beauchamp, could do was raise the county militia for Wiltshire, where his father, Hertford, was lord lieutenant (it was probably this that accounted for the rumour reported in March 1603 that Hertford and Beauchamp were in arms and on the point of revolt).[46] As a none too subtle reminder, while Elizabeth lay dying James assembled his Scottish forces near the border, the news of which caused the English commander of Berwick Fort to write urgently to London announcing that an invasion was imminent. But, of course, the Scottish army was not actually needed. As if by magic it dissolved overnight, after the king received secret communiqués from both Cecil and Northumberland urging him not to use force lest it provoke opposition, and assuring him that everything was in hand down south.[47] In the end the English kingdom was his because the council and its representatives controlled the armed forces, the local trained bands (some 26,000 part-time soldiers).[48] In England and Wales effective resistance to him was unlikely.

But what about the other component of James's prospective Tudor inheritance, the kingdom of Ireland? Long before 1603 it had been a maxim of British and European politics that anyone intending to invade England or to seize its throne would be well advised to consider using Ireland as a stepping-stone. To quote the contemporary proverb: 'He who would England win must with Ireland begin'.[49] Throughout the sixteenth century fears over security lay at the heart of England's Irish policy, and it was largely in order to defend England that so much effort was expended in garrisoning the country with more and more troops and interfering (often brutally) in the affairs of the Irish lordships. But with the growth of English power on the island from the 1540s a new problem materialized – the emergence of the army of Ireland as the single greatest force in the Tudor state.[50] From 1580 the Irish wars usually necessitated a full-time army of nearly 3,000 men, rising to far more through levies and

---

45 Geoffrey Parker, *The army of Flanders and the Spanish Road, 1567–1659* (Cambridge, 1972), pp 247–51. 46 Joel Hurstfield, 'County government: Wiltshire, *c.*1530–*c.*1660', in idem, *Freedom, corruption and government*, p. 238. The rumour of an impending Seymour revolt was spread by the French ambassador: *CSPV, 1603–07*, p. 3. 47 Nicholls, *Gunpowder plot*, pp 113–14; HMC, *Salisbury MSS*, xii, *1603*, p. 699. 48 Williams, *The later Tudors*, pp 535–6. 49 J.J. Silke, *Kinsale: the Spanish intervention in Ireland at the end of the Elizabethan wars* (Liverpool, 1970), p. 76. See also Hiram Morgan, 'British policies before the British state', in Brendan Bradshaw and John Morrill (eds), *The British problem, c.1534–1707: state formation in the Atlantic Archipelago* (Basingstoke, 1996), p. 67. 50 Ciaran Brady, 'England's defence and Ireland's reform: the dilemma of the Irish viceroys, 1541–1641', in Bradshaw & Morrill (eds), *The British problem*, pp 89–117; Hiram Morgan, 'Overmighty officers: the Irish lord deputyship in the early modern British state', *History Ireland*, 7:4 (Winter 1999), 17–21.

conscription depending on the seriousness of the conflict in which it was engaged. Crucially for the impending royal succession, the intensification of warfare that occurred during the 1590s saw troop numbers leap to unprecedented heights. When the earl of Essex arrived as English governor, or viceroy, of the kingdom in 1599 he took charge of a force of 16,000 foot and 1,300 horse.[51] Across the entire British Isles there was nothing like it.

That the Irish army made a potential kingmaker of the viceroy, its commander-in-chief, was obvious. Essex's abortive coup-attempt of February 1601, in which he had hoped to destroy Cecil, Nottingham and the rest of his enemies in England, had originally been conceived on behalf of King James and had expected to attract Irish military support. Perhaps had Essex attempted it two years earlier, while he had charge of the Irish army, it might actually have succeeded in its object to force Elizabeth and her council to name James as her heir. Indeed, it may even have succeeded as late as December 1600, at which time Essex still thought that the enterprise enjoyed the support of his successor as Irish viceroy, his friend Lord Mountjoy. In the event, the withdrawal of Mountjoy's support ensured the scheme was doomed to failure, and King James was for a time compromised, as following the revolt the extent of his contacts with Essex became known.[52]

Though aware that security and military issues had brought Ireland to James's attention as king of Scotland, nonetheless historians of the 1603 union of crowns have consistently ignored the country's strategic importance to him at the time of the succession.[53] Written from the false premise that it was only the Irish rebels under Aodh Ó Néill, the earl of Tyrone, who worried the king, most accounts of the Jacobean succession contend that following the English victory at Kinsale and the subsequent routing of the Irish rebel confederacy, the country posed no threat to the incoming monarch. Yet it was from the English stationed in Ireland, not the Irish, that James had most cause to fear. Furthermore, a close examination of the Irish dimension of James's political strategy helps to explain one of the key mysteries of the Jacobean succession – how Sir Robert Cecil was persuaded to embrace King James's cause in 1600–1, having previously opposed it.

James VI was more concerned by Ireland and its strategic position in the British Isles than has hitherto been acknowledged. For many years he

51 Cyril Falls, *Elizabeth's Irish wars* (London, 1950), p. 232.   52 *CSPV, 1592–1603*, p. 450.
53 The most recent example of this is A.D. Nicholls, *The Jacobean union: a reconsideration of British civil policies under the Early Stuarts* (London, 1999), in which Ireland is not mentioned at all in a chapter dealing with the security question (ch. 3).

had been sending agents there, partly to gather intelligence, but also, as Elizabeth declined, to establish his presence and make useful contacts for the day when finally he would make his bid to succeed her. Though he employed others, two of his Scottish agents are known to scholars, largely because of their association with the founding of Trinity College, Dublin – the future Viscount Clandeboye, James Hamilton, and the subject of the remainder of this paper, James Fullerton. Because Hamilton went on to become one of the leading Scotsmen in Ireland after 1603,[54] as a colonial adventurer and a patron of Presbyterianism in Ulster, Fullerton – his friend and colleague at Trinity – has largely been forgotten. This is regrettable. Before the Jacobean succession was secured, and for some years afterwards, it was Fullerton, not Hamilton, who was by far the most important of the king's representatives in Ireland.[55] Through a close scrutiny of his movements it is possible to see behind the 'official' version of events leading up to March 1603, and gain an impression of the occasionally acute sense of insecurity that affected King James's ambitions to succeed.[56]

III

The main reason why Fullerton has not received much attention from historians is the fact that, like all secret agents and 'intelligencers', his activities are but fitfully recorded. Just three letters that are either in his hand or else signed by him have survived from before 1603.[57] Such meetings as he had with senior government officials or major political personages in Ireland, England or Scotland were informal, not meant to be written down. To further cover his tracks he used at least two aliases, in Scotland in 1595 arranging to be addressed in correspondence as 'William Oliphant' (after a well-known lawyer),[58] while in 1600–1 he appeared in

---

54 For Hamilton, see esp. T.F. Henderson, 'James Hamilton, Viscount Clandeboy (1559–1643)', *DNB*, viii, pp 1062–3; Michael Perceval-Maxwell, *The Scottish migration to Ulster in the reign of James I* (Belfast, 1999), pp 1, 51–8, 234–45; and now R.J. Hunter, 'James Hamilton, first Viscount Claneboye (1560–1644)', *ODNB* (Oxford, 2004). 55 David Edwards, 'Scottish officials and secular government in Early Stewart Ireland' (forthcoming). 56 Suffice it to say that I do not agree with the view of James's most recent biographer that he was confident he had it sown up (Jenny Wormald, 'James VI and I', *ODNB*). 57 There are two letters from June 1595, given a full description in *Cal. Scottish Papers, 1593–5* (Edinburgh, 1936), pp 586–7, 627–8, and a brief treatment in *CSPS, 1589–1603* (London, 1858), pp 679, 685. The remaining letter, of April 1597, was co-written with Walter Travers: HMC, *Salisbury MSS*, vii, *1597* (London, 1899), pp 151–2. 58 *Cal. Scottish Papers, 1593–5*, p. 628.

London as a 'Mr Figg'.[59] The rest of the time he masked his actions behind the cloak of his everyday work as a scholar and university man.

It has been claimed that his family origins were 'humble',[60] but this is misleading. The Fullertons might not have been nobles, but they were hardly peasants. An established landowning lineage, they had been settled in Ayrshire since at least the early fourteenth century, from the reign of King Robert I, 'the Bruce' (whom, reputedly, they had helped to the Scottish throne).[61] While not of the head branch that resided at Craighall near Kyle Stewart, the family of James Fullerton was of gentry status all the same, possessing a small estate at Dreghorne, situated between the coastal towns of Irvine and Ayr. In recognition of their respectable social standing, James's father, John Fullerton, and his elder brother, also called John, are each referred to as 'laird of Dreghorne' in the contemporary registers of the Scottish council.[62] Writing from Ayr about his brother the laird in 1595, James described him as 'a man of good credit and estimation in this country'.[63] The head branch at Craighall clearly agreed. While James Fullerton was still a young man his sister, Agnes, was deemed a suitable marriage partner for the chief, 'Fullerton of that ilk', and went to live at Craighall.[64] Undoubtedly, Fullerton's background aided his later career. Had he not been from recognizable stock, it would have been virtually impossible for him to gain entry to the inner sanctum of government buildings or noble houses in Dublin and London, let alone effect decisions on King James's behalf among sections of the English and Irish political elite.

He and his family had strong Protestant credentials. As he told the English agent in Edinburgh during the 1590s, prior to taking his uncle as her second husband, his aunt, Margaret Chalmers, had been married to James Boyd of Trochrig, the late archbishop of Glasgow (d. 1581).[65] Archbishop Boyd had been one of the founders of Protestantism in Stewart Scotland. In the 1570s, influenced by Andrew Melville, he had helped to draft the Second Book of Discipline that tried to push the national church towards Geneva-style Presbyterianism. In addition to his archiepiscopal duties he had served briefly as church moderator.[66] Being associated with

59 Ibid., *1597–1603*, p. 683; HMC, *Salisbury MSS*, xiv: *Addenda, 1596–1603* (London, 1923), pp 171–2. 60 George Hill (ed.), *The Montgomery manuscripts* (Belfast, 1869), p. 30n; Bruce (ed.), *Correspondence of James VI*, p. xliii. 61 Ibid., pp 79–80n; *Burke's landed gentry* (18th ed., London, 1972), iii, pp 353–4, sub 'Fullerton of Norwood Grange'. 62 *RPCS*, v, *1592–99*, pp 652, 717; ibid., vi, *1599–1604*, pp 56, 743. 63 *Cal. Scottish Papers*, xi, *1593–95*, p. 627. 64 *Burke's landed gentry* (18th ed., London, 1972), iii, p. 354. 65 *Cal. Scottish Papers*, xi, *1593–95*, p. 587. 66 Hew Scott, *Fasti Ecclesiae Scoticanae* (2nd ed., Edinburgh, 1928), vii, pp 321, 439.

Boyd was a boon to Fullerton, and he seems to have stayed close to the archbishop's family, lodging with his Aunt Margaret when in Ayr.[67]

Fullerton was an accomplished scholar. In the late 1570s he had studied under Andrew Melville at Glasgow University, receiving his laureate in 1581, and he quickly earned a lasting reputation as an outstanding Latinist and grammarian.[68] It is not recorded what he thought of Melville's controversial views on presbyteries, episcopacy, and church-state relations, but throughout his life he consistently praised Melville as an educationalist, and remained in close contact with him even when the latter was in disgrace.[69] Fullerton's links to his former teacher were reinforced in 1587, when he sought a companion with whom to travel overseas. He chose James Hamilton, the son of an Ayrshire clergyman, from the village of Dunlop. A little younger than Fullerton, Hamilton had studied under Melville at St Andrew's University in the mid-1580s, and had just entered the teaching profession in Glasgow.[70] Encountering storms in the Irish Sea, the ship in which they sailed was damaged, and put in to Dublin for repairs. Perhaps because the weather did not improve (the Irish annals note 1587 as cold, wet and stormy),[71] or else for some other reason, they decided to abandon their journey and stay in Dublin after Fullerton was offered a job as a Latin schoolmaster. Hamilton agreed to serve as his usher, or general assistant.[72] To enable them to take up their posts and receive their pay 'free of servitude', they were each naturalized, made denizens, sometime afterwards.[73]

The school was an official municipal project, and Fullerton negotiated his salary of £20 (stg) per annum, plus subsistence expenses, directly from Dublin Corporation.[74] Significantly, his recruitment was a coup for the clique of native Protestants that only recently, with English help, had begun exercising a controlling influence over the affairs of the predominantly Catholic capital city.[75] As a city schoolmaster Fullerton suddenly

67 *Cal. Scottish papers*, xi, *1593–95*, p. 587.   68 See C.R. Elrington's 'Life of Ussher', in *The whole works of the Most Rev. James Ussher*, ed. C.R. Elrington and J.H. Todd, 17 vols (Dublin, 1847–64), i, p. 3.   69 Thomas McCrie, *The life of Andrew Melville: containing illustrations of the ecclesiastical and literary history of Scotland, during the latter part of the sixteenth and beginning of the seventeenth century*, 2nd ed., 2 vols (Edinburgh, 1824), ii, pp 294n, 410, 530.   70 Henderson, 'James Hamilton', p. 1062; T.K. Lowry (ed.), *The Hamilton manuscripts* (Belfast, 1867), p. 4.   71 Ibid., pp 3–4; *ALC*, ii, s.a. 1587.   72 Not the other way round, as some writers have it: Bruce (ed.), *Correspondence of James VI*, pp xliii–xliv; Akrigg, *Jacobean pageant*, p. 1; Perceval-Maxwell, *Scottish migration*, p. 1. This error seems to be derived from Thomas Birch, *Life of Henry, prince of Wales* (London, 1760).   73 NAI, Ferguson MSS, vol. 18: Repertory to the Memoranda Rolls, Edward VI-Eliz. I, pp 131, 140. Fullerton is given as 'James Foolerton' in his denization certificate.   74 J.T. Gilbert (ed.), *Calendar of ancient records of Dublin* (19 vols, Dublin 1889–1944), ii, p. 219.   75 For the growth of protestant power in the city, see Colm Lennon, *The lords of Dublin in the age of reformation* (Dublin, 1989), pp 136–9.

became important to the future prospects of Irish Protestantism. From his schoolhouse in Ship Street Great he provided an educational foundation for the sons of rich, upwardly mobile, aldermanic families whom the English government intended would rule the city in the greater Protestant interest in the years to come. His most famous pupil was James Ussher, the future archbishop of Armagh, who attended Ship Street for five years, from 1589–90 (aged eight) to 1593–4 (aged thirteen).[76] In later years Ussher stated that the 'advantage of his education from these men [Fullerton and Hamilton]' had been providential, one of God's special favours to him.[77] For the two Scotsmen who ran it, the Latin school was a place full of promise, a point of contact with the members of a powerful and privileged community that controlled the affairs of the third most important centre of the Tudor dominions, behind London and York.

Several Irish historians have claimed that, from the very beginning, Fullerton's teaching was in fact a front for clandestine political activities, contending that he and Hamilton had actually been sent to Dublin by James VI to serve as his secret agents.[78] No evidence can be found to support this view. Rather, the two near-contemporary memorials of the teachers to have survived, dating from the late seventeenth century – Richard Parr's *Life of James Ussher* (1686) and a manuscript history of the Hamiltons of Ulster – both agree that Fullerton and Hamilton arrived in Dublin by accident. According to Parr, in 1587 the Scotsmen had turned up in the city 'by chance', while it is the author of the Hamilton history who records the tradition of their being forced by stormy weather to take refuge in Dublin port.[79] Examining these sources, it is hard not to agree with scholars such the Ulster antiquarian, Revd George Hill, or, more recently, Alan Ford, who have pronounced as 'improbable' and 'without foundation' the idea that King James *sent* Fullerton and Hamilton to Dublin as spies.[80]

However, while clearly the two teachers did not travel to Ireland as secret agents, it seems they did become agents soon after their arrival. As the author of the Hamilton family history observed, when the Latin

---

76 Ussher, *Whole works*, ed. Elrington & Todd, i, p. 4.   77 Richard Parr, *The life of the most reverend father in God, James Ussher, late lord archbishop of Armagh* (London, 1686), p. 3.   78 In the mid-nineteenth century the most influential exponent of the 'school-as-front, teacher-as-spy' interpretation was Sir John Gilbert: J.T. Gilbert, *A history of the city of Dublin* (3 vols, Dublin, 1849–54), ii, pp 263–4. See also Elrington's comments in Ussher, *Whole works*, i, pp 2–3nn. It has since been repeated in Henderson, 'James Hamilton' and G.A. Hayes-McCoy, *Scots mercenary forces in Ireland, 1565–1603* (Dublin, 1937), p. 193.   79 Parr, *Life of James Ussher*, p. 3; Lowry (ed.), *The Hamilton MSS*, pp 4–5.   80 Hill, *The Montgomery manuscripts*, p. 31n; Alan Ford, 'The origins of Irish dissent', in Kevin Herlihy (ed.), *The religion of Irish dissent, 1650–1800* (Dublin, 1996), p. 13n.

school opened Fullerton and Hamilton were 'called' by James VI to 'convers[e] with the nobility and gentry of Ireland, for the king's service'. In particular, they were to promote 'the knowledge and right of King James's interest and title to the crown of England [and Ireland]'.[81] Given what we know of the Ship Street school, in which Fullerton did not begin teaching until autumn 1588,[82] the king must have hired them sometime shortly before, on learning of their unexpected arrival in Dublin the previous year.

The year 1588 might seem rather too early for King James to be pressing his claim to the English and Irish thrones. Queen Elizabeth was still in her prime, and in all the standard histories of the succession James's schemes and intrigues with members of the Elizabethan elite are usually traced to a few years later, to the mid-1590s. Yet it has been recently shown that the Scottish king first made contact with the earl of Essex in 1588, and had established friendly relations within a year.[83] There were, moreover, compelling reasons for him to begin pressing for recognition as Elizabeth's successor so soon. First and foremost, while it angered him greatly, the execution in 1587 of his Catholic mother, Queen Mary, removed the single greatest obstacle to the Stewart royal cause in England and Ireland, and cleared the way for him to re-present it as a Protestant venture. The arrival of Fullerton and Hamilton in Dublin therefore created a useful opportunity to recruit Irish and English supporters there. Second, for more immediate diplomatic reasons King James needed servants in the Irish capital by 1588. In 1586 a mutual defence pact, the Treaty of Berwick, had been signed between England and Scotland. To honour his promise to prevent the inhabitants of the Western Isles and the Highlands from aiding Irish rebels in Ulster and Connacht, and so make the English better disposed towards him, James required representatives in Ireland who could gather intelligence and assist the English military officials there.[84]

In this light, it is interesting that, besides their teaching,[85] the only reference to Fullerton or Hamilton between 1587 and 1594 records Fullerton as becoming involved in the affairs of native clansmen in Connacht. In March 1593 he acted as a guarantor to secure the pardon of more than 140 inhabitants of counties Galway and Roscommon. The

81 Lowry (ed.), *The Hamilton MSS*, p. 4.   82 Gilbert (ed.), *Calendar of ancient records*, ii, p. 219. 83 P.E.J. Hammer, *The polarisation of Elizabethan politics: the political career of Robert Devereux, 2nd Earl of Essex, 1585–1597* (Cambridge, 1999), pp 91–2.   84 Hayes-McCoy, *Scots mercenary forces*, pp 177–8; Nicholls, *The Jacobean union*, p. 28.   85 Their teaching duties are regularly noted in Dublin Corporation records, through salary and expenses payments to Fullerton: Gilbert (ed.), *Calendar of ancient records*, ii, pp 226, 245, 249, 256.

document is silent on the reason for the pardon.[86] In the event of the recipients failing to honour its terms, Fullerton was liable to pay fines on their behalf amounting to almost £35 (stg), a large sum, almost twice his annual teacher's salary. To have properly secured the pardon without risk of financial embarrassment he would have needed an additional source of income; as an agent of James VI he may well have had access to extra funds.

In 1594 Fullerton and Hamilton were elected fellows of Trinity College, Dublin, ostensibly in recognition of their growing reputation as scholars and teachers, and henceforth they drew their salary and expenses from the new university.[87] In part, they probably owed their new employment to the string-pulling influence of Alderman Walter Ball, a great supporter of the new university who had been instrumental in setting the two Scots up in the municipal Latin school six years earlier.[88] The fact that Trinity had a new provost, Walter Travers, was also relevant. Travers was a Cambridge Presbyterian and an old associate of Andrew Melville. In 1587 he had drafted a 'Book of Discipline' for English Protestantism that was clearly inspired by the Melvillian Scottish model co-authored by Archbishop Boyd, Fullerton's kinsman, a few years earlier.[89] No wonder Travers favoured Fullerton and Hamilton.[90] Given their background, they were ideally suited to his vision of Trinity as a Calvinist academy. For their part, in time the two new fellows were able to turn the provost's pro-Scottish religious and cultural leanings to more immediate political use.

IV

The fellowships given to Fullerton and Hamilton brought administrative responsibilities, including the requirement that they travel widely on college business (as part of a never-ending search for funds). Crucially, their travels not only encompassed various areas of Ireland, but England

86 *Irish fiants*, Eliz. I, iii, no. 5802.   87 Among the Laing Papers in Edinburgh there is a short account of their Trinity careers, compiled in 1816 from manuscript sources, some of which do not seem to have survived: Edinburgh University Library, MS La.II.646/24.   88 Lennon, *The lords of Dublin*, p. 137.   89 Alan Ford, 'Walter Travers (1548?–1635)', *ODNB*; Helga Robinson-Hammerstein, 'Archbishop Adam Loftus: the first provost of Trinity College, Dublin', in eadem (ed.), *European universities in the age of reformation and counter reformation* (Dublin, 1998), pp 49–51.   90 Their exposure to Ramist educational principles while studying under Melville in Scotland was another factor: Elizabethanne Boran, 'Ramism in Trinity College, Dublin, in the early seventeenth century', in M. Feingold, J.S. Freedman and W. Rother (eds), *The influence of Petrus Ramus: studies in sixteenth and seventeenth century philosophy and sciences* (Basel, 2001), p. 189.

and Scotland too. Practically at once their potential as agents of the Scottish king was activated. Before the end of March 1595, barely a year into his fellowship, Fullerton departed from Dublin and crossed the Irish Sea, fetching up in Glasgow early in May. From his lodgings in the city he wrote a letter that provides our first real beam of light into his secret other life. Written to George Nicolson, an English agent in Scotland, its contents say nothing about universities or education, but instead deal exclusively with soldiers, guns and powerful noblemen in Ireland and western Scotland. Moreover, to judge from the tone of the letter, it clearly was not the first time Fullerton had communicated with Nicolson on such matters – that is to say, the letter was part of ongoing secret contact hardly any of which is recorded.[91] Although he had been out of Dublin since at least 31 March, Fullerton shows himself to be aware of subsequent developments, such as the capture and execution of the Leinster rebel Walter Reagh Fitzgerald (7 April).[92] Plainly, Hamilton and possibly others were sending messages to him in Scotland to keep him up to date. There would have been no point in him receiving such news unless his purpose was to pass it on.

The bulk of the letter deals with a joint Anglo-Scottish plan to cut off the supply of arms and men from Scotland and the Isles to the recently revolted Ulster chieftain, Aodh Ó Néill, second earl of Tyrone – supplies which, reports stated, had been coming across the North Channel in increasing quantities. Fullerton was not confident the traffic could be stopped, but explained that he would utilize his local family connections in Ayrshire and southwest Scotland to make Ó Néill's supply-line less productive. Already, he said, he had involved the laird of Minto, the provost of Glasgow, and the captain of Dumbarton in the scheme, getting them to agree to try to prevent the movement of 'unlawful' (unlicensed) shipments to Ireland. The letter ends with Fullerton announcing he is about to go to Ayr town to stay with his aunt and that he would remain there until it was time for his 'sudden departure'. Where he meant to go is not stated, but the fact that he intended leaving abruptly suggests either that it would soon be too dangerous for him to remain around Ayr (before he was discovered?), or else that his destination after he left the port town was so important that no-one must think he was going there until after he had gone, and had a head-start on any would-be pursuers.[93]

91 *Cal. Scottish papers*, xi, *1593–95*, pp 586–7; *CSPS, 1589–1603*, p. 679.   92 For Fitzgerald's capture and its importance in the Irish war, see David Edwards, 'In Tyrone's shadow: Feagh McHugh O'Byrne, forgotten leader of the Nine Years War', in Conor O'Brien (ed.), *Feagh McHugh O'Byrne: the Wicklow Firebrand* (Rathdrum Historical Soc., Rathdrum, 1998), p. 232. 93 As note 91 above.

Fullerton's second letter to Nicolson, written eight weeks later, on 30
June 1595,[94] says little about his movements in the interim. Chiefly
concerned with secrecy, it is dated at Ayr, and outlines the arrangements
Fullerton had made with his brother the laird of Dreghorne for the
passage of letters back and forth to Nicolson in Edinburgh. It is here that
we first learn that Fullerton had adopted the alias 'William Oliphant',
'which [being] a lawyer's name ... if men intercept [the letters] they may
be thought to be instructions for the lawyer in matters of law'.[95]
Fortunately, the letter is not totally silent about his activities. At the end
Fullerton reports his 'pleasure' that no less than five ships were now
patrolling the North Channel, frustrating the efforts of the Gaelic Scots
and Islanders who hoped to cross over to Ulster. Reading between the
lines, it is possible to speculate that part of the brief for Fullerton's
undercover work must have entailed his finding trustworthy shipmasters
on the west coast to carry out the patrols. If this was the case, as seems
very likely, it suggests the maritime community around Ayr and elsewhere
was opposed to closing down the lucrative military trade with Ireland:
they cared little for helping the English.

The importance of these patrols is often overlooked. When Aodh Ó
Néill of Tyrone finally rose in revolt in May 1595 the English feared he
would be able to draw upon Scotland at will and thus overwhelm the
crown forces before the arrival of adequate reinforcements. On 13 June
such fears seemed justified when Ó Néill destroyed an English relief
expedition at the battle of Clontibret. On hearing the news of Tyrone's
victory, the viceroy, Sir William Russell, stated that unless steps were
taken at once to block off his supplies from Scotland there was nothing to
stop the earl overrunning the Pale and driving the English out of much of
the country.[96] Yet within just a few weeks the danger was over. In addition
to Fullerton, who apparently operated mainly in southwest Scotland, the
English were assisted in cutting off Ó Néill's Scottish supplies by the earl
of Argyll and Sir Lachlann Mac Gill'Eathain (MacLean), operating
further to the north. It is not known whether Fullerton had contacted
these lords when planning his 'sudden departure' from Ayr earlier in the
summer, but to a certain extent it is irrelevant. What really matters is the
impact of the various patrols and other measures that they implemented,
either separately or in concert. As the English soon learned, within barely

94 *Cal. Scottish Papers*, xi, *1593–5*, pp 627–8; *CSPS, 1589–1603*, p. 685.   95 The choice of
'William Oliphant' as Fullerton's alias coincides with some legal business entered into by his
brother the laird at precisely this time, becoming a surety before the Scottish council for his
Chalmers kin and others in their feud with a neighbour: *RPCS*, v, *1592–99*, p. 652.   96 E.g.,
CSPI, 1592–6, p. 337.

a month of his victory at Clontibret, it was being reported across Ulster that Ó Néill's expected Scottish levies had failed to materialize, and that he was 'out of hope' of getting any for the foreseeable future.[97] The reports were accurate: in Ayr, and probably in other south-western Scottish ports, traffic with Ireland suddenly stopped in mid-summer.[98] As a result, by the beginning of September it was estimated there were not one hundred Scots in all of Ulster and Connacht.[99] Instead of advancing, Tyrone was forced to delay, until all advantage had gone.[1]

Fullerton reveals himself in the two letters as a careful and prudent agent of the Scottish crown. He betrays none of the excitability or melodrama that characterized other, less effective, intelligencers of the time. Instead of trying to attract greater patronage by scaremongering or blowing his own trumpet, Fullerton had a quiet, understated approach, concentrating on reporting his movements as economically as possible to Nicolson, his contact. Although (as he had predicted in his second letter) Scottish supplies to Aodh Ó Néill resumed the following year, simply changing route,[2] nonetheless his efforts in the North Channel in the summer of 1595 proved of lasting worth for King James. The English had seen the benefits of close cooperation with the king of Scotland, and learned, moreover, that the king was prepared to be their friend. More personally, Fullerton had identified himself as one of King James's most trustworthy representatives. Even before he had left Scotland and returned to Dublin, his was the main Scottish name to be mentioned in English diplomatic despatches as Nicolson and the English ambassador, Sir Robert Bowes, kept London abreast of developments. Especially significant for his future prospects of helping to advance the succession, Fullerton's care and ability was brought to the attention of the English secretary of state, Sir Robert Cecil.[3] The Scot had made an important leap. In 1595 it was Cecil's great enemy, the earl of Essex, who chiefly championed King James's right to the English and Irish thrones. By entering Cecil's orbit, Fullerton had opened a potential channel of communication to those of Elizabeth's ministers most likely to oppose his master's claim. This would pay dividends later.

Intriguingly, Fullerton's lengthy absence from Trinity College during the spring and summer of 1595 in no way damaged his standing in the Dublin college. Surviving evidence about his travels on Trinity's behalf is

97 Ibid., pp 345–6. **98** Carnegie Library, Ayr: Ayr Burgh Archives, B6/29/1 (the Ayr 'Cocket Book', 1577–1632), shows a total shutdown of trade with Ireland throughout 1595 and early 1596. **99** CSPI, 1592–6. **1** Hiram Morgan, *Tyrone's rebellion: the outbreak of the Nine Years War in Tudor Ireland* (Dublin, 1993), pp 178–92 for an analysis of Ó Néill's strength (and weakness). **2** *CSPI, 1592–6*, pp 479, 522. **3** *Cal. Scottish Papers*, xi, *1593–95*, p. 630.

silent about his Scottish sojourn; perhaps he had not claimed to be serving the college by his absence: hence its omission from the records. Whatever the case, when he is next mentioned as present in Trinity, in November 1595, he appeared in a very senior capacity, as the third most important officer of the college behind the provost. Early the following year he was appointed college bursar.[4] Seamlessly he had slipped back into 'normal' university life.

He does not appear to have broken cover again for a few years. In April 1597 he accompanied Provost Travers to London, but beyond petitioning Secretary Cecil for extra revenue for Trinity, and probably meeting the secretary, it is not known what he did during his time there.[5] It is clear from one episode, however, that his official position at Trinity notwithstanding, it was becoming increasingly common knowledge in Scotland that he and Hamilton were King James's men in Ireland, and that Scottish messages to London were best forwarded via Dublin, through their hands. In October 1598, as George Nicolson described it to Cecil, 'a [Scottish] gentleman of better birth than wit or discretion', having intercepted some Spanish letters about the Irish rebels, had sent them *openly* to Fullerton and Hamilton at Trinity College to be forwarded by them to the viceroy and council at Dublin Castle. It was just the sort of thoughtless action dreaded by all 'secret' agents. As well as risking publicizing the discovery of the Spanish letters, it clearly advertized the fact that the two Scottish academics were known to be suitable couriers of politically sensitive material between Scotland and England. Judging from the tone of the letter it is clear Nicolson assumed that Secretary Cecil shared his view that Fullerton and his colleague were valuable, and should not be so exposed.[6] The Cecilian link was growing.

If he was to continue being useful to James with the English, Fullerton's only option was to move. When he next turns up in extant documents, in December 1599, he was back in Scotland. He appears to have given up his position at Trinity College Dublin to enter the king's service more formally, as all subsequent references to him before 1603 have him either in Edinburgh or Glasgow when he was not in southern England. Hamilton, who succeeded him as bursar of Trinity in 1598, stayed on in Dublin until the summer of 1600, and probably returned there in mid-1601.[7] It was Fullerton's political skill (particularly his fact-

---

4 TCD, MUN/P/1/19, a reference I owe to Dr Elizabethanne Boran; see also Edinburgh University Library, La. II 646/24.   5 HMC, *Salisbury MSS*, vii, 1597, pp 151–2. This, the third and final letter by Fullerton before 1603, and co-authored by Travers, seems to be a preliminary request for a meeting.   6 *Cal. Scottish Papers*, xiii, *1597–1603*, p. 326.   7 Hunter, 'James Hamilton'; Edinburgh University Library, MS La.II.646/24.

finding ability), rather than his academic gifts that ensured King James kept him close at hand. Accordingly, when Elizabeth I wrote to James late in 1599 expressing her indignation that a book about the succession written by the recently deceased English MP, Peter Wentworth,[8] had been published in Edinburgh, the king turned to Fullerton to discover who was responsible. He soon tracked down the culprits, who had published the book reckoning that it would sell so quickly in Scotland, England and Ireland that the print-run would be entirely sold out before it could be traced back to them. They reckoned wrong. After a visit from Fullerton, the book's compositor fled Edinburgh, fearing he 'would be put to the walls' (shot) if he stayed. Fullerton's prompt action was reported by George Nicolson, whose letter on the affair brought the Scot once more to the attention of Secretary Cecil.[9]

V

It was not until 1600–1 that Fullerton's mettle was fully tested. The disgrace and fall of the earl of Essex following his sudden departure from Ireland in September 1599 had greatly jeopardized the Stewart royal claim in England. As the case of Wentworth's book indicated, already the question of the royal succession was becoming increasingly vexed. It was especially heated in London. Just days before Essex's fateful decision to leave his post in Ireland, Cecil's principal ally, Charles Howard, earl of Nottingham and lord admiral of England, had declared himself totally opposed to King James's cause during an argument over dinner in the English capital. It was also reported that fights and scuffles had broken out at Elizabeth's court between those who supported Essex and the Scottish king, and those who did not.[10] Essex's unexpected arrival from Ireland added immeasurably to the tension. His banishment from the queen's presence and subsequent disgrace left no-one convinced that his bolt was truly shot, least of all his supporters, who began planning a pro-Stewart coup on his behalf. A key conspirator at this stage was the new Irish viceroy, Mountjoy, who in February 1600 sent King James a message proposing what has been called 'a joint military *démarche*' between the armies of Scotland and Ireland to restore Essex to supremacy at Whitehall and secure the English and Irish crowns for James. James tried to respond,

---

8 Though not named in the source, this can only be Wentworth's 1593 treatise, *A pithie exhortation to her majesties for establishing her successor to the crowne* [STC no. 25245]. Wentworth had died in prison in 1596.   9 *Cal. Scottish Papers*, xiii, *1597–1603*, p. 583.   10 William Fraser, *Memoirs of the Maxwells of Pollok* (2 vols, Edinburgh, 1863), ii, p. 35.

but as Maurice Lee has shown, he was unable to persuade the Scottish Convention of Estates to grant him the necessary money.[11] Consequently, fearing that Essex's overthrow might lead to the collapse of his claim, over the following months the king became steadily more anxious, eventually deciding as a matter of urgency that instead of pursuing an aggressive line towards England through Ireland, he must be moderate, and secure new English backers.

Fullerton's connections with Sir Robert Cecil now became significant. Simply put, the English secretary of state had to be courted. It was already widely believed that he leaned towards recognizing the Spanish Infanta, Isabella; the fact that in May 1600 he began exploring the possibility of peace with Spain added immeasurably to James's fears.[12] Accordingly, plans were laid to send both Fullerton and Hamilton (recently arrived in Edinburgh from Dublin) to London. Fullerton's contact, Nicolson, prepared the way. On 11 August he wrote to Cecil informing him that the two Scottish academics were coming.[13] Although Hamilton was to present himself openly as King James's London agent, officially sent south to oversee the payment of the annual English subsidy to his master, in reality the subsidy was but an excuse, its collection being handled by others, such as David Foulis and Archibald Johnstone.[14] The real purpose of his journey was to contact Cecil, and to that end Nicolson arranged that the English secretary prepare for negotiations by entering a secret symbol for Hamilton into his cipher book.[15] Hamilton had reached London by 26 August at the latest, on which date his presence there was reported to Sir Robert Sidney, the English commander in the Low Countries.[16] Because they were arrested at Durham, we know that Hamilton employed two Scotsmen, John Hay and Robert Montgomery, to carry messages to Edinburgh and back;[17] judging from later evidence it is likely that he and Fullerton used an English Protestant writer named Francis Herring to carry messages to Cecil on King James's behalf, a service Herring performed, as he later recalled, 'not without risk of personal danger'.[18]

The most clandestine role in the negotiations seems to have fallen to Fullerton. Nicolson having arranged that Cecil deal with him in correspondence as 'Mr Figg', Fullerton also travelled to London, but unlike

11 Lee, *The 'inevitable' union*, p. 103.   12 Ibid., pp 106–7.   13 *Cal. Scottish Papers*, xiii, *1597–1603*, p. 683.   14 Julian Goodare, 'James VI's English subsidy', in Goodare & Lynch (eds), *Reign of James VI*, p. 115.   15 As n.5 p. 208.   16 *Report on the manuscripts of Lord De L'Isle and Dudley, preserved at Penshurst*, ed. C.L. Kingsford, 6 vols (London, 1925–66), ii, p. 480.   17 Joseph Bain (ed.), *The border papers* (2 vols, Edinburgh, 1896), ii, pp 680–1.   18 HMC, *Salisbury MSS*, XXIV, *Addenda, 1605–1668*, p. 256. Herring is best known for publishing a wildly anti-Catholic tract in 1610: Antonia Fraser, *The Gunpowder Plot: terror and faith in 1605* (London, 1996), pp 280–1.

Hamilton he went secretly. So well did he cover his tracks that his time in the English capital was only recorded after he returned to Edinburgh to report on Hamilton's progress, about the beginning of October. Unusually for Fullerton, he could not contain his excitement. Contact had not just been made with Cecil, but also with other important Englishmen. On being interviewed by the king he reportedly boasted that Hamilton had made 'twenty thousand friends' for the Stewart cause, having reached an understanding with 'all the best of the [English] council', leading nobles and 'other great personages' of the realm, so that in time the king could expect 'great things to pass'.[19] Everything, apparently, was settled. Now that Essex was discredited and powerless, Cecil and others of Elizabeth's privy council were willing to recognize James as Queen Elizabeth's heir. Fullerton's excitement was understandable: his links to Cecil had helped make it possible.

There is not much doubt that Ireland and the huge English army stationed there featured in the negotiations. In the first place, when Nicolson was helping Cecil to set up the talks, arranging secret identities for Fullerton and Hamilton, he instructed the secretary to use one other code in the communications about their visit – 'Ireland by this *', an asterisk.[20] Secondly, it is only after the Hamilton/Fullerton mission to London in August 1600 that communications between Secretary Cecil and Lord Mountjoy, the pro-Stewart Irish viceroy, and former Essex associate, began to move very edgily from mutual dislike towards grudging cooperation.[21]

The spectre of the earl of Essex hung over the London agreement, so much so that as long as the earl remained alive James VI and Cecil could not fully commit to each other. Great dissimulators both, Cecil feared (not entirely incorrectly) that James would be his 'true friend' only until Essex's fortunes revived, while James fretted that Cecil was playing him for a fool, luring him (through Fullerton and Hamilton) into a trap designed to keep Essex weak before supporting another royal claimant. The long silences necessitated by secrecy did not help; nor did ongoing contact with Essex's followers, who clearly had a vested interest in sowing seeds of doubt about Cecil in James's mind. In order to reassure the king Fullerton was despatched to London before Christmas 1600 to communicate with the secretary anew. A letter by Sir Henry Brouncker on

---

19 *Cal. Scottish Papers*, xiii, *1597–1603*, p. 712. 20 Ibid., p. 683. 21 They continued to mistrust each other for some considerable time, until June 1601, after which Mountjoy finally accepted that Cecil was prepared to co-operate with him: John MacLean (ed.), *Letters from Sir Robert Cecil to Sir George Carew* (Camden Soc., o.s. 88, London, 1864), p. 84.

15 December records his visit. Writing to Cecil, Brouncker describes Fullerton as 'a man long known to me', yet the fact that he wrote as if the Scot was a stranger to the secretary shows only that he knew neither as well as he thought![22] Relations inched forward. Having been 'introduced' to Cecil by Brouncker, Fullerton returned to Edinburgh late in January 1601 to assure the king that all was fine.[23] However, sometime after his arrival he would have learned that while he had been in London there had been a dramatic development elsewhere, one that hardly inspired total confidence in Cecil's promises of friendship. In Ireland, apparently about Christmas time, and for reasons that remain shrouded in mystery, Lord Mountjoy had decided to abandon Essex to his fate after being approached about a new plot.[24] Mountjoy's decision in effect temporarily removed the Irish army from the political equation, so that, at last, Cecil had his hands free. But without the threat from Ireland could the English secretary be trusted? Had Fullerton made a terrible miscalculation?

About the beginning of February 1601 the continuing uncertainty became too much for James VI. Convinced that Cecil had outwitted them all, the king lashed out at the servants he deemed responsible – Fullerton and Hamilton. Presumably for having met with so many English ministers and lords, and being indiscreet, Hamilton bore the main brunt of the royal wrath. As George Nicolson described it to Cecil: 'Mr James Hamilton is in great hatred', and ominously it was understood that the king intended having charges brought against him. Fullerton fared slightly better: 'Mr James Fullerton is presently out of taste, yet not charged with offence'. Either on or just before 7 February Hamilton contacted Nicolson before making his escape south to London.[25] He was fortunate – and Fullerton too – that he arrived just in time to witness the Essex rebellion and its bloody aftermath. Able to report on the trial and execution of the earl, his messages to Edinburgh went some way towards easing the king's fear of Cecil. Essex, he said, was wrong about Cecil; the secretary did not favour the Infanta, nor had he ever.[26] Finally accepting that Sir Robert was probably well disposed towards him, all the same James could not forgive Hamilton his past actions. When Hamilton returned to Scotland in March he was dropped as a royal agent,[27] and returned to Dublin. Henceforth, and for the remainder of Queen Elizabeth's life, James Fullerton would act alone 'as the [Scottish] king's great dealer in intelligence', with a substantial salary of £100 (stg) per annum.[28]

22 HMC, *Salisbury MSS*, x, *1600*, p. 421.   23 *Cal. Scottish papers*, xiii, *1597–1603*, p. 763.
24 Bruce (ed.), *Correspondence of James VI*, pp 102–4; HMC, *Salisbury MSS*, xxiii, *Addenda 1562–1605*, p. 87.   25 *Cal. Scottish papers*, xiii, *1597–1603*, p. 767.   26 HMC, *Salisbury MSS*, xiv, *Addenda, 1596–1603*, pp 171–2.   27 *Cal. Scottish papers*, xiii, *1597–1603*, p. 778.   28 Ibid., p. 1051.

Though he had managed to retain the king's trust, and had secured a major position in the Stewart state, Fullerton was unable to relax. With Essex gone, and Cecil apparently won over to the king's cause and prepared to cooperate with Mountjoy in Ireland, there was nothing to do except wait for Elizabeth to die. By the summer of 1602 reports of Elizabeth's continuing good health were not welcome in Scotland. King James's secret correspondence with Cecil and the earl of Northumberland stressed patience above all other virtues, but the king grew increasingly fidgety. As before, he was inclined to doubt his English 'friends', all the more so as letters from servants in London such as Sir David Murray identified potentially threatening developments there. Thus in June 1602 Murray informed the earl of Mar that the countess of Kildare 'knew not what reckoning to make of Cecil', and that two of Elizabeth's chief courtiers, Lord Cobham and Sir Walter Raleigh, were conspiring against the king's friend, the Irish viceroy, Mountjoy. Cobham, indeed, seemed to be getting the upper hand at Elizabeth's court. His advice to the old queen that she refuse King James's offer of Scottish military aid to Mountjoy in Ireland was successful largely because he dared to link it to the succession question, a subject usually carefully avoided by Elizabeth's courtiers. Denouncing Mountjoy for being prepared to endanger the queen by yielding to the king of Scots, Cobham's intervention over the war in Ireland seemed to signal that the succession was not yet settled, and that James would face serious opposition when Elizabeth died.[29] By the end of September, unnerved by the rise of Cobham, the king lashed out at Fullerton, threatening to take back his salary as chief intelligencer as he had 'done no service for it'.[30]

Once more Fullerton headed to London, his intention being to get Cecil and others to send reassuring messages to James, before crossing over to France 'to see what he can learn to flatter the king'.[31] In the event a French voyage was unnecessary. By late 1602 Elizabeth at last began to fade. As her godson Sir John Harington told his wife 'Our dear queen doth now bear show of human infirmity', and onlookers paid close attention to the slightest sign of her mental and physical decline, which manifested itself through forgetfulness and melancholy as well as pain and tiredness.[32] Fullerton next appears in surviving records in August 1603, five months after Elizabeth's death and his master's triumphant accession. Having recently returned to Ireland to take up an important government

---

29 Edmund Goldsmid (ed.), *The secret correspondence of Sir Robert Cecil with James VI of Scotland* (3 vols, Edinburgh, 1887), ii, p. 44.   30 *Cal. Scottish papers*, xiii, *1597–1603*, p. 1051.   31 Ibid.   32 Neale, *Queen Elizabeth I*, p. 394.

position, as muster-master general and clerk of the cheque,[33] it seems he had been present about London all through the final stages of the succession drama, invisible, looking on, as Cecil (his English patron) eased King James's path. Apart from being knighted, he kept out of view before receiving his Irish appointment.

VI

Unaware of his career outside England, some English historians have assumed that Sir James Fullerton was just one of many Scotsmen on the make in 1603, and followed the new king southwards looking to enrich himself through service at the new Anglo-Scottish court being assembled at Whitehall.[34] The fact that he was already in London, having helped to secure the king's succession, and that he subsequently sought his advancement by leaving England to return to Ireland has been overlooked. This oversight needs to be corrected not only for the sake of greater historical accuracy, but because, as before March 1603, Fullerton's activities after that date highlight aspects of the Jacobean succession that challenge current orthodoxy. His behaviour in Ireland shows that King James felt his second new kingdom needed careful handling, lest it present a threat. Contrary to a common assumption, the political and military security of the Stewart succession was not yet completely settled.

As Mark Nicholls has revealed in a series of groundbreaking investigations, in the weeks and months that followed James's ascent, sections of the English political nation were far from content with their new king. Catholics were to the fore, disgruntled that all the fair words about tolerance that they had received from James before 1603 were forgotten now that the monarch had obtained his goal. A conspiracy largely inspired by the priest William Watson, known as the Bye Plot, soon ensued, in which the conspirators intended to kidnap the king and force him to grant toleration. The plotters were greatly boosted by the decision of the Protestant nobleman, Lord Grey de Wilton, to act as their leader. A second conspiracy, the Main Plot, was more serious again. Organized around the courtiers Lord Cobham and Sir Walter Raleigh, this was intended to dethrone James in favour of Arabella Stewart and to exterminate the king and his family.[35] In the event, neither plot made much

33 *CSPI, 1603–6*, p. 191; Hughes, *Patentee officers of Ireland, 1173–1826* (Dublin, 1960); NAI, Catalogue of Fiants, James I, no. 1514.   34 Pauline Gregg, *King Charles I* (London, 1981; rpr. ed. 2000), p. 24.   35 Nicholls, 'Two Winchester trials'; idem, 'Treason's reward: the punishment of conspirators in the Bye Plot of 1603', *Historical Jn.*, 38:4 (1995), 821–42.

progress, each being discovered by government agents, but this should not be allowed to conceal something rarely acknowledged by historians: King James was *not* universally accepted as Elizabeth I's successor.

Moreover, based on the evidence that his officials unearthed, the king had reason to suspect that his enemies were not confined to England, but existed in the kingdom of Ireland also. Sir Griffin Markham, one of the principal participants in the Bye Plot, had held a military command in Ireland for some years prior to 1603.[36] The question facing the king was: how many of Sir Griffin's fellow officers shared his distaste for the new regime, and were they prepared to take action? Of equal concern in this regard was the claim made by Cobham's brother, George Brooke, shortly before his execution, that one of those favoured by the plotters was the outgoing lord president of Munster, Sir George Carew.[37] Though Secretary Cecil would have assured the king that Carew, his friend, was totally reliable, James must nonetheless have wondered how the president was linked to such dastardly people. From his own experience he knew that Carew had identified himself as a great enemy of Mountjoy in 1600 when the latter had advertised his support for the Stewart succession. Could Carew really be trusted? And even if he could, how reliable was the English army in Munster, a part of Ireland that was beyond Mountjoy's control because of its status as a presidential jurisdiction? For that matter, how many of the English soldiers settled there were friends of Raleigh, formerly a captain and great landowner in the province?

It is against this background that the appointment of Sir James Fullerton as muster-master general of Ireland and clerk of the cheque was made. Sir Ralph Lane had filled the post prior to the Scot's nomination, and though old and in poor health, Lane was still alive when Fullerton arrived in Dublin to replace him. Lane was a close friend of Sir Walter Raleigh, with whom, famously, he had crossed the Atlantic and founded the colony of Virginia in the 1580s.[38] Fullerton assumed the muster-mastership shortly after the Bye and Main plots had been discovered, enjoying full responsibility for the mustering, or formal assembly, of the English army in the country and the inspection of its men. Most importantly, as part of his duties he was authorized to oversee the demobilization of most of the army's forces and the decommissioning of its weapons. It is usually assumed that King James wanted the Irish army demobilized in order to save money. While this undoubtedly was a key motivation, so too,

---

36 Ibid., 828. A 'Captain Markham' was active in southern Ireland as early as May 1589, either Sir Griffin or a kinsman of his (*Irish fiants*, Eliz. I, no. 5329).   37 Nicholls, 'Treason's reward', 821n.   38 W.M. Billings, 'Sir Ralph Lane (d. 1603), soldier and colonist', *ODNB*.

plainly, was royal security. Had cost-cutting been the only consideration, the king could have appointed almost anyone as muster-master general, or else left Sir Ralph Lane undisturbed. The fact that he chose a fellow Scot for the post (and one greatly experienced in cloak-and-dagger operations to boot), requiring him to oversee the disarming and cashiering of thousands of Englishmen, is highly suggestive.

Between May and November 1603 Fullerton oversaw the first wave of demobilization, assisted by Ralph Birkenshaw, the English comptroller of musters.[39] He stopped just before the Bye and Main conspirators were brought to trial at Winchester, having laid off 25 companies and their commanding officers (about 2,500 men),[40] before leaving for court in company with James Hamilton.[41] Hamilton was also involved in the demobilization. Like Fullerton he too had recently received a military appointment, being made constable of Trim Castle, one of the principal royal fortresses outside Dublin, and a place where arms were stored.[42] Almost certainly the arms and ammunition taken from the cashiered companies were delivered into his custody, to prevent it falling into the wrong hands. At least three of Raleigh's former associates were among the first batch to be stood down: Sir Alexander Clifford, Sir Simon Killigrew, and Sir George Lane (Sir Ralph's kinsman).[43]

Fullerton and his helpers completed their task the following year, by which time they had stood down three-quarters of the entire English force. As Fullerton informed Sir Thomas Lake on 24 November 1604, since his arrival in Ireland to take up his post he had overseen the reduction of the royal army from 12,000 foot and 1,000 horse, to just 3,000 foot and 400 horse at his departure.[44] His letter to Lake chiefly concerns the financial losses he had accrued through his service, and says nothing of any operational difficulties that he may have experienced, but from other sources it is clear that he had at one time feared his actions would encounter stiff resistance. In June 1604, to avert opposition from the troops, he had been granted a commission of martial law, empowering him to execute without trial anyone who resisted his orders, or whom he suspected might do so (in Ireland martial law often involved pre-emptive executions, in contrast to England and Wales, where it was a reactive measure only).[45] His

---

39 For Birkenshaw, see Hiram Morgan, 'Birchensha's discourse', in idem (ed.), *The battle of Kinsale* (Dublin, 2004), pp 391–2.   40 PRO, SP 63/215/113 (=*CSPI, 1603–6*, pp 109–11). 41 They were at court by 19 November, when Sir Geoffrey Fenton wrote to Cecil about them (PRO, SP 63/215/110).   42 *CSPI, 1611–14*, p. 114.   43 Clifford had served under Raleigh at Cadiz in 1596, and Killigrew was a kinsman of Raleigh's old ally Sir William Killigrew: see Edward Edwards, *The life of Sir Walter Raleigh* (2 vols, London, 1868).   44 *CSPI, 1603–6*, p. 211. 45 NAI, Chancery Rolls Office, Catalogue of Fiants, vol. II: Elizabeth I and James I, p. 689 (no.

enjoyment of martial power, for use against Englishmen, was controversial. It would be twenty years before another Scot obtained a like commission in Ireland.[46]

The muster-mastership was not the only post Fullerton occupied during this time. Midway through 1604 he had been among those senior crown officials who sat in judgement of the case of William Miagh, the recorder of Cork, in the court of Castle Chamber in Dublin. It is easy to understand Fullerton's involvement. Miagh, a staunch Catholic disappointed by the king's maintenance of Protestantism, stood charged of 'contradicting His Majesty's title to the crown of this realm [Ireland] and levying war against His Majesty'.[47] Less obvious is the reason for Fullerton's subsequent elevation to a place on the council of Munster. His authority as muster-master general was countrywide – he did not need a special appointment to operate in Munster. It is possible, therefore, that his joining the provincial council was a means for King James to spy on the other officials there, to be sure that those who had worked under Sir George Carew, the recently departed president, were in no way associated with Sir Walter Raleigh and other conspirators in England (as Carew himself was, albeit remotely). Whatever the reason, Fullerton spent August and September 1604 touring through the province with Carew's replacement, Sir Henry Brouncker.[48]

VII

It was only when the demobilization was complete that Fullerton left Ireland and returned to London in search of a position at court. Through the assistance of King James's new secretary of state, Sir Thomas Lake, his return was notified to the monarch, and after waiting a few months his petition for reward was accommodated, and then in some style. Without having to relinquish his Irish posts, in 1605–6 Fullerton obtained not one, but two, important court appointments. He was made a gentleman of the royal bedchamber, a position worth £100 (stg) per annum that would bring him close to James on a daily basis, and he also became a personal servant of the king's younger son, the duke of York, Prince Charles (worth £33 6s. 8d. per annum).[49] He did not owe his promotion to his teaching

1055). For martial law see David Edwards, 'Beyond reform: martial law and the Tudor reconquest of Ireland', *History Ireland*, 5:2 (Summer 1997), 16–21.   46 Edwards, 'Scottish officials'.   47 *Earl of Egmont manuscripts*, HMC, 3 vols (London, 1920–3), i, p. 28.   48 BL Harleian MS 697, ff 15r, 22v, 24r, 26v, 29v, 34v; NLI, Sarsfield Papers, D. 25,963–4.   49 HMC, *Salisbury MSS*, xxiv, *Addenda 1605–1668*, pp 62, 66.

ability. The prince already had a tutor in Sir Thomas Murray.[50] Rather, it was his experience in security matters that specially qualified him. Late in 1605 there was a pressing need for increased royal security, with the discovery of the 'Gunpowder' plot to blow up the king and his eldest son, Prince Henry, in parliament, and kidnap Prince Charles.[51]

Curiously, Charles's biographers have ignored this threat, but then until very recently it was customary for political and constitutional historians to dismiss as not very serious all the various plots against the fledgling Stewart regime, on the retrospective basis that none of them succeeded. Needless to say, King James could not afford to be so dismissive. Perceiving real danger to his family in the English capital he reacted by appointing a Scottish security expert of proven ability and absolute loyalty – Fullerton – to take care of his younger son and attend regularly about his own royal person.

The importance of Fullerton's new task was confirmed seven years later, in 1612, when Prince Henry suddenly died, and Charles became heir-apparent to the three kingdoms. Hitherto, Fullerton had continued to occasionally involve himself in Irish government, as a member of the Irish privy council and an organizer of the Ulster Plantation.[52] With Prince Henry's death he finally sundered all involvement in Irish affairs. Despite the comments of some, it is not 'surprising' at all that he subsequently emerged as one of the lesser royal favourites at court. The very future of the Stewart monarchy was in his care, in the person of Charles, and far from being inexplicable his promotion to major court positions about the prince during the 1610s and 1620s was entirely understandable given his record of service. Indeed, to an extent that is often forgotten, the great positions he attained – groom of the privy stool to Charles, and first gentleman of his bedchamber[53] – were security postings first and foremost, ceremonial postings second. To sum up, having assisted in securing the succession of James VI & I in 1603, after 1612 Sir James Fullerton was given responsibility for ensuring that the next phase of the succession would proceed smoothly, by acting as chief bodyguard to King James's heir, Prince Charles.

That Charles continued to rely on Fullerton after succeeding his father as king in 1625, and this despite the opposition of Buckingham, the chief royal favourite,[54] is testament to the esteem in which Fullerton was held,

50 Carleton, *Charles I*, pp 15–16.   51 Nicholls, *Gunpowder Plot*, pp 21–2.   52 e.g., *RPCS*, viii, *1607–10*, pp 497–8; *CSPI, 1603–6*, p. 388; ibid., *1606–8*, pp 9, 92; ibid., *1608–10*, pp 4, 33–4. 53 Aylmer, *The king's servants*, p. 317; N.E. McClure (ed.), *The letters of John Chamberlain* (2 vols, Philadelphia, 1939), ii, p. 58.   54 *Supplementary report on the manuscripts of the earl of Mar and Kellie preserved at Alloa House, Clacmannanshire*, ed. Henry Paton (HMC, London, 1930) p. 234; *De L'Isle & Dudley MSS*, v, p. 441.

reflecting the young monarch's sense of gratitude to someone who had looked after him for so long. Had Charles's biographers investigated Fullerton's origins as a royal security agent, in Dublin and London before 1603, they might have realized how insecure the house of Stewart had once been. Since the 1590s fear of enemies (real and imagined) had been very much part of the world of King James and Prince Charles. The Stewart succession might look easy in retrospect; it was anything but at the time.